Humanity and Nature in Economic Thought

Humanity and Nature in Economic Thought: Searching for the Organic Origins of the Economy argues that organic elements seen as incompatible with rational homo economicus have been left out of, or downplayed in, mainstream histories of economic thought.

The chapters show that organic aspects (that is, aspects related to sensitive, cognitive or social human qualities) were present in the economic ideas of a wide range of important thinkers including Hume, Smith, Malthus, Mill, Marshall, Keynes, Hayek and the Polanyi brothers. Moreover, the contributors to this thought-provoking volume reveal in turn that these aspects were crucial to how these key figures thought about the economy.

This stimulating collection of essays will be of interest to advanced students and scholars of the history of economic thought, economic philosophy, heterodox economics, moral philosophy and intellectual history.

Gábor Bíró is an Assistant Professor and Vice Chair of the Department of Philosophy and History of Science at the Budapest University of Technology and Economics, and a Research Fellow of the MTA Lendület Morals and Science Research Group at the Research Centre for the Humanities, Budapest, Hungary. He was awarded the History of Economics Society 'Craufurd Goodwin Best Article Prize' in 2021 for his paper on Michael Polanyi and the first economics film, published in the *Journal of the History of Economic Thought*.

Routledge Studies in the History of Economics

Foundations of Organisational Economics
Histories and Theories of the Firm and Production
Paul Walker

John Locke and the Bank of England
Claude Roche

Poverty in Contemporary Economic Thought
Edited by Mats Lundahl, Daniel Rauhut and Neelambar Hatti

Thomas Aquinas and the Civil Economy Tradition
The Mediterranean Spirit of Capitalism
Paolo Santori

The Macroeconomics of Malthus
John Pullen

Competition, Value and Distribution in Classical Economics
Studies in Long-Period Analysis
Heinz D. Kurz and Neri Salvadori

David Ricardo. An Intellectual Biography
Sergio Cremaschi

Humanity and Nature in Economic Thought
Searching for the Organic Origins of the Economy
Edited by Gábor Bíró

European and Chinese Histories of Economic Thought
Theories and Images of Good Governance
Edited by Iwo Amelung and Bertram Schefold

For more information about this series, please visit www.routledge.com/series/ SE0341

Humanity and Nature in Economic Thought

Searching for the Organic Origins of the Economy

Edited by
Gábor Bíró

LONDON AND NEW YORK

First published 2022
by Routledge
2 Park Square, Milton Park, Abingdon, Oxon OX14 4RN

and by Routledge
605 Third Avenue, New York, NY 10158

Routledge is an imprint of the Taylor & Francis Group, an informa business

British Library Cataloguing-in-Publication Data
A catalogue record for this book is available from the British Library

Library of Congress Cataloging-in-Publication Data
Names: Bíró, Gábor, editor.
Title: Humanity and nature in economic thought : searching for the organic origins of the economy / edited by Gábor Bíró.
Description: Milton Park, Abingdon, Oxon ; New York, NY : Routledge, 2022. |
Series: Routledge studies in the history of economics | Includes bibliographical references and index.
Identifiers: LCCN 2021025115 (print) | LCCN 2021025116 (ebook)
Subjects: LCSH: Economics--History. | Economic policy.
Classification: LCC HB81 .H86 2022 (print) | LCC HB81 (ebook) |
DDC 330.09/03--dc23
LC record available at https://lccn.loc.gov/2021025115
LC ebook record available at https://lccn.loc.gov/2021025116

ISBN: 978-0-367-68695-6 (hbk)
ISBN: 978-0-367-68697-0 (pbk)
ISBN: 978-1-003-13865-5 (ebk)

DOI: 10.4324/9781003138655

Typeset in Bembo
by Taylor & Francis Books

Contents

Contributors

Gábor Bíró, Budapest University of Technology and Economics; Research Centre for the Humanities, Budapest, Hungary

Tamás Demeter, Corvinus University of Budapest; Research Centre for the Humanities, Budapest, Hungary

Antonello La Vergata, University of Modena and Reggio Emilia, Italy

Helen McCabe, University of Nottingham, UK

Neil B. Niman, University of New Hampshire, USA

Hilton L. Root, George Mason University, USA

Craig Smith, University of Glasgow, UK

Ted Winslow, York University, Canada

Acknowledgements

Contributors to this volume were invited to a conference in Budapest titled *Towards an Organic History of Economic Thought* that was scheduled to happen 6–7th July, 2020. Then something unexpected happened. The global COVID-19 pandemic of 2020–21 forced us to drop the idea of an offline conference and to continue our cooperation online. As an editor, I cannot be grateful enough to the contributors for meeting the deadlines and delivering high-quality chapters in times of unprecedented hardship. The pandemic killed millions of people, made tens of millions lose their job and forced literally everyone to change their daily routine for circa one and a half years. Still, within these grim circumstances, the team of contributors have managed to deliver a volume which, we hope, will inspire further studies into the organic aspects of economic realms.

Special thanks are due to Tamás Demeter, head of the MTA Lendület Morals and Science Research Group for advising me to organize a conference and for endeavouring to host the event which unfortunately could not happen due to the restrictions on international travel from mid-2020. I feel privileged to be able to work with Judit Gróf, who put a tremendous amount of work into organizing the conference. Thanks to her, everything was ready to welcome our distinguished contributors in our spectacular guesthouse at the Buda castle as well as in the research centre. While the conference had to be cancelled, her deeds are still highly appreciated. Special thanks must also go to Péter Hartl and Ádám Tamás Tuboly for their useful advice about organizing the conference and to Deodáth Zuh for his insightful help in finding the proper visuals for the conference poster. While writing the chapters and editing the volume we reached out to many distinguished scholars who generously gave expert advice about how to improve the book or parts of it. Some of them provided extensive reviews or brief reflections, others suggested reviewers to be invited for certain chapters. We are thankful to Duncan Bell, Simon J. Cook, Thomas Dilern, Wendy Donner, Geoffrey Harcourt, Onur Ulas Ince, Roope Kaaronen, Heinz Kurz, Timothy Larsen, Charles Lowney, Christopher Macleod, Inder S. Marwah, Robert Mayhew, Dale E. Miller, Phil Mullins, Maria Pia Paganelli, Spyridon Tegos, Martin Turkis and Charles Wolfe.

I am grateful to Andy Humphries and Natalie Tomlinson, editors of the *Routledge Studies in the History of Economics* for their support of the project from

2020. I could always rely on their insightful guidance and experience when it was most needed. I owe many thanks to Emma Morley, editorial assistant for economics at Routledge. Special thanks must go to Kate Reeves for her dedication and excellent editing, and to Katie Hemmings for her outstanding professional guidance. This book was supported by the MTA Lendület Morals and Science Research Group.

1 Introduction

Gábor Bíró

This book endeavours to show that *organic* aspects were present in the economic ideas of a wide range of important thinkers from David Hume to Karl Polanyi. By organic, authors of this volume mean something that is *related to given sensitive, cognitive or social human qualities.* It seems worthy to note here, at the very beginning of the book, that we do not consider this account to be comprehensive about organic aspects in the history of economic thought. We neither think that all important thinkers are being addressed nor that we discuss all organic aspects of the chosen ideas. The aim is to demonstrate that organic aspects have been inherent parts of how celebrated thinkers addressed economic issues from the end of the eighteenth century, to show that there was an organic pattern which might or might not be used to develop an alternative, organic history of economic thought. This volume does not portray a single alternative organic history of the relevant ideas, but presents various organicities and tries to pave the way for later converging interpretations. But why would someone work on laying down the theoretical foundations of these interpretations?

Artificial intelligence, robots and big data are rising, and by doing so, bringing an unprecedented rise of the quantitative in public thinking. In parallel, qualitative aspects, aspects that are inherent to human feeling, thinking and being are systematically downplayed in most accounts. And, perhaps what is even more troublesome, histories of economic thought have been increasingly accommodated to our highly mathematized present and presumably even more mathematized and computerized future. The history of economic thought has become seen as a history leading to a quantitative, mathematical, data-driven and computerized discipline. Theories, approaches, methods and tools that did not fit to this picture of the discipline as a proto-theory of computers were mostly regarded as irrelevant for serious studies and have been pushed out of the terrain of economic science by the *boundary work* of those focusing more on numbers and devices than on human qualities. This book aims to warn about this unnoticed boundary work by drawing attention to some of the "unfitting" aspects of economic theories that might not only falsify the math-fetish of recent historiographers of economic thought but also flash a common strand in these theories, organicity, that might lead to a very different take on the history of the discipline.

DOI: 10.4324/9781003138655-1

In the second chapter, Demeter traces similarities between the Humean propagation and structuring of mental, economic and political processes. Elective attractions – he claims – are defining in both cases driving processes towards a common end, an organic unity, without being centrally coordinated.

In the third chapter, Craig Smith explores the implications of the changefulness of Adam Smith's moral beliefs for his understanding of the working of the economy. He identifies a gradual, evolutionary view of moral change that refines the traditional interpretation of Smithian moral improvability and the latter's scope for changing large-scale economic processes.

In the fourth chapter, La Vergata discusses the rich social contexts of Malthusianism entering and leaving Darwinism. He portrays various attempts to naturalize society and to moralize nature based on Malthusian ideas and, perhaps, phrases some general lessons about the changefulness of moral valences attached to theories.

In the fifth chapter, McCabe identifies organic elements of Mill's political economy, particularly his understanding of the laws of production and distribution. She explores the influence of the Saint-Simonians and Harriet Taylor on Mill's understanding of social change, which led him to envisage an "organic", socialist, future.

In the sixth chapter, Niman investigates how Alfred Marshall introduced the concept of continuous change as a counterpoint to the static natural theology of his time. He contends that Marshall believed that individuals and social institutions are the product of their choices and as such, they are active contributors to the social fabric and underlying ideological superstructure that exist at a moment in time.

In the seventh chapter, Winslow addresses the psychological roots of Keynes' general theory of capitalism and explains that a specific irrational individual consciousness, the money-making instinct, plays a characteristic role in the Keynesian system.

In the eighth chapter, Root endeavours into the organic origins of Hayekian morality and finds elements that might prove to be useful for contemporary complexity science to understand the moral implications of complex adaptive systems.

In the ninth chapter, Bíró analyses the economic thought of Michael and Karl Polanyi and discovers that while the brothers had radically different ideas about what the economy and its science should look like, they were both working on renaturalizing the economy and rehumanizing society.

2 Sympathies for common ends

The principles of organization in Hume's psychology and political economy[1]

Tamás Demeter

Introduction

David Hume's "science of man" consists of a foundational theory of human cognitive and affective functions. On this basis Hume aspires to provide an overarching account of moral, aesthetic, social, and political (including economic) phenomena. The foundational theory is laid down in the first two books of *A Treatise of Human Nature* (published in 1739), and its applications to various fields of human activity are developed in Book III of the *Treatise* (1740), as well as in his several subsequent essays and dissertations.

Hume's mental universe of cognitive and affective functioning is frequently understood in terms of (typically Newtonian) "mechanics" (e.g. Owen 2009) or "dynamics" (e.g. Stroud 1977: 9; Buckle 2001: 133–137; Collier 2019: 435; for a critique of such views see Demeter 2019a). According to this vision, the mental contents of the Humean mind are inert atomistic elements. As such, they are identifiable in themselves, without reference to other contents, and they lack activity of their own. Their interactions are due to the "gentle force" (T 1.1.4.1) of association whose influence is typically understood in terms of a "push-pull talk" of external forces analogous to Newton's gravity (Fodor 1983: 31–32). Hume's famous principles of association (causation, resemblance, contiguity) are taken to be inferred from observed regularities in human psychological activities. So, they seem to be inductively established law-like generalizations, and as such they can be conceived as analogous to the laws of motion. As mental contents and their interactions are taken to constitute the Humean mind in its entirety, this picture presents human psychology on a par with inanimate nature and the world of inert matter.

There seem to be strong mechanical allusions also in Hume's theory of the passions that play a central role in his theory of motivation. He compares passions to sounds produced by a string instrument that decay slowly – unlike those produced by a wind instrument (T 2.3.9.12). This feature is supposed to be explanatory of why they tend to mingle with different other passions over time. The same analogy is used to clarify the mechanism of sympathy as the communication of affections (T 3.3.1.7). Furthermore, passions seem to be affected by some kind of Newtonian gravity, because they "like other objects,

DOI: 10.4324/9781003138655-2

descend with greater facility than they ascend" (T 2.2.2.19) – meaning in this case that, for Hume, our affections tend to spread more easily from superior to inferior objects than *vice versa*. And then Hume extends this kind of gravity to ideas, turning it into a general feature of perceptions (T 2.3.8.8).

Against this background, a mechanical imagery of social and economic processes may be tempting to discern in Hume. He does indeed claim that "the cohesion of the parts of matter arises from natural and necessary principles" and "we must allow, that human society is founded on like principles" (T 2.3.1.8), and thereby he invites us to read him through a lens of mechanical imagery. If one agrees that the language in which Hume

> describes the motions of the passions as producing the energy or force of motivation, able to exert itself on the passivity of the will, is that of a mechanical model, in which change only occurs through the application of a force strong enough to overcome the resistance of inertia [Packham 2012: 90],

then by natural extension, one can also view the institutions of society, that are themselves products of the passion and not of reason, "much like the mechanical operations of a pocket watch, there are several intricate and interconnected moving parts that coordinate with one another" (Schabas and Wennerlind 2020: 90).

Similar mechanical approaches have been suggested to Hume's economy as well. And indeed, it seems apt to point out that his studies in natural philosophy might have plausibly influenced his account of the "specie-flow mechanism" (Barfoot 1990: 165). It describes the process of how the sudden influx of specie, ungrounded in an increase of productivity, raises the price level in a given economy, and makes imported goods cheaper resulting in the flow of the specie abroad (for a good summary see Schabas and Wennerlind 2020: 144–145). It is tempting to interpret this celebrated insight in a mechanical framework, e.g. by relying on Newton's theory of gravity: the flow of money may be envisaged as subject to tide mechanisms; or represented alternatively in terms of hydrostatic circulation and fluid dynamics, or of a theory of "subtle fluids" such as electricity (Schabas 2004: 70–74). Due to this physical imagery Hume is placed among the first to successfully introduce the idea of an "equilibrium model" into the study of economic phenomena (e.g. Gordon 1991: 126).

In this chapter I intend to suggest that the sources of Hume's conceptual inspiration are more eclectic than the readings emphasizing his allegiance to mechanical imagery suggest. I admit, mechanical imagery is indeed present in Hume's toolkit of metaphors and analogies; it is even locally dominant in certain segments. Yet, its overarching influence on Hume's thought is limited and gives way to an organic and chemically inspired imagery that informs Hume's accounts of mind and of society at large. Here I will argue that while mechanical imagery is discernible in certain parts and parcels of Hume's philosophy, his general conceptual framework is more inclined towards the discourses of qualitative differences in matter and of living nature – especially when he turns to the discussion of interactions of and in complex systems. His accounts of how mental phenomena arise from the interaction of different faculties and how economical phenomena arise from the broader texture of social interaction exhibit remarkable convergences. In order to reveal these consequences, I will highlight the organic and chemical features, at the expense of mechanical imagery, in Hume's way of making sense of people and their interactions.

Affinities and sympathies in the Humean mind

While the *Treatise* provides resources to those wishing to look at the Humean mind as a mechanical unity, a closer look reveals that even the central tenets of the mechanical reading, i.e. conceiving association as analogous with gravity (recently e.g. Morris and Brown 2019; Garrett 2015: 50; de Pierris 2015: 17), and the perceptions as analogous with corpuscles of inert matter (e.g. Stroud 1977: 9; Buckle 2001: 133–137), lend themselves to a chemical interpretation. Hume's famous initial phenomenological distinction in Book I (e.g. T 1.1.1.1, 3, 5) proclaims that impressions (roughly, the matter of experience) and ideas (roughly, the matter of thought) differ only with respect to their degree of force, liveliness, and vivacity, but not in kind or "in nature" (T 1.1.1.5). This is consonant with the mechanical reading, as it suggests that the universe of the mind's perceptions, just like the universe of inert matter, is qualitatively homogeneous. But this phenomenological insight is only a starting point for Hume's project of introducing "the methods of experimental reasoning" into the inquiry of human nature – as the subtitle of the *Treatise* announces. And as it turns out subsequently, experimental reasoning reveals features of the mind and its perceptions that are not readily available in our phenomenology.[2]

In an important passage in Book II, Hume explicitly introduces a distinction *in kind* between impressions and ideas (T 2.2.6.1). The core of this distinction is as follows. Ideas can indeed be conceived as solid, inert, corpuscular elements of the mental universe that keep their identity while forming compounds. Impressions, however, are unstable elements lacking the distinctness of ideas and are prone to lose their identity while entering into compounds. Due to this distinction the dictum of qualitative homogeneity of the mental universe cannot be maintained, especially because Hume derives "some of the most curious phænomena of the human mind" (ibid) from this distinction. For example, this distinction can be seen as already lurking behind the famous case of the missing shade of blue: should ideas lack "solidity", they could also be blended so as to "form a total union", they could also lose their identity, and then the mind could easily produce the idea of the missing shade just by mixing the ideas of the two neighbouring shades – and there would be no need to explore other mechanisms producing the idea of the missing shade.[3]

Consequently, the copying process (introduced in T 1.1.1.3–7) by which impressions are turned into ideas (roughly, percepts into concepts) is not mechanical, but productive: it *transforms* the input impression by changing its *compositional properties*. What holds for copying holds for the reverse process of sympathy with the further complication that this latter process is selectively sensitive to the content of ideas: it only "converts" (e.g. T 2.1.11.3, 2.3.6.8, 3.3.1.7) ideas about others' mental states into the corresponding impression. Copying and sympathy are thus productive processes with opposing directions that induce a qualitative change in the perceptions. Because of this productivity, the processes can be ascribed neither to the self-activity of the perceptions themselves, nor to the external force of association (that does not transform the "nature" of the perceptions involved), but only to the active influence of mental faculties on perceptions.[4]

The resulting difference in compositional properties explains why ideas and impressions can be compounded in different ways. "The mind has the command over all its ideas, and can separate, unite, mix, and vary them" (T A.2), and during these processes, component ideas preserve their discernible identity. But the combination of the passions can follow different principles "as in certain chemical preparations, where the mixture of two clear and transparent liquids produces a third, which is opaque and colour'd" (T 2.3.10.9). Passions are simple impressions (see e.g. T 2.2.1.1) that can combine so that their combination results in a new but still simple impression[5] – i.e. they can be "blended so perfectly together, that each of them may lose itself, and contribute only to vary that uniform impression, which arises from the whole" (T 2.2.6.1).

Consequently, compounded passions may not consist in introspectively distinguishable parts, and their analysis requires methods with which to look beyond their phenomenology. This and other phenomenologically hidden features of the mind and its contents can be revealed only if:

> The same liberty may be permitted to moral, which is allow'd to natural philosophers; and 'tis very usual with the latter to consider any motion as compounded and consisting of two parts separate from each other, tho' at the same time they acknowledge it to be in itself uncompounded and inseparable.
>
> (T 3.2.2.14)

Prima facie, this invocation of the analysis of compound motions might be read as yet another element in a kinematic-mechanical imagery, but that would miss the point. What really matters here is that compound motions are phenomenologically just as united as "a particular colour, taste, and smell are qualities all united together in this apple" (T 1.1.1.2). In this apple "we consider the figure and colour together, since they are in effect the same and undistinguishable", but with some effort we can "distinguish the figure from the colour by a *distinction of reason*" (T 1.1.7.18).[6] This analysis reveals the components of the mental world that are not phenomenologically given – just as the analysis of compound motions.

Hume's principles of association, the principles of composition and connection of both ideas and passions, are also established by an analysis of experience and inferential practices. We cannot experience them directly, but their effects are observable, so Hume can establish association as "a kind of ATTRACTION, which in the mental world will be found to have as extraordinary effects as in the natural, and to show itself in as many and as various forms" (T 1.1.4.6). This sentence is widely interpreted as a hint at Newton's gravity.[7] But Newton was careful to warn in Query 31 of the *Opticks* that there may be several attractive powers beside gravity, and "attraction" signifies:

> only in general any force by which bodies tend towards one another, whatsoever be the cause. For we must learn from the phenomena of nature what bodies attract one another, and what are the laws and properties of the attraction.
>
> (Newton 2004: 132)

Taking a closer look at the passage, the idea of *elective affinities* (or attractions, or rapports) provides a more promising model for understanding Hume's sentence – and the nature of association along with it: elective affinities do indeed have "extraordinary effects" in "various forms" – unlike gravity that has a uniform effect on all bodies throughout the universe.[8]

Elective affinities can be described and classified on the phenomenal level without knowledge of the underlying causes of why they obtain, thereby representing the relative strength of attraction between qualitatively different substances – attractions that are sensitive to the particular (chemical) properties of substances as opposed to those they generally share (i.e. their physical properties). Elective attractions are thus the cement of the chemical universe, but not in a sense modelled on Newtonian gravity: while gravity is a universal attraction irrespective of qualitative differences, elective affinities depend on the particular properties of substances and their relative attractions, and not on the quantity of matter.[9] The business of chemistry founded on this idea is to explore and arrange elective attractions systematically, and to account for various combinations and separations of substances in terms of general principles established by such classifications.

This idea started to gain currency in chemistry from the 1710s under the influence of Newton's *Opticks*, and motivated the compilation of "affinity tables" throughout the eighteenth century.[10] Even if impracticable, it does not take too much effort to entertain the idea of an imaginary Humean "affinity table" of ideas charting the possible associative links and their relative strength among various ideas. This might be tempting, because the principles of association do not hold universally among ideas, they only hold selectively, and there can be ideas that have no associative attractions between them. These are clear disanalogies with gravity.

Furthermore, the relations of contiguity and cause/effect are statistically sensitive, and the underlying statistics makes them selective: these two associative attractions between ideas emerge due to the frequency of co-occurrences, and their strength also depends on this frequency. The frequency of co-occurrence is a relational property of the ideas concerned, while gravity depends on an intrinsic property, namely mass. The relation of resemblance is even more selective: it is sensitive to the content, i.e. to particular properties of perceptions in which they resemble – so much so that when we reflectively compare ideas while reasoning, resemblances "depend entirely on the ideas which we compare together" (T 1.3.1.1). Non-reflective association by resemblance is also sensitive to the particular properties of the ideas, but it also requires the active contribution of memory in "producing the relation of resemblance among the perceptions" (T 1.4.6.18) – i.e. it requires a faculty as an active agent in *producing* the attraction.[11]

The principles of association work differently with respect to the two kinds of perception, i.e. impressions and ideas. Passions can be associated only by resemblance, but not by cause–effect and contiguity relations – unlike ideas that can be associated by all three relations (T 2.1.4.4). The association of passions by resemblance have a peculiar feature: passions can resemble not only through their phenomenology, but also by their intrinsic activity or tendency to change. "One impression may be related to another, not only when their sensations are resembling [...] but also when their impulses or directions are similar and correspondent" (T 2.2.9.2). Ideas, being solid inert conceptual atoms, lack this kind of "bent or tendency", thus they cannot resemble each other in this functional way – and cannot be so associated either.

The chemical imagery of passive and active perceptions transforming and interacting according to quasi-chemical principles fits neatly with Hume's explicit aspiration for an "anatomy of the mind". Hume (T 2.1.12.2) makes it clear that anatomy and physiology are indeed the models of his science of man, and that this project is an inquiry into *hidden composition* and *underlying causes* of psychological processes through the study of manifest psychological and behavioural functioning (T 1.4.6.23, 2.1.1.2, 2.1.12.2, 3.3.6.6, A.2): the delineation of the mind's parts is achieved through the study of its normal functioning, i.e. its physiology. The aim of Hume's anatomy is thus to identify components of the mental architecture, the "organs of the human mind" (T 2.1.5.6, see also T 2.1.5.8, 2.2.11.6), in terms of the powers that *mental faculties* exercise over perceptions – just as we have seen in the case of copying and sympathy.

Hume's analogy of nature

Hume's faculties are functional components of the mind that perform specific tasks on perceptions and interact in cognitive and affective processes – just as bodily organs and their substances (fluids, spirits, etc.) do in a healthy physiology. Accordingly, the Humean mind is an organic (and not mechanical) unity whose identity is "of a like kind with that which we ascribe to vegetables and animal bodies" (T 1.4.6.15). This organization

> is still more remarkable, when we add a *sympathy* of parts to their *common end*, and suppose that they bear to each other, the reciprocal relation of

cause and effect in all their actions and operations. This is the case with all animals and vegetables; where not only the several parts have a reference to some general purpose, but also a mutual dependence on, and connexion with each other.

(T 1.4.6.12, emphasis in the original)

Here "sympathy" does not denote the faculty of the mind that we have encountered above in connection with the transformation of perceptions. In this sense "sympathy" belongs to the same family of concepts as "affinity" and "attraction" (Knight 2003):[12] it denotes the principle of organization that generates a unity from diversely functioning, and qualitatively different parts through reciprocal relations. As in the processes in living bodies, the association and transformation of perceptions are guided by this "reference of the parts to each other, and a combination to some *common end* or purpose" (T 1.4.6.11, emphasis in the original) – namely that of sustaining balanced functioning that focuses the harmonious concert of faculties.[13]

Hume's analogy between the organization and processes of living matter and the mind fits well with Hume's other emphatic (and empathetic) analogy drawn in the same section of the *Treatise*. This second analogy is drawn in the same terms between the mind and a political commonwealth, more specifically: a republic. In the Humean mind, perceptions "pass, re-pass, glide away, and mingle in an infinite variety of postures and situations. There is properly no *simplicity* in it at one time, nor *identity* in different" (T 1.4.6.4), and similarly "in a very few years both vegetables and animals endure a *total* change, yet we still attribute identity to them, while their form, size, and substance are entirely alter'd" (T 1.4.6.12). Members of societies organized by republican institutions, just like minds and organic bodies, are united by "reciprocal ties" and "give rise to other persons, who propagate the same republic in the incessant changes of its parts" (T 1.4.6.19). The "members" as well as the "laws and constitutions" of a commonwealth may change, just as a person's perceptions and dispositions, and some principles of the mind are also changeable (see T 1.4.4.1).

In all these cases, components and principles of organization can change to some extent, depending on the nature of the components: the chemical and functional composition of organic bodies; the nature of the mind's perceptions and faculties; the laws and members of political commonwealths. Yet, in all these cases the whole remains a unity due to the causal history of its parts and their reciprocal operations toward a common end.[14] This teleological organization does not mean reflective and conscious teleology on the components' parts: the components themselves cannot or need not be aware of their common end in either of these cases, yet their reciprocal causality drives them toward it. The components respond to external stimuli according to their nature and tendency, and thus perform a functional role that cannot or need not be transparent to them. This is obvious in plants and animal anatomy, but this feature is also present in the Humean mind that lacks a central overseeing faculty.[15]

Similarly, political commonwealths are not and cannot be governed by their members' sense of the public good as it is "too disinterested, and too difficult to support", but it can be done "by other passions, and animate them with a spirit of avarice and industry, art and luxury" (E-OC: 263). For regulating the conduct of its members, it is enough to introduce the institution of property, i.e. a rule for "the stability of possession" in society: "after the agreement for the fixing and observing of this rule, there remains little or nothing to be done towards settling a perfect harmony and concord" (T 3.2.2.12). The establishment of this institution governs the conduct of the members of society towards their common end of peaceful, harmonious and cooperative coexistence without their knowledge and intentions – and even without the knowledge and intention of those who established the institution of property that is "of course advantageous to the public; tho' it be not intended for that purpose by the inventors" (T 3.2.6.6).

It is sometimes noted that the formation of Hume's conventions and institutions is an organic process (e.g. Wennerlind 2008: 107). It is much less transparent, however, that essentially the same imagery of affinities and sympathy hides behind Hume's account of institutions as behind his view of the organization of living bodies and the mind. This can be aptly called a Humean "analogy of nature": Humean nature is "very consonant and conformable to her self"[16] – throughout world of living matter, the mind and political commonwealths. Hume's basic example of an emerging convention invokes "two men, who pull the oars of a boat". Their actions rely on a "common sense of interest" and "have a reference to those of the other" (T 3.2.2.10) – so they are united by "reciprocal ties" (T 1.4.6.19) and a "common end" in the same manner as "animals and vegetables" and the mind itself (T 1.4.6.11, 12, 15). Humean conventions solve coordination problems, i.e. problems arising in non-competitive social situations where the parties are "sensible of a like interest" in each other (T 3.2.2.10) – as in organic bodies, we can observe here "a *sympathy* of parts to their *common end*" (T 1.4.6.12).

This sympathy of the interacting parties "produces a suitable resolution and behaviour" (T 3.2.2.10) as a result of which a convention "arises gradually, and acquires force by a slow progression, and by our repeated experience of the inconveniencies of transgressing it" (T 3.2.2.10, see also T 3.2.3.3). Conventions are thus stabilized through trial-and-error mechanisms: we learn that we are better off conforming to them than deserting. Utility ensures conformity – not coercion, and not the explicit exchange of promises (T 3.2.2.10), i.e. not contracts, because at bottom they are also regulated by convention. Hume instantly extends this model of organic constitution to more complex conventions regulating the "stability of possession", the emergence of language and of money (T 3.2.2.10), and in the next step to justice, right, and obligation (T 3.2.2.11) – that is to the foundational institutions of society, economy, and politics.

As "circumstances, which are fitted to work on the mind as motives or reasons" are subject to change, and as these circumstances are the "moral causes" that "render a peculiar set of manners habitual to us" (E-NC: 198), conventions and institutions are subject to change with the circumstances. This process has a peculiar Humean dialectic that informs social and economic developments. Circumstances beget certain institutions, and we get used to them due to their utility and, gradually, their history. We also form institutions (of education, politics, and communication) that transmit opinions and habits necessary for the maintenance of the institutional system both within society and from one generation to another. This transmission takes place via the mechanism of "sympathy" (introduced above in section 2), which is a form of psychological "contagion" in the community (T 3.3.3.5).[17] Just like the parts of living organisms, institutions, opinion, and habit have a reciprocal influence on each other. Institutions influence opinion, but if opinion changes along with a change in circumstances, habits, manners, and institutions change too. Our conformity to the rules of our institutions rests on "a common sense of interests", and we are indeed "much governed by interest; yet even interest itself, and all human affairs, are entirely governed by *opinion*" (E-BG: 51) transmitted by institutions and socialization. These various elements of the socio-economic conglomerate, depending on their given historical form and their changes, can exhibit different attractions, sympathies, and affinities to the other elements, and thereby they can influence the course of social and economic development. This is the background to a Humean account of "commercial society", or "capitalism" as it is better known today.

Weber's elective affinities

The idea of sympathies and elective affinities between qualitatively different socio-economical elements contributed distinctively to the historiography of economics through Max Weber's account of the connections between certain forms of Protestantism and Western capitalism. Margaret Schabas (2020), albeit not from this angle, has pointed out some convergences between Hume's views on the economic significance of religious differences in Europe, and the position Weber articulated in *The Protestant Ethic and the Spirit of Capitalism*. Schabas draws attention to the neglected significance of religion in Hume's economic thought and presents him as a "proto-Weberian". On her account, the core of Weber's thesis consists in a linear causal link connecting the Reformation as the cause to the unfolding of capitalism as the effect. She claims that for Weber the Reformation was "a necessary condition for the advent of capitalism" (Schabas 2020: 193, 204), and therefore she finds Weber's chronology problematic, because as she rightly points out, "capitalist practices had taken hold […] before the Reformation and, moreover, could be found in Catholic republics" (ibid: 194).[18] And although she finds that Hume "fell short of" a similar claim (ibid: 193), she still presents Hume's arguments as foreshadowing Weber's thesis so understood.

While I think there are indeed intriguing convergences between Hume and Weber in this context, I also think that these are more properly seen if we join ranks with those emphasizing the significance of concepts such as "affinity" (*Verwandschaft*) and "elective affinity" (*Wahlverwandtschaft*) in Weber – instead of linear causality. These terms were originally translated by Talcott Parsons (in 1930) as "correlation", "relationship", and "intimate" or "inner relationship",[19] but this choice of words disguises Weber's crucial allusions to a chemical and organic imagery plausibly inspired by Goethe's *Elective Affinities* (*Die Wahlver-vandschaften*).[20] Goethe's novel might have been "the last gasp of sympathy, in the form of elective affinity" (Knight 2003: 30) as far as chemistry is concerned, but the grip of this imagery on Weber's vision of socio-economic relations was still strong enough. As I see it, it is this imagery, rather than linear causality running from Protestantism to capitalism, that provides the connective link between Hume's and Weber's outlook concerning large-scale transformations leading to capitalism (in Weber's vocabulary) or to commercial society (in Hume's vocabulary).[21]

Weber's imagery, through Goethe, has common roots with that of Hume's in eighteenth-century theories of elective affinity,[22] but the elective affinities they detected in the background of economic development are rather different. As Andrew McKinnon argues, Weber's "affinity" means a "sympathy of one thing for another, whether abstract or concrete" that can be revealed from "a comparison between different ideal types" (McKinnon 2010: 117). One way this affinity can arise is common genealogy, and this is how Weber presents the relation between monastic-type asceticism and its descendant, the Calvinist type. This affinity is exhibited in a common focus on "the destruction of spontaneous, impulsive enjoyment" by bringing "order into the conduct of its adherents" (Weber 2001: 73). But their affinity does not mean identity, because "Catholicism had restricted the methodical life to monastic cells" (ibid: 73), while Protestantism brought this form of life into the world of common life. Thereby, asceticism was turned into a "worldly asceticism, which everywhere first seeks for tasks and then carries them out carefully and systematically" (ibid: 87) in order to find assurance about the prospects of one's salvation in worldly success.[23] The similarities here are so strong, and the line of descent is so clear, that later Weber would proclaim this to be the *par excellence* case of affinity *simpliciter*.

> if the kinds of "spirit" in each of these two contrasting principles of life regulation are not to be judged as inwardly and essentially parallel and akin to each other, I do not know when one should ever speak of an "affinity".
>
> (Chalcraft and Harrington 2001: 114)

While in Weber's terminology "affinity" is a passive similarity that might obtain between seemingly radically different phenomena that analysis can reveal and requires an explanation, "elective affinity" is an active attraction between the phenomena concerned, and it is also a possible explanation (just as common genealogy) of why a given form of "affinity" obtains. "So if an inner affinity between the old Protestant spirit and modern capitalist culture is to be found", then the project of *The Protestant Ethic* is to explain it by their elective affinities. There are no affinities between them with respect to the "materialistic or at least antiascetic enjoyment of life", or to "what is today called 'progress'", but they can be explained in terms of "purely *religious* features" (Weber 2002: 7). And this is the explanation that Weber offers here.

"Elective affinity" appears at an emphatic place in *The Protestant Ethic*, namely in the concluding paragraph of Part I.[24] Instead of linear causality, the term implies "an *interactive* causal relationship, in which two patterns of action and belief *reinforce* each other" (Ringer 1997: 154). This is only hinted at in this last paragraph as a "tremendous confusion of interdependent/reciprocal influences" (Weber 2001: 49 or Weber 2002: 36 – depending on the translation one prefers) between the material conditions, the institutions, and the circulating ideas in the age of Reformation. And indeed, in Part II, Weber's analysis amounts to more than just showing how Protestantism facilitates capitalism – he also argues that capitalism favours some forms of Protestantism more than others, and *vice versa*. Calvinism, for example, has stronger elective affinities (*wahlverwandter*) with "hard legalism and the active enterprise of bourgeois-capitalistic entrepreneurs",[25] than with the virtues of a "faithful" worker or a "patriarchal employer" that are, as Weber sees it, "favoured by Pietism" (Weber 2001: 88). Not only does Calvinism foster attitudes more suitable for modern capitalism than Pietism, but modern capitalism rewards attitudes that conform to Calvinism rather than Pietism. It is due to the elective affinity of Calvinism and capitalism that Pietism diminishes to a form of "religious dilettantism for the leisure classes" (ibid: 89).

The contrast between Pietism and Calvinism relies on a distinction between the "form" and "spirit" of capitalism that Weber spells out responding to criticism: "A given historical form of 'capitalism' can be filled with very different types of 'spirit'", and the form can stand in different degrees of "'elective affinities' to certain historical types of spirit: the 'spirit' may be more or less adequate to the 'form'". Form and spirit "tend to adapt to each other" and where they exhibit "a particularly high 'degree of adequacy' [...] there ensues a development of (even inwardly) unbroken unity" (Weber 2002: 263). With this conceptual machinery Weber reveals the "elective affinity of Calvinism to [Western] capitalism (and also of Quakerism and similar sects)" (Chalcraft and Harrington 2001: 107), so the "degree of adequacy" between Western capitalism and other Protestant sects, as well as Catholicism, is significantly smaller.

The Protestant Ethic is thus a story of the mutually reinforcing processes of the development of certain forms of Protestantism and modern capitalism driven by their elective affinities. There were reformist religious movements before the age of Reformation, and there were several Protestant sects. There were also forms of capitalist economic activity before the advent of modern capitalism. One can plausibly see these processes as unfolding independently up to the point where their "spirit" started to converge.[26] This was the Weberian moment when capitalist economic activities, that were only tolerated, but not approved (and sometimes indeed prohibited) by the Catholic Church, encountered Protestant asceticism that "created that machinery's positive ethic: it created the 'soul' it needed to unite 'spirit' with 'form'" (Chalcraft and Harrington 2001: 130). By turning labour into calling and vocation, and success in it into a reassuring indication of salvation pre-destined by God, Protestantism configured belief systems so that

> a religious value was placed on ceaseless, constant, systematic labor in a secular calling as the very highest ascetic path and at the same time the surest and most visible proof of regeneration and the genuineness of faith. This was inevitably the most powerful lever imaginable with which to bring about the spread of that philosophy of life which we have here termed the "spirit" of capitalism. And if that restraint on consumption is combined with the free-dom to strive for profit, the result produced will inevitably be the creation of capital through the ascetic compulsion to save.
>
> (Weber 2002: 116–117)

Against the background of Weber's socio-economic chemistry, I agree with Schabas that there are proto-Weberian tendencies in Hume's account of com-mercial society (i.e. capitalism), but I detect those tendencies in Hume's outlook and language rather than in the historical role he ascribes to Protestantism. Hume is a proto-Weberian more in his approach to socio-economic phenomena rather than in the substance of his historical diagnosis: Hume, as a consequence of his "analogy of nature", operates with a conceptual apparatus that is similar in several respects to Weber's approach – but the elective affinities that Hume reveals are rather different.

Affinities for commercial society

Weber and Hume may be seen as converging on several conceptual and methodological points. "Spirit" (and "genius") in Hume is a generic term fre-quently invoked as an explanatory category in his political and economic essays, and in *The History of England*. The spirit of an age, a society (a people or nation), a religious sect, or an individual consists of tastes, sentiments, and opi-nions, and this spirit figures as a cause in both sociological and psychological contexts. As such, it is a "moral cause" capable of changing manners and habits. Although Hume mentions institutions, ways of conduct, economic and poli-tical conditions among the primary examples of a "moral cause", spirit should also figure among them, because, for example, "The genius of a particular sect or religion is also apt to mould the manners of a people" (E-NC: 207).

While spirit is a social and psychological cause, its emergence and change are also effects of various moral causes. A rough outline of a Humean story of the unfolding capitalist (commercial) spirit can be explicated from two sources:[27] certain universal features of human nature and certain changes in moral causes.[28] People are not self-sufficient (e.g. T 2.2.4.4), and different people have different talents allowing for different degrees of perfection in different occupations – this natural situation already necessitates "mutual exchange and commerce" (T 3.2.4.1), i.e. some basic form of division of labour, and the exchange of the products of one's labour. What is true about individuals is equally true about countries, because different parts of the world supply different products and "Nature, by giving a diversity of geniuses, climates, and soils, to different nations, has secured their mutual intercourse and commerce" (E-JT 329).

Another natural condition is *avarice*, "or the desire of gain". It is an "obstinate" (E-CL: 93) and "universal passion, which operates at all times, in all places, and upon all persons" (E-AS: 113). What gain is, however, depends on what an individual perceives as his interest, and that perception depends on his opinion (recall E-BG: 51), which is a consequence of "moral causes" such as manners, institutions, and the spirit of the age. Therefore, monarchical institutions and spirit are not favourable for a commercial society: there commerce is "less honourable", because a

> subordination of ranks is absolutely necessary to the support of monarchy. Birth, titles, and place, must be honoured above industry and riches. And while these notions prevail, all the considerable traders will be tempted to throw up their commerce, in order to purchase some of those employments, to which privileges and honours are annexed.
>
> (E-CL: 93)

Under a republican government, however, one's way of securing gain must be different: it leads through making "himself *useful*, by his industry, capacity, or knowledge" (E-AS: 126). Opinions and sentiments change along with institutions, and *vice versa*. A republican government attracts virtues favourable in a commercial society rather than in a feudal court. And commercial society is more strongly attracted to republican than monarchical institutions: its members "covet equal laws, which may secure their property, and preserve them from monarchical as well as aristocratic tyranny" (E-RA: 278) – and this security inspires and helps to maintain the spirit of industry (e.g. E-CL 94, E-AS 125). With the republican emphasis on utility, commerce and industry become honourable and desirable, so avarice, whose objects were ranks and titles in a monarchy, emerges here as "the spur of industry" (E-CL: 93). No surprise, then, from Hume's angle, that Catholic republics were also in the forefront of capitalist development (cf. Schabas 2020: 194).

When commerce starts to flourish, it "rouses men from their indolence" because it reveals previously unknown pleasures and profits, and the success of some in this enterprise motivates others to imitate them (E-OC: 264). So, commerce spreads the spirit of industry "by conveying it readily from one member of the state to another" (E-Int: 301). Humean industry, i.e. "the systematic, methodical, and ingenious application of human labor" (Schabas and Wennerlind 2020: 119), has at least two sets of consequences arising from two different kinds of enjoyment. When the spirit of industry flourishes, "men are kept in perpetual occupation, and enjoy, as their reward, the occupation itself, as well as those pleasures which are the fruit of their labour" (E-RA: 270).

Due to the latter kind of enjoyment, industry is "*linked together by an indissoluble chain*" with knowledge and humanity, so industrious ages are also "more polished" and "more luxurious" ages (E-RA: 271, emphasis added) that are characterized by general refinement and politeness. The elements of the compound in this respect are connected by so strong an attraction that "we cannot reasonably expect that a piece of woollen cloth will be wrought to perfection in a nation which is ignorant of astronomy or where ethics are neglected" (E-RA: 270–271). The surplus from increased productivity boosts the arts and sciences, whose development further increases productivity and refines manners. The indissolubility of this compound can be aptly ascribed to strong elective affinities:[29] the reciprocal, selective attraction of these elements is a crucial driving force of the qualitative socio-economical changes leading to the advent of commercial society – and to public good.

Beyond pleasures and profits, the psychological reward arising from "the occupation itself" is no less crucial a driving force: striving for this satisfaction is responsible for the accumulation of capital. Economic activity is one way of satisfying the "constant and insatiable" craving of the human mind "for exercise and employment" (E-Int: 300).[30] As Axel Gelfert (2013: 729–730) pointed out, economic activity in this respect is not different from curiosity-driven inquiry in mathematics and philosophy, or one could add, not even from hunting (see T 2.3.10.8). In these exercises, one derives pleasure from the activity, but in order for the activity to be pleasurable the aim one pursues "must also be of some importance" (T 2.3.10.4).

Economic activity is a gain-driven activity: if someone is engaged in lucrative enterprises, and

> especially if the profit be attached to every particular exertion of industry, he has gain so often in his eye, that he acquires, by degrees, a passion for it, and knows no such pleasure as that of seeing the daily encrease of his fortune.
>
> (E-Int: 301)

The character of this passion is similar to the passion for gaming (T 2.2.4.4, 2.3.10.9), but its effects are different, because it increases industry that, in turn, incites a further passion: "It is an infallible consequence of all industrious professions, to beget frugality, and make the love of gain prevail over the love of pleasure" (E-Int: 301). So, the (seemingly) ascetic behaviour of Hume's capitalist is not rooted in his striving for reassurance of his state of grace, and his restraint in consumption is due not to religiously prescribed duty – but to the pleasure that arises from feeding his avarice.

Neither Humean way of generating capital has affinities to the innerworldly ascetic Protestant virtues of Weber's early capitalists. On the one hand, generating capital through an increased "stock of labour of all kinds", including the labour "employed for the ease and satisfaction of individuals" (E-Com: 262), amounts to an "irrational use of wealth" – by the standards of such a prominent Quaker as Robert Barclay (Weber 2001: 115). On the other hand, satisfying one's desire or love for gain is "the pursuit of riches for their own sake", and it is condemned by Protestant asceticism as "impulsive avarice" (ibid: 116). In a society where everyone is "a monk all his life" and pursues his "ascetic ideals within mundane occupations" (ibid: 74), the public good cannot be served, and the political commonwealth cannot be maintained:

> The encrease and consumption of all the commodities, which serve to the ornament and pleasure of life, are advantageous to society; because, at the same time that they multiply those innocent gratifications to individuals, they are a kind of *storehouse* of labour, which, in the exigencies of state, may be turned to the public service. In a nation, where there is no demand for such superfluities, men sink into indolence, lose all enjoyment of life, and are useless to the public, which cannot maintain or support its fleets and armies, from the industry of such slothful members.
>
> (E-RA: 272)

Without consumption no component of the indissoluble compound can develop – there is no improvement in industry without similar improvement in knowledge. It is thus more beneficial to individuals, societies, and their economies if economic agents are motivated and regulated in accordance with human nature, than with a system founded on "monkish virtues" that "neither advance a man's fortune in the world, nor render him a more valuable member of society" (EPM 9.3).

Conclusion

The conceptual imagery of Hume's political economy exhibits certain proto-Weberian affinities in its chemical tuning – even if Hume's storyline of the emergence of a commercial society locates the elements and their attractions, sympathies, and chemical bonds differently from Weber's on the rise of capitalism. This chemical imagery in political economy is congruent with Hume's understanding of living nature and the mind, and it is also amended with a teleological outlook that similarly characterizes both. According to Hume's "analogy of nature", living bodies, the mind, and political commonwealths known as republics are functionally structured organic unities whose parts interact on an analogy with the teleological functioning of living nature.

The processes of the Humean mind are propagated and structured by elective attractions among perceptions and by qualitative transformations that mental faculties instigate, whose common end is to sustain balanced functioning – as in plants and animals. There is no overseeing mental faculty that can ensure this harmonious concert, though. The economic and political processes are similarly propagated and structured by the "indissoluble" bonds between industry, knowledge, and humanity, and by elective affinities between commercial society and republican institutions. In Hume's eyes, these processes are driving toward the common end of public good without being centrally coordinated – just like the healthy processes in a living body and in the mind.

Notes

1 I am grateful to Gábor Bíró: without his encouragement this chapter would not have been written. I am also grateful for Margaret Schabas' comments. Her paper (Schabas 2020) was indispensable for the argument advanced here. I also thank Catherine Dromelet, Gergely Kertész, Dávid Kollár, Iván Szelényi, Gábor Zemplén, and Deodáth Zuh for their comments and discussion. This chapter contributes to the research programme of MTA Lendület Morals and Science Research Group.

2 On these aspects of Hume's method see Demeter 2012 and 2020.

3 One such mechanism is suggested by Buckle 2001: 138–139, but see Schliesser 2004 for an opposite evaluation of Newton's relevance for Hume's project and the missing shade of blue, and Kervick's (2018) discussion of Schliesser's views.

4 This also means they cannot be processes of association, because association is a principle of connectivity and constituency, not of transformation in kind. Consequently, not all the processes of the Humean mind are associative, yet it is common to think that the principles of association provide all the analytical and explanatory toolkit that Hume deploys in his theory of mental and behavioural phenomena, and to claim that Hume "strongly suggests that all the various and complicated operations of the mind can be completely accounted for in terms of those three principles alone" (Stroud 1977: 36, or more recently Carruthers 2006: 293, Biro 2009: 43). This view is consonant with the denial of a substantive faculty psychology in Hume. For some recent expressions of this view see e.g. Cohon 2008: 66–70, Alanen 2014: 4, de Pierris 2015: 221–222), and so on. Garrett (2015, ch. 3) takes a more friendly look at the idea of a Humean faculty psychology, and so do I in Demeter 2016, 2019c, 2021.

5 For a classic discussion see Árdal 1966: ch.1.

6 Of course, this analysis can be performed without philosophical preparations and intentions. The experimental method of reasoning is continuous with everyday inferential practices, but it is conducted reflectively and systematically. See e.g. Demeter 2012: 580, 586–587 and Qu 2018: 455–458.

7 Recently e.g. Garrett 2015: 50; de Pierris 2015: 17; for a critique see Demeter 2014 and 2021.

8 For a discussion see Demeter 2014.

9 See Schofield 1969: 218; Klein and Lefèvre 2007: 38, 47, 56.

10 See e.g. Levere 2001: 45–48; Kim 2003: esp. 113–114, 126, 134–139; for the Scottish context see Donovan 1975.

11 For more details about how Hume can be fitted into the context of eighteenth-century Scottish chemistry see Demeter 2014 and 2016.

12 As Charles Wolfe (2014: 251) points out, the idea of affinity around this time was sometimes explicitly taken to have its roots in "the older idea of *sympathies*", and this genealogy of "affinity" suggests "a commitment to the unbroken continuity of matter" – or to put it differently, as a materialist version of the analogy of nature. It is also worth reminding in this context that Leibniz and his followers accused Newton of introducing an "occult quality" in the form of gravitational attraction. As to how this charge could be substantiated, see Henry 1994 and Schliesser 2010.

13 Hume's outlook can find its place in the context of contemporary Scottish debates in physiology. William Porterfield (1735: 161–167) critically discusses explanations of coordinated eye movements based on a "supposed sympathy of our Eyes" that obtains "without having Recourse to any Meeting, Communication or Conjunction of the nervous Fibres in the *Sensorium*" (ibid: 163). Robert Whytt (1751) later relies on a similar concept while explaining the coordination of distantly located organs of the body, and ascribes this sympathy to "something equally present in these several places, i.e. to the mind or sentient principle" (ibid: 182). Hume's "sympathy" is immune to such criticism as it emphasizes the connection and

reciprocal causation of sympathizing parts. For useful discussions of "sympathy" in the Scottish and broader European context and its various senses see Lawrence 1979 and Forget 2003.

14 Alanen (2014) is illuminating with respect to the commonwealth analogy in the discussion of passions, but she does not discuss Hume's organic overtones, and relies on a thoroughly associationist reading of Hume. Packham (2012: ch. 3) highlights the affinities of the political and the organic, but she reads Hume as committed to a mechanistic imagery.

15 Humean reason, that famously is and ought to be a slave of the passions (T 2.3.3.4), cannot play this role; Humean will is an "internal impression", not a faculty (T 2.3.1.2, see e.g. Demeter 2019b); and conscience does not have a role to play in Hume (unlike in e.g. Butler, see Penelhum 1985: 35–38).

16 I am, of course, invoking here Query 31 of Newton's *Opticks* (Newton, 2004: 132), that echoes Rule 3 from the "Rules for the Study of Natural Philosophy" in the *Principia* (ibid: 87). More specifically, I am invoking Newton's dictum in the second sense that de Pierris (2015: 179) suggests: "different generalizations obtained by induction and the principle of the uniformity of nature in different realms can now be unified with one another under an even more comprehensive generalization."

17 On the transmission of beliefs by sympathy see Berry 2018; Taylor 2015: 59–65. Demeter (2019c) offers a case study on the role of sympathy in the generation of mathematical knowledge.

18 I do not think that linear causal readings are tenable here. The last paragraph of Part I of *The Protestant Ethic* concisely makes it clear that Weber does not think the Reformation was a necessary condition for the emergence of capitalism (Weber 2001: 49).

19 See Ghosh 1994, and "Translator's note" in Chalcraft and Harrington 2001. In the following discussion I take the liberty of quoting the English translation (Weber 2001, 2002 and Chalcraft and Harrington 2001) that seems best at conveying Weber's meaning in a given context. Schabas draws on the Parsons translation, and bases her reading of Hume on the concept of a Weberian "correlation", instead of an "elective affinity" between Protestantism and capitalism (Schabas 2020: 153).

20 For an enlightening discussion and further references see Howe 1978, and more recently McKinnon 2010.

21 I agree with Schabas and Wennerlind's (2020: 1) usage that suggests the two terms mean roughly the same. For a crisp and clear summary of what "commercial society" meant for the Scots see Berry 2013: 76–78.

22 On Goethe's connections see Adler 1990; on Hume see Demeter 2017.

23 For Weber's summary of the differences between Catholic monastic and Protestant asceticism, see Chalcraft and Harrington 2001: 114.

24 See Weber 2001: 49–50, but as I mentioned above, the two occurrences of "*Wahlverwandschaften*" here (Weber 2006: 75) are translated as "correlations" and "relationships". The 2002 translation by Peter Baehr and Gordon C. Wells gives the term more helpfully as "elective affinities" (Weber 2002: 36).

25 For the term "*wahlverwandter*" see Weber 2016: 126. Neither English version keeps the allusion to *elective* affinities. In Parsons' translation the two sets of attitudes are "more closely related" (Weber 2001: 88); as Baehr and Wells render it, they "have a closer affinity" (Weber 2002: 95).

26 Ringer (1997: 88–91) argues convincingly that we should understand Weber's explanatory strategy as invoking the interaction between two causal processes rather than events.

27 Here I am reconstructing a "philosophical" version that can be read off Hume. There is an alternative, "historical" version that could be based on *The History of England*. That narrative could start with the emerging practice under Edward IV that became a law under Henry VII "by which the nobility and gentry acquired a power

of breaking the ancient entails, and of alienating their estates" (HE 3:77). One could point out, that "one great cause of the low state of industry during this period" was the monarchical element in the government (HE 3:79). The narrative could continue with the emerging "habits of luxury" and "new methods of expence", the consequently emerging and flourishing "mechanics and merchants", and the increasing economic power of "the middle rank of men" (HE 4:384), as a result of which under Edward VI "a spirit of industry began to appear in the kingdom" (HE 3:387). One version of a similar narrative with more details is offered in Berry 2018: 199–203.

28   On the nature and limits of Hume's universalism see Berry 2007.

29   Just as the opposite compound of "ignorance, sloth, and barbarism" (E-JT: 328). For a helpful discussion see Berry 2018.

30   Andrew Cunningham (2007) sees this self-driven character of the Humean mind, its craving for activity, as a sign of "a vitalist theory of mind" congruent with eighteenth-century theories of active, living matter. He connects Hume's account with subsequently emerging physiological theories of Louis La Caze, John Brown, and William Cullen. Catherine Wilson 2016 also argues that Hume was favourably disposed to post-Newtonian "vital materialism", and so do I in Demeter 2016.

References

Primary sources

David Hume

E *Essays, Moral, Political, and Literary*, ed. E.F. Miller, Indianapolis: Hackett, 1987.

E-AS, "Of the Rise and Progress of the Arts and Sciences"

E-BG, "Whether the British Government Inclines More to Absolute Monarchy or to a Republic"

E-CL, "Of Civil Liberty"

E-Com, "Of Commerce"

E-Int, "Of Interest"

E-JT, "Of the Jealousy of Trade"

E-NC, "Of National Characters"

E-OC, "Of Commerce"

E-RA, "Of Refinement in the Arts"

EPM*An Enquiry concerning the Principles of Morals*, ed. T. Beauchamp, Oxford: Clarendon Press, 1998.

HE*The History of England from the Invasion of Julius Caesar to the Revolution in 1688*, 6 vols, foreword by W.B. Todd, Indianapolis: Liberty Fund, 1983.

T*A Treatise of Human Nature*, 2 vols., eds D.F. Norton and M.J. Norton, Oxford: Clarendon Press, 2007.

Other primary sources

Chalcraft, David J. and Harrington, Austin (eds). 2001. *The Protestant Ethic Debate: Max Weber's Replies to His Critics, 1907–1910*, Liverpool: Liverpool University Press. doi:10.5949/UPO9781846313868.

Porterfield, William. 1735. "Essay concerning the Motions of Our Eyes," Part I: "Of Their External Motions," in *Medical Essays and Observations*, vol. 3, Edinburgh, 160–261.

Weber, Max. 2001. *The Protestant Ethic and the Spirit of Capitalism*, translated by T. Parsons, London: Routledge. doi:10.4324/9780203995808.

Weber, Max. 2002. *The Protestant Ethic and the Spirit of Capitalism*, translated by P. Baehr and G.C. Wells, New York: Penguin.

Weber, Max. 2016. *Die protestantische Ethik und der Geist des Kapitalismus*, Wiesbaden: Springer VS. doi:10.1007/978-973-658-07432-6.

Whytt, Robert. 1751. *An Essay on the Vital and Involuntary Motions of Animals*, Edinburgh: Hamilton, Balfour, and Neill.

Secondary literature

Adler, Jeremy. 1990. "Goethe's Use of Chemical Theory in his *Elective Affinities*" in Andrew Cunningham, Nicholas Jardine (eds), *Romanticism and the Sciences*, Cambridge: Cambridge University Press, 267–279.

Alanen, Lili. 2014. "Personal Identity, Passions, and 'the True Idea of the Human Mind'", *Hume Studies*, 40/1, 3–28. doi:10.1353/hms.2014.0013.

Árdal, S. Páll. 1966. *Passion and Value in Hume's Treatise*. Edinburgh: Edinburgh University Press.

Barfoot, Michael. 1990. "Hume and the Culture of Science in the Early Eighteenth Century" in M.A. Stewart, *Studies in the Philosophy of Scottish Enlightenment*, Oxford: Clarendon Press, 151–190.

Berry, Christopher J. 2007. "Hume's Universalism: The Science of Man and the Anthropological Point of View", *British Journal for the History of Philosophy*, 15/3, 535–550. doi:10.1080/09608780701444980.

Berry, Christopher J. 2013. *The Idea of Commercial Society in the Scottish Enlightenment*, Edinburgh: Edinburgh University Press. doi:10.3366/edinburgh/9780748645329.001.0001.

Berry, Christopher J. 2018. "Hume and the Customary Causes of Industry, Knowledge, and Humanity" in *Essays on Hume, Smith and the Scottish Enlightenment*, Edinburgh: Edinburgh University Press. doi:10.3366/edinburgh/9781474415019.003.0011.

Biro, John. 2009. "Hume's New Science of the Mind" in D. Norton, J. Taylor (eds), *The Cambridge Companion to Hume*, 2nd ed., Cambridge: Cambridge University Press, 40–69.

Buckle, Stephen. 2001. *Hume's Enlightenment Tract: The Unity and Purpose of An Enquiry concerning Human Understanding*. Oxford: Clarendon Press. doi:10.1093/acprof:oso/9780199271146.001.0001.

Carruthers, Peter. 2006. *The Architecture of the Mind. Massive Modularity and the Flexibility of Thought*. Oxford: Clarendon Press. doi:10.1093/acprof:oso/9780199207077.001.0001.

Cohon, Rachel. 2008. *Hume's Morality: Feeling and Fabrication*. Oxford: Clarendon Press. doi:10.1093/acprof:oso/9780199268443.001.0001.

Collier, Mark. 2019. "Hume's Legacy: A Cognitive Science Perspective" in A. Coventry, A. Sager (eds), *The Humean Mind*, London: Routledge, 434–445.

Cunningham, Andrew S. 2007. "Hume's Vitalism and Its Implications", *British Journal for the History of Philosophy*, 15/1, 59–73. doi:10.1080/09608780601087962.

de Pierris, Graciela. 2015. *Ideas, Evidence, and Method: Hume's Skepticism and Naturalism concerning Knowledge and Causation*. Oxford: Oxford University Press. doi:10.1093/acprof:oso/9780198716785.001.0001.

Demeter, Tamás. 2012. "Hume's Experimental Method", *British Journal for the History of Philosophy*, 20/3, 577–599. doi:10.1080/09608788.2012.670842.

Demeter, Tamás. 2014. "Enlarging the Bounds of Moral Philosophy: Newton's Method and Hume's Science of Man" in Z. Biener, E. Schliesser (eds), *Newton and Empiricism*, New York: Oxford University Press, 171–204. doi:10.1093/acprof:oso/9780199337095.003.0008.

Demeter, Tamás. 2016. *David Hume and the Culture of Scottish Newtonianism: Methodology and Ideology in Enlightenment Inquiry*, Leiden: Brill.

Demeter, Tamás. 2017. "A Chemistry of Human Nature: Chemical Imagery in Hume's Treatise", *Early Science and Medicine*, 22/2–3, 208–228. doi:10.1163/15733823–15702223p05.

Demeter, Tamás. 2019a. "Hume's Science of Mind and Newtonianism" in E. Schliesser, C. Smeenk (eds), *The Oxford Handbook of Newton*. doi:10.1093/oxfordhb/9780199930418.013.19.

Demeter, Tamás. 2019b. "Hume on Moral Responsibility and Free Will" in A. Coventry, A. Sager (eds), *The Humean Mind*, London: Routledge, 223–235. doi:10.4324/9781138323032–18.

Demeter, Tamás. 2019c. "Hume on the Social Construction of Mathematical Knowledge", *Synthese*, 196, 3615–3631. doi:10.1007/s11229-11017-1655-x.

Demeter, Tamás. 2020. "The Science in Hume's Science of Man", *Journal of Scottish Philosophy*, 18/3, 257–271. doi:10.3366/jsp.2020.0276.

Demeter, Tamás. 2021. "Fodor's Guide to the Humean Mind", *Synthese*, doi:10.1007/s11229-11021-03028-03024.

Donovan, Arthur. 1975. *Philosophical Chemistry in the Scottish Enlightenment*. Edinburgh: Edinburgh University Press.

Fodor, Jerry. 1983. *The Modularity of Mind*. Cambridge, MA: MIT Press.

Forget, Evelyn L. 2003. "Evocations of Sympathy: Sympathetic Imagery in Eighteenth-Century Social Theory and Physiology", *History of Political Economy* 35, annual supplement, 282–308. doi:10.1215/00182702-00182735-Suppl_1-282.

Garrett, Don. 2015. *Hume*. London: Routledge.

Gelfert, Axel. 2013. "Hume on Curiosity", *British Journal for the History of Philosophy*, 21/4, 711–732. doi:10.1080/09608788.2013.792238.

Ghosh, Peter. 1994. "Some Problems with Talcott Parsons' Version of 'The Protestant Ethic'", *Archives Européennes de Sociologie*, 35/1, 104–123.

Gordon, Scott. 1991. *The History and Philosophy of Social Science*, London: Routledge.

Henry, John. 1994. "'Pray Do Not Ascribe That Notion to Me': God and Newton's Gravity", in J.E. Force, R.H. Popkin (eds), *The Books of Nature and Scripture: Recent Essays on Natural Philosophy, Theology and Biblical Criticism in the Netherlands of Spinoza's Time and the British Isles of Newton's Time*, Dordrecht: Kluwer, 123–147.

Howe, Richard Herbert. 1978. "Max Weber's Elective Affinities: Sociology within the Bounds of Pure Reason", *American Journal of Sociology*, 78/2, 366–385.

Kervick, Dan. 2018. "Hume's Colors and Newton's Colored Lights", *Journal of Scottish Philosophy*, 16/1, 1–18. doi:10.3366/jsp.2018.0180.

Kim, Mi Gyung. 2003. *Affinity, that Elusive Dream: A Genealogy of the Chemical Revolution*. Cambridge, MA: MIT Press.

Klein, Ursula and Lefèvre, Wolfgang. 2007. *Materials in Eighteenth Century Science: A Historical Ontology*, Cambridge, MA: MIT Press.

Knight, David. 2003. "Sympathy, Attraction, and Elective Affinity", *XVII–XVIII. Bulletin de la société d'études anglo-américaines des XVIIe et XVIIIe siècles*, 56, 21–30. doi:10.3406/xvii.2003.1814.

Lawrence, Christopher. 1979. "The Nervous System and Society in the Scottish Enlightenment" in B. Barnes, S. Shapin (eds), *Natural Order: Historical Studies of Scientific Culture*, London: Routledge, 19–40.

Levere, Trevor Harvey. 2001. *Transforming Matter: A History of Chemistry from Alchemy to the Buckyball*, Baltimore: Johns Hopkins University Press.

McKinnon, Andrew M. 2010. "Elective Affinities of the Protestant Ethic: Weber and the Chemistry of Capitalism", *Sociological Theory*, 28/1, 108–126. doi:10.1111/j.1467-9558.2009.01367.x.

Morris, William Edward and Brown, Charlotte R. 2019. "David Hume" in E. Zalta (ed.), *Stanford Encyclopedia of Philosophy* (Spring 2020 Edition). https://plato.stanford.edu/archives/spr2020/entries/hume/.

Newton, Isaac and Janiak, Andrew. 2004. *Isaac Newton: Philosophical Writings*. Cambridge: Cambridge University Press.

Owen, David. 2009. "Hume and the Mechanics of Mind: Impressions, Ideas, and Association" in D. Norton, J. Taylor (eds), *The Cambridge Companion to Hume*, 2nd ed., Cambridge: Cambridge University Press, 70–104.

Packham, Catherine. 2012. *Eighteenth-Century Vitalism: Bodies, Culture, Politics*. Basingstoke: Palgrave. doi:10.1057/9780230368392.

Penelhum, Terence. 1985. *Butler*, London: Routledge.

Qu, Hsueh. 2018. "Hume's (ad hoc?) Appeal to the Calm Passions", *Archiv für die Geschichte der Philosophie*, 100/4, 444–469. doi:10.1515/agph-2018-4003.

Ringer, Fritz. 1997. *Max Weber's Methodology: The Unification of the Cultural and Social Sciences*, Cambridge, MA: Harvard University Press.

Schabas, Margaret. 2004. *The Natural Origins of Economics*, Chicago: University of Chicago Press.

Schabas, Margaret. 2020. "David Hume as a Proto-Weberian: Commerce, Protestantism, and Secular Culture", *Social Philosophy and Policy*, 37/1, 190–212. doi:10.1017/S0265052520000114.

Schabas, Margaret and Wennerlind, Carl. 2020. *A Philosophers' Economist: Hume and the Rise of Capitalism*, Chicago: University of Chicago Press.

Schliesser, Eric. 2004. "Hume's Missing Shade of Blue Reconsidered from a Newtonian Perspective", *Journal of Scottish Philosophy*, 2/2, 164–175. doi:10.3366/jsp.2004.2.2.164.

Schliesser, Eric. 2010. "Without God: Gravity as a Relational Property of Matter in Newton" in P.R. Anstey, D. Jalobeanu (eds), *Vanishing Matter and the Laws of Nature: Descartes and Beyond*, London: Routledge, 80–100. doi:10.4324/9780203833384.

Schofield, Robert E. 1969. *Mechanism and Materialism: British Natural Philosophy in an Age of Reason*, Princeton: Princeton University Press.

Stroud, Barry. 1977. *Hume*. London: Routledge.

Taylor, Jacqueline. 2015. *Reflecting Subjects. Passions, Sympathy, and Society in Hume's Philosophy*. Oxford: Oxford University Press.

Wennerlind, Carl. 2008. "An Artificial Virtue and the Oil of Commerce: A Synthetic View of Hume's Theory of Money" in C. Wennerlind, M. Schabas (eds), *David Hume's Political Economy*, London: Routledge, 105–126.

Wilson, Catherine. 2016. "Hume and Vital Materialism", *British Journal for the History of Philosophy*, 24/5, 1002–1021. doi:10.1080/09608788.2016.1149444.

Wolfe, Charles T. 2014. "On the Role of Newtonian Analogies in Eighteenth-Century Life Science" in Z. Biener, E. Schliesser (eds), *Newton and Empiricism*, New York: Oxford University Press, 223–261. doi:10.1093/acprof:oso/9780199337095.003.0010.

3 Adam Smith on organic change in moral beliefs

Craig Smith

Introduction

That Adam Smith's economic and moral theories complement each other and are characterised by a fascination with the phenomenon of unintended order is now a well-established view.[1] The aim of this chapter is to argue that we can further appreciate how *The Theory of Moral Sentiments* and the *Wealth of Nations* complement each other by examining their use of an organic account of changes in the moral beliefs and institutions that develop alongside a commercial society. The chapter builds on the work of Maria Pia Paganelli who has explored how Smith's evolutionary explanation of moral change makes a generalised connection between the increase of wealth and the refinement of moral behaviour based on individual mutual adjustment on a personal level.[2]

This chapter takes this organic account of changes in moral beliefs and places it in direct contrast to the deliberative consideration of moral issues by philosophers. Acceptance of the reality of an organic and evolutionary account of how beliefs shift over time invites scepticism about the detached consideration of moral issues. This will be illustrated by considering the specific example of Smith's discussion of the Graeco-Roman practice of infanticide. Infanticide allows us to examine his theory of moral change and how it relates to the generation of wealth; more importantly it will illustrate a direct connection between the normative value of commercial society outlined in the introduction to the *Wealth of Nations* and the organic theory of morality in *The Theory of Moral Sentiments*.[3] Smith considered it a matter of progress that infanticide was no longer widespread in "civilized and thriving nations" (Smith 1976b: 10), and his explanation of why that happened focuses on the individual experience of emotional reflection and moral judgment.

Mechanical versus organic imagery in Smith's work

Recent scholarly literature has had much to add to our understanding of the use of mechanistic concepts and images in Adam Smith's work. Eric Schliesser (2005) and Leonidas Montes (2013) have done much to stress the sophistication of Smith's methodological debt to Isaac Newton and the influence of

DOI: 10.4324/9781003138655-3

gravitational and mechanistic images in Smith's presentation of his ideas.[4] This has been complemented by Tony Aspromourgos's (2012) work on mechanical images and by Nicholas Phillipson's (2010) exploration of Smith's interest in mathematics and geometry. Less attention has been paid to Smith's interest in vitalism and physiological concepts, though Smith himself stated that he had engaged in the study of botany during the writing of *Wealth of Nations* (Ross 2010: 241–432).[5]

The aim of this chapter is not to challenge the importance of mechanical imagery in Smith, nor is it to assert the dominance of organic imagery. Instead, taking its lead from the aims of this collection, it intends to explore how Smith draws on the sensitive, cognitive, and social qualities of humans, how he makes them central to his theory, and how they form the basis of an evolutionary and gradualist approach to moral judgment. To do this the chapter will explore the two layers of Smith's account of social change in commercial society: the macro level layer of unintended consequences at the institutional level and the micro layer of unintended consequences at the level of individual moral judgments, which combine to provide an endogenous, evolutionary, and organic account of commercial morality. For the purposes of this chapter the focus will be on the micro level, but a brief outline of the macro level of institutions should be given first.

The evolution of institutions

The first layer of explanation, unintended consequences and institutions, is instantly familiar to readers of Smith.[6] It is pervasive in his work, particularly in the account of the fall of feudalism and the rise of commerce that appears across his writings. Through "conjectural history" Smith developed a stadial theory of cultural change which accounted for difference through time by reference to the changing economic condition of the country. The stadial analysis that is developed by Smith has become known as the "four stages" theory.[7] Within this stadial analysis Smith provides a detailed evolutionary account of the move from agriculture to commerce in Europe.

In Book III Chapter I of the *Wealth of Nations* Smith analyses how the "natural" progress of opulence (Smith 1976b: 377) in the relationship between town and country was reversed in the politics of Europe. His classic analysis outlines how there was a gradual shift in the feudal power balance between King, Lords, and Burghers (Smith 1976b: 401–2), and how this led to "Order and good government, and along with them the liberty and security of the individuals" (Smith 1976b: 405) being established in the cities before the countryside. The account is one where micro level changes in behaviour accumulated to transform the macro level institutional order of Europe in a process that, once begun, became self-reinforcing.[8]

As a result of this process, the rule of law, stable property rights, and political stability spread from the towns to the country, leading to his famous observation that: "commerce and manufactures gradually introduced order and good government, and with them, the liberty and security of individuals, among the inhabitants of the country" (Smith 1976b: 412). This, in turn, paved the way for trade to develop and for the division of labour to begin to unfold, with the subsequent exponential growth in living standards. Investment, driven by capital accumulation from parsimony and prudent economic conduct, laid the foundation for the immense difference between civilised and uncivilised nations.

Central to Smith's analysis of the economic growth that this transformation sets loose is a series of normative assessments as to why this is to the material advantage of all of the citizens of a commercial society. Smith's oft-noted use of the example of the ordinary labourer and the African King in Book I Chapter I of the *Wealth of Nations* neatly illustrates this, but commentators often overlook the short "Introduction" to the book where the same point is given an additional moral edge. Here Smith argues that savage nations "are so miserably poor, that from mere want, they are frequently reduced, or, at least, think themselves reduced, to the necessity sometimes of directly destroying, and sometimes of abandoning their infants, their old people, and those afflicted with lingering diseases, to perish with hunger, or to be devoured by wild beasts" (Smith 1976b: 10). Whatever other disadvantages commercial societies labour under, they are, in Smith's view, increasingly immune to such moral enormity driven by absolute want. High infant mortality and deliberate infanticide are features of undeveloped economies and uncivilised nations.

Smith attributes this to the ubiquitous "desire of bettering our condition" (Smith 1976b: 341), and he is clear that part of this desire is the desire to raise children. If "[e]very man is rich or poor according to the degree in which he can afford to enjoy the necessaries, conveniencies, and amusements of human life" (Smith 1976b: 47), then the ability of people to make a more comfortable life for themselves and their families is central to Smith's account of the benefits of a growing commercial society. In Book I Chapter VIII he makes this account explicit by linking the unintended macro level outcome of population growth – "The most decisive mark of the prosperity of any country is the increase of the number of its inhabitants" (Smith 1976b: 87–8) – to the liberal reward of labour and its capacity to allow a wider part of the population to maintain a family (Smith 1976b: 98).[9]

Smith tracks the impact of wage levels on population across growing, stagnant, and shrinking economies, observing that:

> The liberal reward of labour, therefore, as it is the necessary effect, so it is the natural symptom of increasing national wealth. The scanty maintenance of the labouring poor, on the other hand, is the natural symptom that things are at a stand, and their starving condition that they are going fast backwards.
>
> (Smith 1976b: 91)

Along the way he observes two particular cases that illustrate his point. The first is China where the horrific description of the poverty suffered by ordinary people culminates in a description of the pervasive recourse to infanticide. As Smith would have it:

> Marriage is encouraged in China, not by the profitableness of children, but by the liberty of destroying them. In all great towns several are every night exposed in the street, or drowned like puppies in the water. The performance of this horrid office is even said to be the avowed business by which some people earn their subsistence.
>
> (Smith 1976b: 89–90)

Smith's second example of the impact of a lack of growth on population and infant mortality is the Highlands of Scotland. Smith notes that it is not uncommon "in the Highlands of Scotland for a mother who has borne twenty children not to have two alive" (Smith 1976b: 97). The point here appears to be less about infanticide and more about high infant mortality in places where subsistence is scarce. This, of course, is important to Smith's overall analysis in Book I as the Highlands are precisely the example he drew upon to note the absence of the division of labour that results from a limited extent of the market (Smith 1976b: 31).[10] For Smith the division of labour is civilisation, and its absence is characteristic of savage societies.[11] This leads to the observation that:

> in civilized society it is only among the inferior ranks of people that the scantiness of subsistence can set limits to the further multiplication of the human species; and it can do so in no other way than by destroying a great part of the children which their fruitful marriages produce.
>
> (Smith 1976b: 97–8)

In a civilised commercial society infanticide and high infant mortality are features of only the poorest and most isolated communities where the limited extent of the market engenders poverty.[12]

From this we can see that Smith's analysis of the importance of rising living standards places the decline in infant mortality and the abandonment of infanticide at the heart of his account of commercial society. But Smith does not stop there, because infanticide and infant mortality also appear in his account of how moral beliefs change over time in *The Theory of Moral Sentiments*. To make this clear we can examine a brief outline of Smith's micro level account of how macro level moral beliefs emerge organically from individual moral judgments.

Moral change in the *Moral Sentiments*

Smith's primary aim with *The Theory of Moral Sentiments* is to provide a naturalised account of the development of shared moral beliefs. A key part of this is a quite deliberate diminution of the role of both religion and philosophy, a point to which we will return. The main steps in Smith's account are familiar, but worth sketching to emphasise how moral beliefs evolve in an organic fashion.[13]

The Theory of Moral Sentiments represents a part of Smith's wider, unified, project of providing a scientific social theory. Such a theory is based on a number of key assumptions. The most important of these is that there exists a universal human nature which is, at base, unchanging.[14] These "known principles of human nature" (Smith 1980: 293) are to be drawn from the careful observation of historical experience. Smith's conception of a universal human nature was not, however, a species of crude ahistoricism or cultural insensitivity. On the contrary, he made it the centre of his study to examine the differences that arise in human actions through time and across cultures. The key to his theory of the moral sentiments is sympathy.

Smithian sympathy is "fellow-feeling" (Smith 1976a: 10) with any emotion. It is a feature of human nature, a universal fact of human psychology and not a principle that allows us to prefer one action as more "sympathetic" than others (Berry 1997: 157). Moral judgment, on this account, is not to be understood as a detached process of rational argumentation, rather it is an emotional and imaginative experience where we reflect on what to do in the light of past moral judgments. Man "longs for that relief which nothing can afford him but the entire concord of the affections of the spectators with his own" (Smith 1976a: 122) such that we have an in-built desire to please our fellows that leads to a situation where: "Humanity does not desire to be great, but to be beloved" (Smith 1976a: 166).[15]

Thus we are led to desire not just to be loved, respected, and approved of, but to become that which is worthy of love, respect, and approval: to be praised and to be praiseworthy. As a result our morality is shaped on a personal level as we interact with others in our everyday lives. "Society and conversation" (Smith 1976a: 23) are the media by which we reflect upon and adjust our behaviour. However, as no individual can experience in exact detail the feelings of another, what we do as an act of sympathy is imagine what we would feel in a like situation: imagining from our own experience and our observation of the situation what they are going through.[16] We are then free to make judgments as to the propriety of their behaviour by resting our approval on its similarity to what we imagine that we would feel in their position.

Such imaginative sympathy is necessarily of a lesser degree of emotional strength than that experienced by the person in question. As a consequence, individuals limit their emotional responses to bring them closer to that weaker "tone" (Smith 1976a: 22) experienced by spectators. This is achieved by constructing a mental image of what an impartial spectator would think of our actions and then using this as a guide to what is acceptable or would be approved of by others.[17] By seeking to match the "pitch" (Smith 1976a: 27) of emotions to that of spectators we develop an equilibrium notion of propriety: a set of conventional attitudes that guide our actions on a level which will be acceptable to those around us. What Smith stresses here is that we begin to restrict our own behaviour even in the absence of actual spectators. We internalise our standard of impartiality and become "the impartial spectator of our own character and conduct" (Smith 1976a: 114), restricting our behaviour to what we have come to understand as acceptable. This is the guide to behaviour that has become known as conscience, "the man within the breast, the great judge and arbiter" (Smith 1976a: 130). We are capable of assessing our behaviour both before and after an action through the internalisation of conscience. This moves morality a step beyond relying on the *post facto* judgments of actual spectators.

Smith goes on to explain how such inter-subjective standards come to form the basis of custom and shape the "general style of character and behaviour" (Smith 1976a: 209) of a social group. To achieve this, he draws on a further aspect of the universal human nature: habit. Habits are acquired through practice, yielding a constant conjunction in the mind; and this conjunction is strengthened, growing "more and more rivetted and confirmed" (Smith 1976a: 41), through repetition. Habits, drawn from experience, act as a non-deliberative guide to our behaviour; they allow us to form expectations around which we are able to order our actions. Sociable individuals come to form unwritten or non-deliberatively generated conventions which develop into customary modes of behaviour as they are repeated. We judge others' behaviour according to how it fits our habitually formed expectation of what a person in their position usually does, and we become unsettled if they act in an unexpected manner. Our sympathy with their action is in a great measure dependent on a comparison with our habitual standards. We draw on our experience of society to assign standards of appropriate behaviour, but more than this, our own behaviour and our judgment of it, is shaped by a like socialisation.

Circumstances habituate us and guide our behaviour just as they guide our standards of appropriate behaviour in others. Custom, and the conventions that develop with it, are formed in a large part by context and, as we shall see later, this is of central importance to Smith's notion of social change through time. Ideas and practices become general by custom, that is to say that constant repetition leads to conventional expectations and relations developing amongst a people. Thus generalised moral principles are drawn from the repetition of actual, individual, moral judgments in everyday life: the judgment is "antecedent" (Smith 1976a: 159–60) to the rule. It is the experience-based judgment of the spectator and not the "abstruse syllogisms of a quibbling dialectic" (Smith 1976a: 145) that should be trusted as our guide.

The experience of moral judgment is, according to Smith, the reflection on our moral sentiments through the lens of the impartial spectator who embodies our sense of propriety. One consequence of this is that for Smith the moral judgments made by individuals are embedded within the societies that produce those individuals (Forman-Barzilai 2010). However, Smith did not think that this committed his theory to an account of morality as conformity to existing social norms. The account of the impartial spectator involves a reflection on the behaviour of ourselves and others, and Smith thought that the authority of conscience was such that it would support us in standing up to the disapproval of actual spectators (Smith 1976a: 131).[18] Smith's approach to social explanation and his account of the diversity of moral beliefs across time and space suggest that he was well aware of the variation in moral beliefs between different societies and sought to account for this diversity by examining the interaction of a universal human nature with different social circumstances.

The "stickiness" of custom

Moral value systems are produced inter-subjectively or inter-personally and are the unintended consequences of particular moral judgments undertaken in our day-to-day experience. Such customary behaviour affects subsequent actions and our judgments of them. It is in this manner, and not through philosophical analysis, that "accepted" or rather expected conventions of human behaviour develop. However as Smith is keen to note, such socialisation pertains within cultures, and as a result the formation of our character within a given cultural or national tradition can affect our judgments of other traditions and cultures.[19] What this shows us is that context has a vital role to play in the formation of habits and customary behaviour. Humans are socialised within the context of particular circumstances, within a particular society whose attitudes have been in turn formed by the particular circumstances that the people have experienced.[20] He writes: "The different situations of different ages and countries are apt ... to give different characters to the generality of those who live in them" (Smith 1976a: 204). The moral conventions that exist in a society are the result of a habituated balance of utility and emotion within the specific context of that society.

Thus, for Smith, a savage becomes inured to hardship and his behaviour becomes shaped by his circumstances. As he puts it: "His circumstances not only habituate him to every sort of distress, but teach him to give way to none of the passions which that distress is apt to excite" (Smith 1976a: 205).[21] The precariousness of the savage's situation leads him to stifle his humanity, to deaden his emotional responses, in order to survive and to secure subsistence. So experience teaches a savage the most profitable way to act. He is socialised by the example of others who have similarly learned from experience those practices necessary for survival.[22] This is not to say that a savage lacks particular emotional elements of human nature. Smith's point is rather that circumstances can be such that we "smother" or "conceal" (Smith 1976a: 208) elements of our nature in order to secure survival.

Adaptation to external circumstances accounts for much of the diversity to be found among peoples. But the circumstances in which individuals find themselves are not solely physical or economic in their nature. They are also moral. Humans exist in a social context, and experience those conventions of behaviour that have been formed by their predecessors and contemporaries. Individuals become socialised into a culture and habitually accept these conventions taking on the general "character" (Smith 1976a: 204) of their nation. This process, however, does not imply either an explicit agreement with, or endorsement of, these practices by each individual. We are dealing with habitual acceptance of circumstances: thus the habits of others become part of the circumstances to which we become habituated as we are socialised.[23] We need not have any conscious notion of the utility of these practices, but our propensity to form habits and desire for social acceptance lead us to accept them without any great thought.

Customary behaviour, insofar as it shapes part of the circumstances in which we find ourselves, becomes hard to change, like the "stickiness" of institutions observed by Christopher J. Berry.[24] Individuals continue to act in a habitual fashion even after the circumstances from which that habit arose have changed. There is a problem here. A custom is a habituated practice drawn from everyday experience and shared by a group of individuals in a certain set of circumstances. But the strength of habit and custom, added to by long practise, socialisation, and emotional attachment, is such that even after those circumstances shift the behaviour pattern lingers on. Smith's account of moral change needs to outline how consultation with the impartial spectator in a particular instance of moral judgment contributes to a macro level change in habituated moral beliefs. And in his discussion of infanticide he does just that.

Infanticide in *The Theory of Moral Sentiments*

The explanation that Smith provides for the origin of infanticide is grounded in a response to population growth in a situation of severely limited physical resources.[25] This form of behaviour, which Smith believes is contrary to human nature and feeling, arose in times of "the most savage barbarity" (Smith 1976a: 210) and became habitually accepted. Individuals put aside their horror in reaction to their circumstances, and the repetition of this practice rendered it a custom which became accepted by the people as a whole. In Smith's view such behaviour is understandable in situations of extreme indigence, but when the circumstances of subsistence change the practice continues as it has become ingrained. As he puts it:

> In the latter ages of Greece, however, the same thing was permitted from views of remote interest or convenience, which could by no means excuse it. Uninterrupted custom had by this time so thoroughly authorised the practice, that not only the loose maxims of the world tolerated this barbarous prerogative, but even the doctrine of philosophers, which ought to have been more just and accurate, was led away by the established custom.
> (Smith 1976a: 210)[26]

Smith recognises that a society whose general character is marked by a casual lack of concern for human life cannot long survive improvements in economic circumstances, arguing that no society can subsist in widespread customary practices that go against the tenor of human sentiment and feeling. However he does recognise that an anomaly such as infanticide can survive as a "particular usage" (Smith 1976a: 211). This is because it is possible for a custom to pervert our view of propriety away from our natural emotions in a limited field. As he puts it: "but the sentiments of moral approbation and disapprobation, are founded on the strongest and most vigorous passions of human nature; and though they may be somewhat warpt, cannot be entirely perverted" (Smith 1976a: 200).

If we apply the model of how moral beliefs evolve in an organic fashion to the "particular usage" of infanticide we see that Smith is able to provide us with an explanation as to how the custom came to pass out of use, and how people freed themselves from socialised acceptance of the custom. Smith's theory suggests that people gradually became aware of the incongruity of infanticide with the feelings of concern for children that are part of human nature, they came to be repelled by it, and as their material condition became more secure, rejected it as a practice to deal with issues of population.

Such a process relies, on at least some level, on a deliberative calculation – a weighing up of the pros and cons of the practice – which balances sentiment with circumstance. What is significant for Smith's theory though is that such deliberative judgments would occur in relation to particular cases of infanticide. They do not refer to a process of the rational examination of the practice as a social phenomenon, but rather to a feeling of repulsion leading to a belief that particular instances of the practice are unacceptable. The moral philosopher is of little use in this account of moral change. Instead Smith deploys an individualistic micro level explanation to account for the macro level change in moral attitudes. Just as he downplays the role of deliberative behaviour in the fall of feudalism, so his approach here, applied to infanticide, would view its decline as an unintended consequence of the mutual adjustment of individuals whose judgments are directed at particular cases of infanticide; rather than the result of the deliberate attempts of philosophers to critique the practice or of the legislative efforts of politicians and lawyers to prohibit it.

Through the interaction of human nature with external circumstances a group of people develop conventional forms of behaviour that are prudent given their particular circumstances, chiefly those relating to subsistence, which then become habitually accepted and form a standard of propriety in the emotional assessment of moral behaviour (infanticide becomes acceptable behaviour in situations of extreme material privation as individuals suppress their natural emotions in order to secure survival). Over time these practices become customary and individuals are socialised into the acceptance of them as the correct form of behaviour (infanticide is authorised by custom). When circumstances alter, as manifested by the increased security of subsistence, the previous practices continue to be upheld (as they were in Athens) but become subject to gradual and incremental change. As subsistence becomes more secure we move away from the immediacy of savage times and are free to give wider reign to the sympathetic and emotional aspects of human nature.[27]

With wealth comes the ease to allow our feelings a wider role in our judgment of action. As Smith puts it:

A polished people being accustomed to give way, in some measure, to the movements of nature, become frank, open and sincere. Barbarians, on the contrary, being obliged to smother and conceal the appearance of every passion, necessarily acquire the habits of falsehood and dissimulation.

(Smith 1976a: 208)

Or again when he notes: "A humane and polished people, who have more sensibility to the passions of others, can more readily enter into an animated and passionate behaviour" (Smith 1976a: 207).

Individual actors make decisions to cease the practice of infanticide based on their examination of their changed economic position and the incongruity of infanticide with the universal human emotional attachment to children. Infanticide becomes both economically unnecessary and emotionally unacceptable as people move beyond secure subsistence. The specific individuals who cease to engage in infanticide then internalise this stance through the impartial spectator and begin to form the opinion that the spectator would not approve of infanticide as either prudent or fitting with propriety. This internalisation through conscience leads these individuals to judge the behaviour of others within the group as unacceptable when they engage in infanticide. They express "sympathetic indignation" (Smith 1976a: 76) and make actual judgments of the behaviour of those who continue to follow the old custom regarding the "particular usage" of infanticide. Gradually, as more individuals become aware of the incongruity, those who continue the practice begin to feel the disapprobation of increasing numbers of their fellows, in particular those individuals who are close to them; they consult their consciences and make judgments that their behaviour in this particular instance is no longer socially acceptable. Thus as subsistence is secured and the disapprobation of their fellows reflects the change in propriety, they too come to internalise the new standard of behaviour.[28]

The internalisation of the new standard of propriety as an aspect of individual conscience derived from the experience of judgments of particular cases of infanticide allows Smith to explain how, over a period of time, the practice gradually falls from use, comes to be considered as improper and anachronistic, and there is a gradual shift in the conventional forms of behaviour within the group. The new convention becomes habitually accepted, generalised, and forms the basis of individual emotional assessments of proper behaviour. Individuals become socialised to accept the new standard of propriety and there is an organic change in moral attitudes. The whole model is marked by the organic and individualistic nature of its account of changes in moral attitudes. It also provides an account of the difference in attitudes held by succeeding generations. Though habit and custom deepen the acceptance of general behaviour they also allow for subtle shifts over time in the case of "particular usages". Thus when one generation ceases a practice from fear of the disapprobation of their fellows in particular cases, the next will internalise this as the accepted standard of decent behaviour and be repulsed by their ancestors' behaviour. As

Smith notes: "we are all apt to think well and commend the customs of the times we live in and to prefer them to all others" (Smith 1982: 112).[29]

Moral philosophy versus moral judgments

The example of infanticide has shown us that Smith's theory of the moral changes brought about by the increasing wealth of commercial society is conducted through the medium of individual instances of actual moral judgment. The practice of infanticide ceases in an evolutionary fashion, as Smith's organic account reveals to us. But Smith is not quite finished with this account. The endogenous nature of moral change has a further lesson to teach us. This is a lesson about the effective power of moral philosophy.

We noted above that Smith took a dim view of ancient philosophers' attempts to discuss infanticide, wondering how such humane thinkers could be so badly wrong about the enormity of the practice. The philosophers in question are Plato[30] and Aristotle[31] and Smith appears to be arguing that both of them are providing rationalised justifications of infanticide based on claims of the utility of the practice. Smith clearly thought this an example of a phenomenon that he described in scathing terms in the *Wealth of Nations*: "Gross sophistry has scarce ever had any influence upon the opinions of mankind, except in matters of philosophy and speculation; and in these it has frequently had the greatest" (Smith 1976b: 769). In the case of this "particular usage" the humane philosophers have allowed their attempt to reason concerning it to lead them away from the most basic human sensibility. This is a common enough vice among philosophers, as Smith puts it: "Nor can any thing more evidently demonstrate, how easily the learned give up the evidence of their senses to preserve the coherence of the ideas of their imagination" (Smith 1980: 77).

Smith peppers *The Theory of Moral Sentiments* with a series of unflattering comments about the place of philosophy in human life. For example in Part I Chapter I (Smith 1976a: 21) there is an extended discussion over the fact that philosophical differences are less animating to us than the absence of fellow-feeling, and shortly afterwards he describes how it is the society of everyday life rather than philosophy that soothes the mind (Smith 1976a: 23), while later still he observes that philosophers are bad company as they are too preoccupied by their own studies (Smith 1976a: 34). But perhaps most interesting are his comments that his examples are chosen from everyday life precisely to avoid our view of them being perverted by "wrong systems" (Smith 1976a: 17) or by a "refinement of philosophy" (Smith 1976a: 287). The whole recurring line of argument suggests that we can overestimate the role of philosophical reasoning in our behaviour (Smith 1976a: 87). These arguments culminate in the famous passage on the "man of system", where Smith charts the political consequences of an excessive commitment to enforcing a desired moral or philosophical system on a society of individuals who have their own views on such matters (Smith 1976a: 233–4).[32]

The empiricism of Smith's method and the pragmatism of his policy advice have long been noted, but what is less often noted is his argument that the process of civilisation is typified by individual-level sympathetic interaction and socialisation rather than deliberative philosophy. Though this should come as no surprise, as early as the *Lectures on Rhetoric and Belles Lettres* Smith was clear enough on his view, arguing: "What is founded on practice and experience must be better adapted to particular cases than that which is derived from theory only" (Smith 1983: 174). It is a view that becomes even more prominent in *The Theory of Moral Sentiments* where Smith argues that rules of moral behaviour pre-date philosophy. Humans develop the capacity to organically evolve their beliefs systems before they develop philosophical analysis. As he puts it:

> And thus religion, even in its rudest form, gave a sanction to the rules of morality, long before the age of artificial reasoning and philosophy. That the terrors of religion should thus enforce the natural sense of duty, was of too much importance to the happiness of mankind, for nature to leave it dependent upon the slowness and uncertainty of philosophical researches.
>
> (Smith 1976a: 164)

And it is also worth noting that Smith is suggesting that while moral rules are naturally associated with religion, they do not arise from religion. Instead they arise from particular instances of humans judging other humans and gradually become general rules – it is only after this that they come to be associated with the Deity.

Smith's project, like that of Hume before him, is based on the view that a successful theory of what we ought to do (a normative theory) must be based on an accurate understanding of human moral psychology. A "rational" system that provides an argument in favour of a particular normative position will fail if that argument is based on a partial understanding of how our moral thought process actually operates. Smith's point is that the way we make moral decisions is more psychologically complex than the reasoning of philosophers would suggest. And here we see that the desire for answers misleads philosophers who are desperate to create a system. In the *History of Astronomy* he criticises earlier philosophy for "grasping at an account of all things before it had got full satisfaction with regard to any one, hurried on to build, in imagination, the immense fabric of the universe" (Smith 1980: 107–8).

Moral change is not the result of abstract consideration of the "good": it is the product of everyday interaction and judgment. Changes in moral perspective are better accounted for through an organic and evolutionary development from actual instances of judgment. So powerful did Smith think this process to be that he cautioned against the designs of the "man of system", arguing instead that would-be moral reformers should not try to overturn the organic process through which human opinions shift. Instead the true man of public spirit: "When he cannot conquer the rooted prejudices of the people by reason and persuasion, he will not attempt to subdue them by force" (Smith 1976a: 233). Deliberate political reform is constrained by the operation of the organic development of changes in moral beliefs.

Conclusion

By examining Smith's model of the origin and evolution of moral beliefs as examples of the unintended generation of order a clear link can be drawn between economic progress and moral refinement.

When subsistence is secured, humanity is free to develop industry, science, and the arts, in short all of the "progressive" (Smith 1976b: 192–3) aspects of its nature that "ennoble and embellish human life" (Smith 1976a: 183). While Smith is not arguing that wealth necessarily leads to happiness or virtue, indeed he suggests it often adds to the stress of our lives, what he is suggesting is that security of subsistence and a gradual diffusion of wealth are prerequisites for progress in other fields. Smith's account of changes in moral belief is gradual, evolutionary, and organic. It downplays the deliberative and relies instead on the gradual loosening of the emotional constraints that extreme poverty puts on humanity. A society without infanticide and with lower infant mortality is a better society, it is, to use that favourite word of the Scottish Enlightenment, an improvement over what came before. In the *Wealth of Nations* Smith describes how "the vanity of the philosopher" (Smith 1976b: 29) prevents him from seeing that he is a product of his education and socialisation rather than a "natural" superior to the street-porter. In his organic and evolutionary explanation of the decline of infanticide as a cardinal example of the civilising benefits of commercial modernity, privileging as it does the actual judgments of individuals above the abstract arguments of philosophers, Smith seems to be suggesting that when it comes to moral improvement, philosophers are usually late to the party.

Notes

1   See James Otteson (2002), Samuel Fleischacker (2003), and Charles Griswold (1999).
2   See Paganelli (2018, 2020).
3   Smith, Hume, and Ferguson all make reference to this ancient practice as an example of how a morally reprehensible behaviour can become accepted by even relatively advanced people. See Smith (1976a: 209–11), Hume (1985: 398–9) and Ferguson (1995: 135). Smith also discusses the authority of the father over the child at Rome in his *Lectures on Jurisprudence* (1982: 172–5, 449).
4   Newtonian method is "most Philosophical" and Descartes "very Dubious" (Smith 1983: 146).
5   For Smith as vitalist thinker see Catherine Packham (2002) and P.H. Reill (2005). For a more critical view see Charles Wolfe (2018).
6   See Hont's (2015) recent account of Smith's historically attuned theory of political economy.
7   See Höpfl (1978) for a detailed discussion of the "conjectural history" of the shift "from savages to Scotsmen".

 8 See *Wealth of Nations* III.iv. (Smith 1976b: 418–23) for the account of the fall of feudalism and unintended consequences.
 9 For a discussion of this see Paganelli (forthcoming).
10 Spengler (1983) notes that Smith regards the decline of infant mortality as an indicator of economic progress.
11 As he puts it: "In an uncivilized nation, and where labour is undivided" (Smith 1982: 489, 521).
12 Smith's views on infanticide and moral improvement form an important part of Eric Schliesser's (2017) analysis of Smith's blending of the roles of systematic philosopher and policy advocate.
13 For a more comprehensive outline of Smith theory see Fricke (2013).
14 Smith notes that the science of man is impossible without such a conception of a universal human nature. He argues: "Things of so fleeting a nature can never be the objects of science, or of any steady or permanent judgment ... The objects of science ... must be permanent, unchangeable, always existent, and liable neither to generation nor corruption, nor alteration of any kind ... Man is perpetually changing every particle of his body ... But humanity, or human nature, is always existent, is always the same, is never generated, and is never corrupted" Smith (1980: 121). For a discussion of Smith's project as a whole see Otteson (2002: 2).
15 Dwyer (1998: 9) argues that Smith's approach here is based on "the idea of a sentimental polity held together, not by the rules of the legislator or the wisdom of the statesman, but by small-scale sympathetic exchanges which gradually linked individuals to the larger national unit."
16 Broadie (2001: 104) and Skinner (1996: 60) both highlight the epistemic role of the impartial spectator in reaction to our limited knowledge. Though an appeal to the impartial spectator is obviously in some sense deliberate and involves conscious reflection, the purpose of this reflection is not the creation of a moral code. In this sense the moral code is an unintended consequence of a series of sympathetic reactions and conscious reflection on particular cases of sympathetic approval.
17 Leading Raphael (2007: 96) to note that Smith's impartial spectator "was meant to be a sociological and psychological explanation of some moral capacities" and not a justificatory moral theory.
18 For an extended discussion of this aspect of Smith's thinking see Hanley (2009).
19 See Smith (1976a: 195) and "In general, the style of manners which takes place in any nation, may commonly upon the whole be said to be that which is most suitable to its situation" (Smith 1976a: 209).
20 What Griswold (1996: 191–2) calls the "contextuality of the moral sentiments".
21 In the *History of Astronomy* Smith argues that the strength of habit is such that it shapes our emotional responses to external phenomena, making us "used" to certain things. He writes: "It is well known that custom deadens the vivacity of both pain and pleasure, abates the grief we should feel for the one, and weakens the joy we should derive from the other. The pain is supported without agony, and the pleasure enjoyed without rapture: because custom and the frequent repetition of any object comes at last to form and bend the mind or organ to that habitual mood and disposition which fits them to receive its impression, without undergoing any very violent change" (Smith 1980: 37). See also Smith (1976a: 30) where he describes how surgeons become accustomed to blood and gore.
22 For Smith's views on savage behaviour see Smith (1980: 48); (1976a: 153, 206–7). This behaviour is not unique to savage states: Smith also applies the analysis to commercial societies through the example of the behaviour of different occupations. Thus customary modes of behaviour become associated with certain professions and this behaviour is determined by the circumstances of the profession, the role played in it by the individual and the response to that role by others. The behaviour we come to associate with clergymen and soldiers is different, as the circumstances of

their professions and their socialisation into the customs of that profession differ. Through sympathy a concept of proper behaviour is formed and a notion of propriety developed according to the circumstances of each occupation. See Smith (1976a: 201–3, 247, 273–4).

23 This focus on the importance of individual situation is a prominent feature of Smith's *Theory of Moral Sentiments*. The passages on stoicism in Smith's work stress an approval for the adaptation by individuals to the concrete reality of their situations. He writes: "The never-failing certainty with which all men, sooner or later, accommodate themselves to whatever becomes their permanent situation, may, perhaps, induce us to think that the Stoics were, at least, thus far very nearly in the right" (Smith 1976a: 149).

24 Berry (2018: 75–87) refers to "institutional stickiness" as a preoccupation of the Scottish Enlightenment.

25 Hume (1985: 398) and Ferguson (1995: 135) make similar points to Smith.

26 What Smith wishes to highlight here is that even in what are considered advanced nations it is possible to identify anomalous practices that stand against the general character of behaviour. He illustrates this by noting that his contemporaries in Europe often criticise the Chinese practice of female foot binding as barbaric, yet just a century before it was considered normal European practice for women to wear binding corsets to alter their body shapes (Smith 1976a: 199). Smith's project is to examine these differences in attitudes and customs and to account for their change through time.

27 As Smith notes: "Hardiness is the character most suitable to the circumstances of a savage; sensibility to those of one who lives in a very civilized society" (Smith 1976a: 209). See Paganelli (2017) for a discussion of Smith's linkage of economic growth and increased sensibility. It should be noted that Smith also deploys this argument to account for the growth of science and the arts as wealth increases. Security of subsistence allows the mind the scope to pursue other interests leading to the rise of civilisation, see Smith (1980: 48).

28 This discussion draws on Smith (2020: 57–9), for a further discussion of infanticide in Smith see Smith (2006: 45–6).

29 Though, as Hope (1989: 86–7) rightly notes, notions of propriety are subject to change, but there are certain actions that are always "humane and decent" because of the universal aspects of human nature.

30 *Republic* 460 c, 461 c, (1974: 241–4).

31 *Politics* 1335 b 20–1, (1995: 293).

32 This is also apparent in his criticism of scholastic philosophy (Smith 1976a: 139; 1976b: 771).

References

Aristotle. 1995. *Politics*, trans. E. Barker, rev. R.F. Stalley, Oxford: Oxford University Press.

Aspromourgos, Tony. 2012. "The Machine in Adam Smith's Economic and Wider Thought", *Journal of the History of Economic Thought*, 34. 4, pp. 475–490. doi:10.1017/S105383721200048X.

Berry, Christopher J. 1997. *Social Theory of the Scottish Enlightenment*, Edinburgh: Edinburgh University Press.

Berry, Christopher J. 2018. *Essays on Hume, Smith and the Scottish Enlightenment*, Edinburgh: Edinburgh University Press.

Broadie, Alexander. 2001. *The Scottish Enlightenment*, Edinburgh: Birlinn.

Dwyer, John. 1998. *The Age of the Passions: An Interpretation of Adam Smith and Scottish Enlightenment Culture*, East Linton: Tuckwell.

Ferguson, Adam. [1767] 1995. *An Essay on the History of Civil Society*, ed. Fania Oz-Salzberger, Cambridge: Cambridge University Press.

Fleischacker, Samuel. 2003. *On Adam Smith's Wealth of Nations: A Philosophical Companion*, Princeton: Princeton University Press.

Fleischacker, Samuel. 2011. "Adam Smith and Cultural Relativism", *Erasmus Journal for Philosophy and Economics*, 4. 2, pp. 20–41. doi:10.23941/ejpe.v4i2.79.

Forman-Barzilai, Fonna. 2010. *Adam Smith and Circles of Sympathy*, Cambridge: Cambridge University Press. doi:10.1017/CBO9780511676352.

Fricke, Christel. 2013. "Adam Smith: The Sympathetic Process and the Origin and Function of Conscience", in C.J. Berry, M.P. Paganelli, and C. Smith (eds), *The Oxford Handbook of Adam Smith*, Oxford: Oxford University Press, pp. 177–200. doi:10.1093/oxfordhb/9780199605064.013.0010.

Golemboski, David. 2018. "The Impartiality of Smith's Spectator: The Problem of Parochialism and the Possibility of Social Critique", *European Journal of Political Theory*, 17. 2, pp. 174–193. doi:10.1177/1474885115572921.

Griswold, Charles. 1996. "Nature and Philosophy: Adam Smith on Stoicism, Aesthetic Reconciliation, and Imagination", *Man and World*, 29, pp. 187–213. doi:10.1007/BF01248555.

Griswold, Charles. 1999. *Adam Smith and the Virtues of Enlightenment*, Cambridge: Cambridge University Press. doi:10.1017/CBO9780511608964.

Hanley, Ryan Patrick. 2009. *Adam Smith and the Character of Virtue*, Cambridge: Cambridge University Press.

Hont, Istvan. 2015. *Politics in a Commercial Society: Jean-Jacques Rousseau and Adam Smith*, ed. B. Kapossy and M. Sonennscher, Cambridge MA: Harvard University Press.

Hope, Valerie M. 1989. *Virtue by Consensus: The Moral Philosophy of Hutcheson, Hume and Adam Smith*, Oxford: Oxford University Press.

Höpfl, H.M. 1978. "From Savage to Scotsman: Conjectural History in the Scottish Enlightenment", *Journal of British Studies*, 27. 2, pp. 19–40.

Hume, David. [1777] 1985. *Essays Moral, Political, and Literary*, ed. Eugene F. Miller, Indianapolis: Liberty Fund.

Kopajtic, Lauren 2019. "The Vicegerent of God? Adam Smith on the Authority of the Impartial Spectator", *Journal of Scottish Philosophy*, 17, pp. 61–78. doi:10.3366/jsp.2019.0224.

Montes, Leonidas. 2013. "Newtonianism and Adam Smith" in C.J. Berry, M.P. Paganelli, and C. Smith (eds), *The Oxford Handbook of Adam Smith*, Oxford: Oxford University Press. doi:10.1093/oxfordhb/9780199605064.013.0003.

Otteson, James. 2002. *Adam Smith's Marketplace of Life*, Cambridge: Cambridge University Press. doi:10.1017/CBO9780511610196.

Packham, Catherine. 2002. "The Physiology of Political Economy: Vitalism and Adam Smith's 'Wealth of Nations'", *Journal of the History of Ideas*, 63. 3, pp. 465–483. doi:10.2307/3654318.

Paganelli, Maria Pia. 2017. "Boys Do Cry: Adam Smith on Wealth and Expressing Emotions", *Journal of Scottish Philosophy*, 15. 1, pp. 1–8. doi:10.3366/jsp.2017.0148.

Paganelli, Maria Pia. 2018. "Adam Smith on the Future of Experimental Evolution and Economics", *Journal of Bioeconomics*, 20, pp. 20–28. doi:10.1007/s10818-10017-9265-9268.

Paganelli, Maria Pia. 2020. "Markets and Morality: Complements or Substitutes", *Erasmus Journal for Philosophy and Economics*, 13. 1, pp. 1–7. doi:10.23941/ejpe.v13i1.466.

Paganelli, Maria Pia. Forthcoming. "Population as a GDP Proxy in Adam Smith", *Journal of Scottish Philosophy*.

Phillipson, Nicholas. 2010. *Adam Smith: An Enlightened Life*, London: Allen Lane. doi:10.1007/s11406-11012-9371-9378.

Plato. 1974. *The Republic*, trans. D. Lee, Harmondsworth: Penguin.

Raphael, D.D. 2007. *The Impartial Spectator*, Oxford: Clarendon Press. doi:10.1093/acprof:oso/9780199213337.001.0001.

Reill, Peter H. 2005. *Vitalizing Nature in the Enlightenment*, Berkeley: University of California Press.

Ross, Ian S. 2010. *The Life of Adam Smith*, 2nd ed., Oxford: Oxford University Press.

Schliesser, Eric. 2005. "Some Principles of Adam Smith's 'Newtonianism' Methods in the Wealth of Nations", *Research in History of Economic Thought and Methodology*, 23A, pp. 35–77. doi:10.1016/S0743-4154(05)23002-X.

Schliesser, Eric. 2017. *Adam Smith: Systematic Philosopher and Public Thinker*, Oxford: Oxford University Press.

Skinner, Andrew S. 1996. *A System of Social Science: Papers Relating to Adam Smith*, 2nd ed., Oxford: Oxford University Press. doi:10.1093/acprof:oso/9780198233343.001.0001.

Smith, Adam [1759] 1976a. *The Theory of Moral Sentiments*, ed. D.D. Raphael, A.L. Macfie, Oxford: Oxford University Press.

Smith, Adam [1776] 1976b. *An Inquiry into the Nature and Causes of the Wealth of Nations*, ed. R.H. Campbell, A.S. Skinner, W.B. Todd, Oxford: Oxford University Press.

Smith, Adam [1795] 1980. *Essays on Philosophical Subjects*, ed. W.P.D. Wightman, Oxford: Oxford University Press.

Smith, Adam [1759] 1982. *Lectures on Jurisprudence*, ed. R.L. Meek, D.D. Raphael & P. G. Stein, Oxford: Oxford University Press.

Smith, Adam [1759] 1983. *Lectures on Rhetoric and Belles Lettres*, ed. J.C. Bryce, Oxford: Oxford University Press.

Smith, Craig 2006. *Adam Smith's Political Philosophy: The Invisible Hand and Spontaneous Order*, London: Routledge.

Smith, Craig 2020. *Adam Smith*. Cambridge: Polity.

Spengler, J.J. 1983. "Adam Smith on Population Growth and Economic Development", in John Cunningham Wood (ed.) *Adam Smith: Critical Assessments*, Volume 3, London: Croom Helm, pp. 395–406.

Wolfe, Charles T. 2018. "Smithian Vitalism?", *Journal of Scottish Philosophy*, 16. 3, pp. 264–271. doi:10.3366/jsp.2018.0211.

4 Malthusianism in and out of Darwinism

Naturalising society and moralising nature?[1]

Antonello La Vergata

Introduction

The present chapter attempts an investigation of the "life" of the Malthus–Darwin connection from Darwin's first reading of Malthus' *Essay* until its full unravelling as a socially and politically contentious nexus around one century later. My main point is that the *moral* side of Malthus' views played from the outset a major role in the debates on what is generally, but rather vaguely, referred to as "social Darwinism", that is the applications (note the plural) of evolution by struggle and selection to society. The *moral* framework of Malthus' argument on population, and his view of human nature in general, influenced the reception of Darwinism, and *vice versa*: Darwinism, or what was meant by the term, was often accepted or rejected according to one's judgement of, or prejudice regarding, its Malthusian component, and its more or less "Malthusian" implications.

Malthus and Darwin

Between 28 September and the first week of October 1838 Charles Darwin read the 1826 edition of Malthus' *Essay on the Principle of Population*. It was to be a decisive moment for the genesis of his theory of natural selection. In his *On the Origin of Species* (1859: 63), Darwin described his view of the struggle for existence as "the doctrine of Malthus applied with manifold force to the whole animal and vegetable kingdoms; for in this case there can be no artificial increase of food, and no prudential restraint from marriage". In a note on the geologist John McCulloch's *Proofs and Illustrations of the Attributes of God* (1837) Darwin used the expression "Malthusian rush for life" to refer to the struggle for existence (cit. in Ospovat 1981: 70). Darwin remained a lifelong Malthusian, and, as we shall see below, he applied Malthusianism to his view of man and society. After reading a harsh review of the *Origin* by the Dublin physiologist and geologist Samuel Haughton, who was also the author of papers applying mathematical techniques to problems in physics, Darwin wrote to his close friends:

> What has Haughton done that he feels so immeasurably superior to all us wretched naturalists & to all political economists, including that great

DOI: 10.4324/9781003138655-4

philosopher Malthus? [...] It consoles me that [he] sneers at Malthus, for that clearly shows, mathematician though he may be, he cannot understand common reasoning. By the way what a discouraging example Malthus is, to show during what long years the plainest case may be represented & misunderstood [...] As he sneers at Malthus, I am content, for it is clear he cannot reason.

(Letters of 5, 6 and 8 June 1860 to J.D. Hooker, C. Lyell and A. Gray, respectively, in Darwin 1985–, 8: 238, 242, 247)

Historians have debated the nature of Darwin's acknowledged indebtedness to Malthus. Was Malthus' role that of a "coagulant" (Hull 1973: 345), a mere catalyst of a process already underway, or the positive contributor of a missing element – in Darwin's own words, "the long sought clue" for a "theory by which to work"? If the latter, was the missing element the importance of the inescapable pressure of population growth in general or, more particularly, the importance of intraspecific competition, that is, between individuals of the same species (Vorzimmer 1969; Herbert 1971)? Some scholars described the impact of reading Malthus as a "sudden revelation" occasioning a "dramatic and sustained" response by Darwin (Kohn 1980: 148), or a "Malthusian revelation" (Richards 1987: 99). Others took it as "merely the culmination in the gradual development of Darwin's thinking, a little nudge that pushed Darwin across a threshold at which he was already standing" (Mayr 1988: 217). Some scholars argued that there were differences between Malthusian and Darwinian struggles: Bowler (1976) pointed out that in Malthus' view intrasocial struggle occurred only in primitive societies, while for others Malthus focused on struggle against the environment.

Also Alfred Russel Wallace, the co-discoverer, so to speak, of natural selection, repeatedly stated that he had been inspired by Malthus' essay when conceiving his own theory on the origin of species in 1858 independently of Darwin (McKinney 1972; Moore 1997). In the words of John Greene (1981: 7):

It is a curious fact that all, or nearly all, of the men who propounded some idea of natural selection in the first half of the nineteenth century were British. Given the international character of science, it seems strange that nature should divulge one of her profoundest secrets only to inhabitants of Great Britain. Yet she did. The fact seems explicable only by assuming that British political economy, based on the idea of the survival of the fittest in the marketplace, and the British competitive ethos generally predisposed Britons to think in terms of competitive struggle in theorizing about plants and animals as well as man.

Robert M. Young marked a turning point in Darwin studies by insisting on a "common context of biological and social theory". Malthus, he argued, was "the source of the view of nature which led to Social Darwinism – the social struggle for existence, the struggle for survival" (Young 1969: 111–112). "Darwinism", he stated, *is* social" (Young 1985a). More particularly:

> the pleasures and pains of utilitarian psychological theory became the rewards and punishments of radical reform movements. In effect, Darwin extended this point of view to the ultimate natural sanctions of survival or extinction. One can also say that Darwinism was an extension of *laissez-faire* economic theory from social science to biology.
>
> (Young 1985b: 3)

Following on the heels of Young, some scholars acknowledged that, "because of the enormous effect of Malthus of Darwin's work, biology remains permanently indebted to the field of political economy, as it does to the ability and willingness of certain individuals like Darwin to transgress the boundaries between fields" (Herbert 1977: 216; cf. Gould 1980: 67–68). Others went so far as to say that the *Origin of Species* itself

> can be characterized as evolutionary thought joining hands with British political economy […] The philosophy of individualism that Darwin subscribed to was […] a characteristic feature of British political economy from Adam Smith to McCulloch […] Darwin's commitment to individualism reflects an indebtedness to the political economists and the Benthamite deductive approach to political economy.
>
> (Schweber 1980: 198; cf. 1977, 1978, 1983, 1985, 1994)

Schweber (1985: 64) also argued that Darwin "obtained useful analogies for understanding the 'natural economy' from the analysis of the marketplace by the 'new' sciences of political economy and agricultural chemistry". In them, together with the writings of Smith and other Scottish authors, he found the idea that benefits could be maximised by competition, and he modelled the principle of divergence accordingly.

Schweber's thesis has been criticised (Ospovat 1981; Conry 1985; Gordon 1989; Tammone 1995; Pearce 2010), but other scholars have pushed the "contextual history" approach even further, alleging that Darwin's family fortunes, class affiliation and political leanings shaped his scientific work. According to Desmond and Moore (1991: 216, 267, 294, 421), as an investor in railways, Darwin confirmed the "Whig Malthusian ideals" of "rising industrialists, free-traders, and Dissenting professionals". He demonstrated that "evolution and utilitarian economics were perfectly attuned", or, in other words, that nature was on "industry's side", which was the side of the "middle-class Malthusians" and "the bosses". According to Janet Browne, Darwin was "so intimately familiar with the ideology of an expanding national power" that "selection by death or survival seemed [to him] an accurate description of what went on. Direct experience of imperial expansion encouraged him to see struggle, war, and extinction as inescapable truths of nature." In short,

"Darwin's social and commercial contexts appear to have both generated and validated his scientific ideas" (1995: 390).

According to some scholars Malthus was the vehicle which allowed an ideology to be downloaded into Darwin's theory, Darwin's mind being a fertile soil for such a transfer, and this set the tone for much subsequent "social Darwinism". What was meant then and what is meant now by this phrase has been the object of a growing body of literature (to name only a few, Hofstadter [1944] 1955; Bannister 1979; Jones 1980; Clark 1984; Bellomy 1984; Weindling 1989; Rupp-Eisenreich 1992; Bernardini 1997; Hawkins 1997; and Weikart 1999) and will not be dealt with in detail here. There were so many and contrasting varieties of social Darwinism that some scholars concluded that, having generated confusion from the outset, the expression would better be avoided by historians (La Vergata 1982, 1985: 961; Bowler 1990).

The interpretation of Darwinism as indebted not only to Malthus but to an entire British tradition and style of thought is as old as Darwinism itself. It was officially sanctioned by some of the contributors to the book celebrating the centenary of Darwin's birth and the fiftieth anniversary of the publication of the *Origin of Species*. J. Arthur Thomson, professor of Natural History at the University of Aberdeen, wrote: "At a time when pressure of population was practically interesting men's minds, Darwin, Wallace, and Spencer were being independently led from a social problem to a biological theory." The severity of industrial competition, and the phenomena of the struggle for existence which economic theory had discerned, had thus come to be temporarily exalted into a complete explanation of organic progress. Thomson quoted his friend, the biologist and town-planner Patrick Geddes: "The substitution of Darwin for Paley" was not "the displacement of an anthropomorphic view by a purely scientific one", but "the replacement of the anthropomorphism of the eighteenth century by that of the nineteenth". However, Thomson commented, the validity of Darwin's theory, "is not affected by what suggested it" (Thomson in Seward 1909: 15).[2]

On the same occasion the professor of philosophy at the University of Copenhagen, Harald Höffding, said that "in accentuating the struggle for life Darwin stands as a characteristically English thinker: he continues a train of ideas which Hobbes and Malthus had already begun". Höffding went on to suggest William of Occam and Duns Scotus, Berkeley and Hume as forerunners, and, in moral philosophy, "the school which is represented by Hutcheson, Hume and Adam Smith". As he was not "a philosopher in the stricter sense of the term", Darwin's "attitude of mind" was all the more representative of "that of the great thinkers of his nation" (Höffding in Seward 1909: 448).

It was probably John Maynard Keynes who pushed the connection between Darwin and the spirit of his age to the extreme, going well beyond the boldest generalisations of any present-day contextualist historian. He deserves to be generously quoted.

> The new ideas [of Darwin] bolstered up the old [of "Paley and his like"].
> The economists were teaching that wealth, commerce, and machinery

were the children of free competition [...]. The human eye was no longer the demonstration of design, miraculously contriving for the best; it was the supreme achievement of chance, operating under the conditions of free competition and *laissez-faire*. The principle of the survival of the fittest could be regarded as a vast generalization of the Ricardian economics [...] Therefore I trace the peculiar unity of the everyday political philosophy of the nineteenth century to the success with which it harmonized and diversified warring schools and united all good things to a single end. Hume and Paley, Burke and Rousseau, Godwin and Malthus, Cobbett and Huskisson, Bentham and Coleridge, Darwin and the Bishop of Oxford, were all, it was discovered, preaching practically the same thing—individualism and laissez-faire. This was the Church of England and those her apostles, whilst the company of the economists were there to prove that the least deviation into impiety involved financial ruin. The parallelism between economic *laissez-faire* and Darwinianism [...] is now seen, as Herbert Spencer was foremost to recognize, to be very close indeed. Darwin invoked sexual love, acting through sexual selection, as an adjutant to natural selection by competition, to direct evolution along lines which should be desirable as well as effective, so the individualist invokes the love of money, acting through the pursuit of profit, as an adjutant to natural selection, to bring about the production on the greatest possible scale of what is most strongly desired as measured by exchange value.

(Keynes [1926] 2004: 31).

This was very eloquent as a eulogy at the grave of *laissez-faire*. As a portrait of an age it is only as true as it is true that terrestrials all look alike to a Martian observer – or to someone sitting on the top of the British Empire.

It is interesting to note that such a view of the relation between Darwin and Malthus was shared by a variety of critics of Darwinism. "English Darwinism exudes something like the stuffy air of English overpopulation, like the small people's smell of indigence and overcrowding", wrote Nietzsche (2001, § 349: 208). The English were definitely "not a philosophical race", and the "English-mechanistic world-stupidification" was responsible for the fact that the "spirit of worthy but mediocre Englishmen – I mean Darwin, John Stuart Mill, and Herbert Spencer – is starting to come to prominence in the middle regions of European taste" (2002, §§ 252–253: 143–145). For Nietzsche, the struggle was not for mere survival, as it was for Darwin, Spencer and their followers, blinded by their shallow mentality, but an aggressive struggle for the expansion of life and power: "the overall condition of life", he said, "is *not* a state of need, a state of hunger, but rather abundance, opulence, even absurd squandering ... You should not confuse Malthus with nature" (2005, IX, § 14: 199). Nietzsche was a figure on his own, but others tapped into the vitalistic strand of German biology to argue that organisms did not passively adapt to external conditions, but were moved by an internal vital impulse to shape their environment actively. British biology, argued the philosopher Max Scheler (1915), was in line with what he called the "British competitive ethos" based on utilitarianism, individualism, a shopkeeper's mentality and, in the last instance, hypocrisy. It was the philosophical basis of what some German intellectuals contemptuously labelled *Manchestertum*. Needless to say, the tendency to see Darwinism as bearing the indelible stamp of British social and intellectual vices reached a peak during the First World War (see for instance Spengler 1918–1923). In a sense, the celebrators of Darwin's Britishness had brought it on themselves: they had served arguments to their opponents on a silver platter by creating a stereotype which could then be easily given a negative connotation.

Energy and improvement

Malthus presented his principle of population as a law of nature, independent of social and political institutions, and it was as a law of nature that Darwin considered it. Malthus, however, was a moralist as well as an economist, and his law was also a *moral* law. This aspect played an important role in his influence on Darwin, but it seems to me to have been underestimated by most scholars, and the reader will excuse me for dwelling on it at some length.

In the first edition of the *Essay* (1798), Malthus' moral message was clear: "evil [including, of course, that generated by the principle of population] exists in the world not to create despair, but activity" (Malthus 1976: 217). The aim of the whole system designed by Providence was "the creation of mind", and, as "the first great awakeners seem to be the wants of the body", the principle of population produced "much partial evil" but "a great overbalance of good". An indolent creature, man must be spurred to exertion by "necessity", which "has been with great truth called the mother of invention" (ibid: 203). Malthus' theodicy incited criticism in Anglican circles, and eventually he dropped the two final chapters of the *Essay* which contained it (LeMahieu 1979; Pullen 1981; Santurri 1982; Waterman 1983, 1991; Harvey-Phillips 1984; B. Young 2000; Cremaschi 2014). Yet the message remained in subsequent editions, although buried under a massive documentation demonstrating the action of the principle from primitive to savage, then to barbarian and finally to civilised nations. In the Appendix to the 1826 edition, the one Darwin read, Malthus wrote:

> If the contemplation of the past history of mankind, from which alone we can judge of the future, renders it almost impossible to feel such a confidence [that a fundamental and very extraordinary improvement in human society is possible], I confess that I had much rather believe that some real and deeply-seated difficulty existed, the constant struggle with which was calculated to rouse the natural inactivity of man, to call forth his faculties, and invigorate his mind; a species of difficulty, which it must be allowed is most eminently and peculiarly suited to a state of probation; than that nearly all the evils of life might with the most perfect facility be removed, but for the perverseness and wickedness of those who influence human institutions.
>
> (Malthus 1826, 2: 471–472)

Although cautiously wrapped in a convoluted prose, expressed as a personal preference, and preceded by an "if", the message would have reached the reader even if Malthus had not openly mentioned the inevitability of a "struggle through [...] scarcity" (ibid: 415), or described the "savage contests" between barbarian invaders and invaded tribes as an instance of "this perpetual struggle for room and food" (ibid, 1: 96).[3] The moral framework of Malthus' argument was still present in the interstices of the edition of the *Essay* that Darwin read.

Let us now read the main part of the famous passage of Darwin's Notebook D where the impact of his reading of Malthus was recorded. Single angled brackets indicate Darwin's deletions. Doubled angled brackets indicate Darwin's insertions.

> 28th [September 1838]. «I do not doubt, every one till he [Malthus] thinks deeply has assumed that increase of animals exactly proportiona[l] to the number that can live.–» [...] Even the energetic language of <Malthus> «Decandoelle»[4] does not convey the warring of the species as inference from Malthus.– «increase of brutes, must be prevented solely by positive checks, excepting that famine may stop desire.–» in nature production does not increase, whilst no check prevail, but the positive check of famine & consequently death..
>
> Population in increase at geometrical ratio in FAR SHORTER time than 25 years— yet until the one sentence of Malthus no one clearly perceived the great check amongst men.— [...] One may say there is a force like a hundred thousand wedges trying force <into> every kind of adapted structure into the gaps <of> in the œconomy of Nature, or rather forming gaps by thrusting out weaker ones. «The final cause of all this wedgings [*sic*], must be to sort out proper structure & adapt it to change.— to do that, for form, which Malthus shows, is the final effect, (by means however of volition) of this populousness, on the energy of Man.
>
> (Notebook D: 134e–135e, in Darwin 1987: 374–376)

In other words: in man, population pressure stimulated "energy" by the constant exertion of faculties; in plants and animals, where there is no preventive check, that is, voluntary abstention from reproduction does not occur due to absence of "volition", and only "positive checks" operate, its "final effect" was the selection ("sorting out") of adapted forms ("proper structure"). In man, the "proper" individuals were those who, according to Malthus, were the morally best, who escaped vice and misery by increasing their "energy"; in animals and plants, the winners (the "wedges" which "thrusted out weaker ones") were the physically adapted. In both cases, it was those who met the requirements that succeeded, and the result was improvement in response to a challenge: improvement of mind and character in man, improvement of adaptation to the economy of nature in animals and plants. A key word in the passage quoted above is "energy", but its importance seems to have been underestimated by commentators. It shows that Darwin saw an analogy ("as inference from Malthus") between a *moral* context and a natural context, in both of which there operated *one* law, which was both natural *and* moral. This enabled him to "translate" a *moral* doctrine into a natural-historical hypothesis on the cause of adaptation. It was not a *direct* transfer of *laissez-faire* competition from economics to nature. It was mediated by a moral view of the economy of both nature and society. We should not forget that according to Malthus men must fight first and foremost with themselves, in order to improve their "mind". The fact that many were called but only a few were elected was a consequence of differential success in the fight against their animal passions, the urge to reproduction in particular. Physical struggle and elimination could then be seen as the equivalent in the natural realm of the spiritual fight in man. Darwin may well have been a Whig and a believer in free competition by family background and political leanings, with his mind "well prepared" to profit from reading Malthus, but this does not necessarily imply that he directly transplanted political economy into nature. The transfer could not occur without the medium of an analogy. And the analogy was made possible by Darwin's fundamental belief in universal laws of nature which manifested themselves in different, but analogous, ways in all orders. In Darwin's eyes, Malthus' principle of population was a law as certain as gravity. A belief in natural-*cum*-moral laws explains why "exertion", "endeavour", "self-help" and the like pervaded the Victorian idea of "progress through struggle", and influenced the way in which the very theory of natural selection for existence was interpreted (Bowler 1990; Ruse 2010). In a word: Darwin was influenced by the *moral* side of Malthus' view of human nature as well as by its numerical argument.

I believe that my interpretation is confirmed by the occurrence of the expressions "final cause" and "final effect" in the same passage. "Final cause" is a teleological term, and Darwin used it elsewhere in his Notebooks.[5] This may have been due to Darwin's writing in a hurry – "final cause" merely, albeit improperly, being the equivalent of "final result". It might be due to a sort of linguistic inertia, as "final cause" was a normal phrase in the natural theology tradition in which Darwin had been educated. But it may also be taken as evidence of the analogy between, or overlapping of, the moral and the natural planes. It fits well with Darwin's image of the economy of nature in 1838. Malthus might well have cast a "melancholy hue" on society and human hopes, but in 1838 in Darwin's view of nature still resonated, in spite of the "war of nature", an echo of the natural theology view that, in Archdeacon William Paley's words, "it is a happy world after all!" (Paley 1802: 400; for a discussion of Darwin's relation to natural theology see Cornell 1987). As Shanahan (2004: 100) aptly remarked, one effect the reading of Malthus did not have on Darwin's theorising was to alter his belief in the perfection of adaptation. Shortly after reading Malthus, Darwin wrote in his notes on McCulloch's *Proofs and Illustrations*: "Now my theory makes all organic beings perfectly adapted to all situations, where in accordance to certain laws they can occur" (Darwin 1987: 633). A long and tortuous process was still necessary before Darwin abandoned perfect adaptation and formulated the "principle of divergence of characters" (in 1856 or 1858, according to different scholars: see Schweber 1977, 1980, 1985; Browne 1980; Ospovat 1981; Kohn 1985).

What I would call "the paradigm of energy and efficiency", or "progress through exertion", operated in Wallace too, indeed to a greater extent and more enduringly than in Darwin. Wallace was not a Whig and an unambiguous supporter of *laissez-faire*, and he eventually embraced a sort of socialism (C. Smith 1992, 2003a, b, 2004a, b; Fichman 2001, 2004; Raby 2001; Shermer 2002; Slotten 2004; Claeys 2008; Stack 2008). Yet he never wavered in his belief that adaptation through exertion led to increasing "harmony" – a key word in his view of nature's economy – between organisms (including man) and the environment. Wallace pushed his belief in harmony – not a static, but a dynamic one, of course – to the point of out-Darwining Darwin by proclaiming that "there is nothing in nature that is not useful", and attributing a positive value to pain in nature – something Darwin never did. Wallace's conversion to spiritualism (C. Smith 2008) merely added one further dimension to his belief, which was there from the beginning, that organic change was progress towards the better, indeed towards, in his own words, "perfection". Wallace's moral view of the economy of nature pervaded his social views.

The snake in Eden

Darwin's main supporter, Thomas Henry Huxley, was a convinced Malthusian. Malthus' conclusions on population, he said, "have never yet been disproved and never will be". There was

> nothing that more appropriately expresses it [the consequences of the excess of the number of organic beings with respect to nutriment] than the phrase, "the struggle for existence"; because it brings before your minds, in a vivid sort of way, some of the simplest possible circumstances connected with it.
>
> (Huxley 1863: 128)

The Malthusian threat was inescapable, like gravity, and Huxley invoked it in his political writings as a scarecrow against both "Anarchy" (by which he meant individualism pushed to extreme) and "Regimentation" (that is despotism and State socialism). Those who reasoned on *a priori* principles (a number of thinkers as diverse as Hobbes, Locke, the *physiocrates*, Morelly, Mably, Rousseau, Stirner, Wilhelm von Humboldt, Dunoyer, Bakunin and Auberon Herbert) ignored that "the political problem of problems is how to deal with over-population, and it faces us on all sides". All "political speculators", whether individualists or socialists, who promised "a millennium of equality and fraternity", were "reckoning sadly without their host, or rather hostess, Dame Nature". It was true that labour is the slave of capital, but it was also true that capital is the slave of labour. "The state of things attributed to the tyranny of the capitalist might far more properly ascribed to the self-enslavement of the wage earners. It is their competition with one another which makes his strength" (Huxley 1893–1894, I: 428–430). Over-population had two sources:

one internal, "by generation", one external, by immigration. "Theoretically", the elimination of want was possible by arresting both. That, Huxley said, was, substantially, the plan of the "Closed Industrial State" set forth by German philosopher Fichte,[6] and there was no other social arrangement by which want could be permanently eliminated.

Against what he called in 1873 the "administrative nihilism" of extreme individualists (which amounted to "reasoned savagery"), Huxley invoked some moderate form of public intervention. This was necessary, he argued, if England was to keep its place in international economic competition. Every year more than 300,000 new claimants "to a share in the common stock of maintenance" (one "about every hundred seconds") were added to the 36,000,000 people living in the British islands. The produce of the soil did not suffice to feed half the population. The other moiety had to be supplied from other countries in exchange for industrial products. But other nations also lay under the same necessity. The ensuing "internecine struggle for existence" required preserving the general good within the nation. But:

> Let us be under no illusions [...]. So long as unlimited multiplication goes on, no social organization which has ever been devised, or is likely to be devised, no fiddle-faddling with the distribution of wealth, will deliver society from the tendency to be destroyed by the reproduction within itself, in its intensest form, of that struggle for existence the limitation of which is the object of society. And however shocking to the moral sense this eternal competition of man against man and of nation against nation may be; however revolting may be the accumulation of misery at the negative pole of society, in contrast with that of monstrous wealth at the positive pole; this state of things must abide, and grow continually worse, so long as Istar holds her way unchecked. It is the true riddle of the Sphinx; and every nation which does not solve it will sooner or later be devoured by the monster itself has generated.
>
> (ibid, II: 210–212)

Or, as Huxley later wrote, even if the most well-meant and ablest social engineering succeeded in creating a new Eden on earth, "the Eden would have its serpent, and a very subtle beast too": the sexual instinct. The tendency to multiply with great rapidity that man shares with the rest of the living world would sooner or later reintroduce the "cosmic" struggle for existence into society. Indeed, "the better the measures of the administrator achieved their object, the more completely the destructive agencies of the state of nature were defeated, the less would that multiplication be checked" (ibid, II: 20–21).

According to Huxley, there were two conditions "of our salvation by works". One was that "our produce shall be better than that of others". That meant using "more knowledge, skill, and industry in producing them, without a proportionate increase in the cost of production", and keeping the rate of wages "within certain limits", as "wages cannot increase beyond a certain proportion without destroying cheapness". The second condition was social stability, which required that the price of labour should not sink "below a certain point". For, when "*la misère* reigns supreme", an explosion is likely to occur in the form of a revolutionary experiment, which sends society back to the chaos of savagery: "the animal man, finding that the ethical man has landed him in such a slough, resumes his ancient sovereignty, and preaches anarchy; which is, substantially, a proposal to reduce the social cosmos to chaos, and begin the brute struggle for existence once again". Huxley claimed that, having "no pretensions to the character of a philanthropist", and "a special horror of all sorts of sentimental rhetoric", he was "merely trying to deal with facts, [...] as a naturalist". And the facts were:

> [that] a certain proportion of the members of every great aggregation of mankind should constantly tend to establish and populate such a Slough of Despond as this is inevitable, so long as some people are by nature idle and vicious, while others are disabled by sickness or accident, or thrown upon the world by the death of their bread-winners.
>
> (ibid: 214–215)

However, no society "in which the elements of decomposition are thus swiftly and surely accumulating can hope to win in the race of industries". Britain was then faced with a dilemma:

> On the one hand, a population the labour of which is sufficiently remun-erated may be physically and morally healthy and socially stable, but may fail in industrial competition by reason of the dearness of its produce. On the other hand, a population the labour of which is insufficiently remun-erated must become physically and morally unhealthy, and socially unstable; and though it may succeed for a while in industrial competition, by reason of the cheapness of its produce, it must in the end fall, through hideous misery and degradation, to utter ruin.
>
> (ibid: 218–219)

As a remedy, Huxley advocated scientific and technical education: "a stable society made up of healthy, vigorous, instructed, and self-ruling people" would secure "the indispensable conditions of permanent industrial development [...] without which [...] the battle of competition cannot be successfully fought (ibid, II: 219). If supported by local taxes raised in industrial districts and attached to factories, schools "under the direction of an employer who desires to train up a supply of intelligent workmen" would not impose a burden on the State. The State "had much better leave purely technical and trade instruction alone". Huxley's personal leanings were "decidedly towards the individualists", but his individualism "should be stronger [...] if it were less vehemently advocated" by "many economists of the individualist school" (ibid, II: 225–226). It was, perhaps, [...] needless, and even tyrannous, to make education compulsory in a sparse agricultural population, living in abundance on the produce of its own soil; but, in a densely populated manufacturing country, struggling for existence with competitors, every ignorant person tends to become a burden upon, and, so far, an infringer of the liberty of, his fellows, and an obstacle to their success. Under such circumstances an education rate is, in fact, a war tax, levied for purposes of defence.

(ibid, II: 228–229)

As a Malthusian individualist, Huxley opposed eugenics. A government guided by "purely scientific considerations" could carry out a "horticultural process" in society by extirpating the "superfluous", that is weeding out "the hopelessly diseased, the infirm aged, the weak or deformed in body or in mind, the excess of infants born", while allowing to reproduce only the best, or most suited to the government's aims. But the gardener-administrator's attempt would eventually be doomed to failure. For our ignorance of all the laws of organic life makes it inadvisable for us to apply a "pigeon fancier policy" to people as we do to calves or roses. Furthermore, a despotic government, whether individual or collective, would attribute to itself a sort of preternatural intelligence, accompanied by the preternatural mercilessness necessary to achieve its objective. It would be at the mercy of demagogue missionaries believing in their own divine right (ibid: 21–23, 33–34).

Critics

Since the beginning, criticisms had been raining on Malthus from many quarters: Anglican members who objected to what seemed the dangerous implications his theodicy, Evangelicals resenting his preference for reason over revelation, Romantic defenders of nature's luxuriance and generosity, radicals like Godwin, free-traders like Cobbett, social critics like Ruskin and Morris (K. Smith 2013; Cremaschi 2014; Mayhew 2014). In the United States his *Essay* was interpreted in a variety of ways during the debate on slavery (Andrews 2020). Likewise, the Malthus–Darwin association was attacked by social critics for favouring materialism, atheism, fatalism and egoism. The critic to whom Darwin reacted the way I mentioned at the beginning of this chapter wrote that Darwin's argument was "borrowed from Malthus' doctrine of Population, and will, no doubt, find acceptance with those Political Economists and Pseudo-Philosophers who reduce all the laws of action and human thought habitually to the lowest and most sordid motives" (Haughton in Hull 1973: 222).

Then there were Marx, Engels and the socialists who followed them. Marx wrote that Darwin's theory was "very important", as it "delivered the death blow to teleology" and provided "the foundation in natural history" of historical materialism and of class struggle (MEW, 30: 131, 578). But, wrote Marx,

it amuses me that he [Darwin] says that he applies the "Malthusian" theory *also* to plants and animals, as though with Mr. Malthus the joke did not consist in that it did *not* apply to plants and animals, but only to humans—with the geometrical progression—in opposition to plants and animals. It is remarkable how among beasts and plants Darwin rediscovers his English society with its division of labour, competition, opening up of new markets, "discoveries" and Malthusian "struggle for existence". It is Hobbes' *bellum omnium contra omnes*, and it is reminiscent of Hegel in the Phenomenology, where civil society figures as "spiritual animal kingdom," while with Darwin the animal kingdom figures as civil society.

> (MEW, 30: 249; cfr. MEGA, II/3.3: 772–773; cit. in Weikart 1999: 26)[7]

And Engels commented sarcastically:

> Darwin did not know what a bitter satire he wrote about humans and especially about his fellow countrymen when he proved that free competition, the struggle for existence, which the economists celebrate as the highest historical achievement, is the normal condition of the *animal kingdom*.
>
> (MEW, 30: 324; MEGA, I/26: 83; tr. Weikart 1999: 69)

Both Marx and Engels poured scorn on those who, like the neo-Kantian philosopher Friedrich Albert Lange and the materialist Ludwig Büchner, endorsed Malthusianism uncritically (Weingart et al. 1988: 116–117; Weikart 1999: 83–101). Malthus remained anathema for Marxists.[8] As to other varieties of socialism, there were differences in different countries (Isemburg 1977; Jones 1980; Pogliano 1983; Clark 1984; Weindling 1989; Bernardini 1997; Weikart 1999; Stack 2003; Hale 2014; Donnini Macciò and Romani 2020; Gehrke 2020).

A number of Russian intellectuals, convinced that their own country was different and needed remedies for its alleged backwardness other than merely transplanting British bourgeois ideas, accused Malthus of naturalising and eternalising the social and historical conditions of England. As Daniel Todes has shown in his excellent *Darwin Without Malthus* (1989), what was a merit for English authors, was generally a defect for Russians.[9] When Russian biologists and political writers (whether conservative or progressivist) accepted Darwinism, they tried to de-Malthusianise it. Some did so by minimising the importance of the struggle for life as an evolutionary factor. Others explicitly rejected Malthusianism as a pernicious doctrine. As the conservative slavophile Nikolaj Jakovlevič Danilevskij wrote in 1885, "Darwinism was a pure English doctrine, with all the particularities of orientation of the English mind, and all the qualities of the English spirit", as exemplified in the cult of "usefulness", on which were founded Benthamite utilitarianism and Spencer's ethics, Hobbes' war of all against all, Adam Smith's, and Malthus' doctrine (cit. in Todes 1989: 41–42). The leading populist thinker Nikolaj Gavrilovič Černyševskij criticised Malthus' theory of population extensively (Markov and Melnik 2020). A Lamarckian evolutionist before 1859, he considered the theory of natural selection irrevocably tainted by its Malthusian origin and content. "Poor Darwin", he wrote, ignored that if you want to use a specialized science [that is, political economy] for your own work you should study it [...] And the result was the same as if Adam Smith had taken it upon himself to write a course in zoology [...] When this foolishness is transferred to human history it becomes bestial, inhuman.

Thus, "the vileness of Malthusianism passed into Darwin's doctrine" (cit. in Todes 1989: 37–38), and the result was "a theory worthy of Torquemada" (Černyševskij 1890: 280, 281. Cf. Venturi 1972, 2: 324–325).

The geographer and anarchist Pëtr Alekseevič Kropotkin's support of "mutual aid" against the "Malthusian war cry 'Woe to the conquered'" made by Darwinians (in spite of their teacher's recognition of the importance of social instincts and "sympathy") is too well-known to be discussed in detail here (Kropotkin 1902; cf. Todes 1989; Dugatkin 2011; Hale 2014). Like many progressive evolutionists in Russia and elsewhere, Kropotkin relied on the "Lamarckian" belief in the direct action of the environment on the organism and in the inheritance of acquired characters to counter the class-biased emphasis on the individualistic effects of natural selection.

"While not necessarily properly read and understood", Malthus was extensively discussed in France (Faccarello 2020: 83; cf. Béjin 1984). The first French translator of the *Origin*, Clémence Royer, celebrated Darwinism as "the universal synthesis of economic laws, the social law *par excellence*, the code of living beings of any race and any epoch". In her long introduction, and in many books and articles in the *Journal des économistes*, she attacked the "blind charity" which Christianity and democracy wanted to turn into a "compulsory brotherhood", thus "sacrificing the strong to the weak, the good to the bad, the beings well-endowed in body and mind to the vicious and sickly" (Royer 1862: lxi). "The law of the strongest" required free competition between individuals as well as between peoples and races. Yet Royer's very enthusiasm for Darwinism led her to reject Malthus' morals and politics. In a sense, she turned Malthus against himself. Darwin's generalisation of Malthus, she wrote,

is by itself sufficient to show with utter clarity how erroneous were the consequences which Malthus himself drew regarding mankind: as it is from the exuberance of a species that its perfectibility derives, to arrest such exuberance would be to oppose a check to its progress. It emerges from Darwin's book that that law which seemed brutal, greedy, ineluctable, and which seemed to accuse nature of avarice, wickedness or impotence, is, rather, the providential law *par excellence*, the law of economy and abundance, the necessary guarantee of well-being and progress of the whole of organic creation.

(Royer 1862: liii)[10]

To Royer, the direct adaptation to circumstances and the inheritance of acquired habits were as important as natural selection, if not more important.

However, she expressed the fear that the hereditary specialisation of habits might, if it became too fixed, lead to stagnation and regression. Competition was the remedy.

For the French liberal historian Edgar Quinet, "Darwin's great work" confirmed the Malthusian law of struggle and the views of those economists for whom competition was necessary for the production of wealth:

> Production of wealth by man, production of organised beings by nature: the same law at different degrees of universal law. Thus, in Darwin's conception, I find, together, Adam Smith and Malthus. Its strength consists in that the whole economic science of England circulates, vegetates and lives, thanks to Darwin, in the organic realms and becomes as it were the soul of nature.
>
> (Quinet 1869–1870, II: 256)

Applied to universal history, the law of evolution demonstrated that man was capable of self-improvement, and that, through the "new knowledge of nature", he could "adapt himself consciously to the order (*ordonnance*) of the universe and complete the edifice within himself as its architect". The evolution of morality ensured progress. Natural selection itself enabled man to take his destiny in his hands, and thus to escape "the divine law of the strongest" (ibid: 189–190, 194–195, 324; cf. Clark 1984: 25; Bernardini 1997: 88–89).

French liberal economists were less dithyrambic. Their reactions to Malthus' *Principles of Political Economy* were generally different from those to his *Essay*. When they discussed his views on population, they also emphasised its moral side, as Faccarello (2020) has shown in his detailed analysis of the reactions of French economists. The best example is probably provided by the Belgian-born Gustave de Molinari, founder and chief editor of the *Journal des économistes*. "As barbarous" as Malthus' doctrine might seem – he wrote in 1849 – "the fact remains that it is the expression of the truth" (cit. ibid: 138).

> Above all – Molinari stated in 1885 – it contained (and this is perhaps its chief merit) a vigorous and strongly motivated claim in favour of individual responsibility [...] If [man] does not fulfil all the obligations implied by self-government, if he does not put a brake on his passions and vices, he and the human beings who depend on him must endure the consequences of his careless and immoral behaviour.
>
> (cit. ibid)

However, most authors considered Malthus' view of human reproduction as too deterministic, and purely physiological. They therefore insisted on the role of education, social factors, technical progress or an increasing efficiency of organisation in agriculture (ibid: 133). Another representative of liberal economics in France, Yves Guyot argued that "for the last century, facts have been giving the lie to the law of Malthus, and showing that *a priori* laws are worth just as little in economic science as anywhere else" (Guyot 1892: 125). Malthus' law "might be reversed":

> The fact is, that there are in our civilisation a great number of persons who choose to limit, and who do limit, the number of their offspring. But the causes which influence them do not come within the domain of economics.
>
> (ibid: 125, 127, 130)

Guyot quoted approvingly parts of a text published by the Malthusian League, which "certain distinguished men, advanced thinkers" had set up in the "prolific country of England" in 1877:

> The prolonged abstinence from marriage which Malthus preached is the source of many diseases and sexual vices; early unions, on the contrary, tend to ensure sexual purity, domestic comfort, social happiness, and individual health; but it is a grave offence for men and women to bring into the world more children than they can suitably lodge, feed, clothe, and educate.[11]

As the new century approached, de-population became an increasing source of national anxiety in France more than in other countries. How could France withstand competition with other nations if the birth-rate was plummeting? An *Association pour l'accroissement de la population française* was established in 1896. Neo-Malthusianism was dangerous, particularly from the perspective of theorists of imperialism like Paul Leroy-Beaulieu (Tapinos 1999).

What about French biologists? Royer's emphasis on the direct adaptation to circumstances and the inheritance of acquired habits reflected an attitude widespread among them, and one which would become stronger as the century advanced, creating a neo-Lamarckian atmosphere (cf. Tort 2008) which was not favourable to what the biologist Ernst Mayr (1988) called Darwin's "population thinking". As a result, Darwinism did not find a fertile ground in France (Stebbins 1972; Conry 1974). A strong and successful tradition in physiological, cytological, embryological and microbiological research joined forces with a determinist environmentalism which privileged the direct influence of circumstances on organic phenomena at all levels of complexity, from cells to species. The role of "chance" was inadmissible in such an experimental-mechanistic approach: it would have been a violation of the fundamental laws of matter and of scientific rigour (Persell 1999).

Those biologists who drew social and political messages from their views of the relations among living beings stressed the importance of association over competition (La Vergata 1992). As the doctor, biologist and politician Jean-Louis de Lanessan (1881, 1903) said, the decisive form of the struggle for existence was not that of individuals against each other, but that against nature, and the "*association pour la lutte*" was its best weapon. Within civilised societies, where brute force had been replaced by mind, social inequalities distorted the effects of selection. As the doctor and anthropologist Paul Topinard said, Malthus' law, should not be confused with Darwin's natural selection. Competition was natural in society, as were intellectual, economic and social inequalities, but this did not mean that it should constitute the sole social and economic law (Clark 1984: 38; cf. 138–149).

In such a context there was no reason for a detailed discussion of the Malthusian grounds for Darwin's theory. No wonder, then, that when French sociologists considered the contribution of biology to the social sciences, they preferred to think of society as an organism (see below). The political context did the rest. The republican ideology that characterised the Third Republic stressed *solidarité* rather than competition (Hayward 1959, 1961).

Moral and physiological laws

What we might call, for commodity's sake, the biological assumptions at the basis of Malthus' principle of population did not go unchallenged either. Not a few criticisms came from a long-standing tradition in which physiological-*cum*-moral mechanisms were thought to ensure equilibrium between fecundity and external circumstances. Most of these counter-arguments were garbed in providential language, but they could be given a naturalistic formulation.[12]

Physiological and moral assumptions, as well as social and political concerns, lay at the basis of Herbert Spencer's "A Theory of Population, Deduced from the General Law of Animal Fertility" (1852), which he republished in the second volume (1867) of his *Principles of Biology* (1864–1867). As a firm believer in the self-adjusting power of "things", he saw universal laws operating infallibly in all spheres of reality. In his theory of population he appealed to the laws of nature as sanctions for the moral and political ideas he had presented in his *Social Statics* (1851), written before he became an evolutionist. Spencer argued that in any individual, whether animal or human, the amount of energy available for reproduction decreases in proportion to the individual's expenditure on maintaining life and developing itself; and, conversely, what is spent in reproduction is subtracted from other activities. Sperm cells, the nerves and the brain contained the same basic chemical substance, and the healthy functioning of the system depended on its well-balanced use. Yet, in order to fight the struggle resulting from population pressure, intelligence and moral sense must be applied with vigour. This causes an improvement of those qualities, and strengthens the nerves and the brain, which, in turn, leads to the establishment of higher, less fecund human types, until a final stage is reached when "the pressure of population [...] must gradually bring itself to an end" (Spencer 1852: 501, 506). Progress was ensured by the same population pressure which seemed to threaten it. "A Godwinian revenge on Malthus, Malthus turned on his head", John D.Y. Peel commented vividly (1971: 139). Spencer's tour de force naturalised Providence in a sort of secular version of natural theology (La Vergata 1990a: 124; 1985).[13]

Whether accepted or criticised, Spencer's theory was taken seriously by a large number of people: doctors, biologists, psychologists, economists and sociologists (La Vergata 2019). Its appeal lay in its promise to account for physiological, moral and social phenomena in terms of the universal and, in the last instance, physical laws of nature, as explained by Spencer in his *First Principles* (1862). Until the 1930s, "mental" or "nervous" strain were still alleged by some demographers, sociologists and economists as a cause of diminishing birth rates, although it was uncertain whether this was due to feebler sexual desire, to energy being diverted from the reproductive system to the brain, to deteriorating seminal liquid, or to a combination of these and other factors (see for instance Hankins 1930: 115–122, 1932: 181–188; cf. Eversley 1959). The frequent failure to distinguish the physiological reproductive capacity from the actual number of children produced aggravated the confusion between biological and social factors. The language of nerves could be used to make forecasts on the future of civilisation which were not as optimistic as Spencer's. "Modern nervosity" and excessive brain activity would become key elements of that typical and pervasive *fin de siècle* syndrome, "degeneration" (Chamberlin and Gilman 1985; Pick 1989), which also included loss of fertility (and of virility in males) among its symptoms.

Spencer's appeal to nature provided reasons for hope to some of those who, soon after reading Darwin's *Origin*, applied his theory to man before Darwin himself did so in *The Descent of Man* (1871), but who did not share the widespread belief that evolution by natural selection ensured further social progress, as it had in early and ancient times. The mill-owner, social critic and political essayist William Rathbone Greg had long opposed the Poor Laws on the grounds that they encouraged laziness, improvidence and vice, thereby abrogating Nature's and Providence's laws of *laissez-faire*, free competition, and supply and demand. The world, he thought, was so made that, if men were morally righteous, they would also be physically happy (Greg 1843, 1849, 1851a, b, 1853, 1854). Malthus was a powerful ally in opposing the Poor Laws, but the law of natural selection he had suggested to Darwin seemed to favour "the multiplication of the race from its least eligible specimens", or the "non-survival of the fittest" (Greg's own expression, modelled on Spencer's "survival of the fittest"). In civilised nations, the educated, healthy and virtuous classes were threatened with being outnumbered by the "unfittest", who multiplied recklessly.[14] As an example, Greg mentioned the fact that "the careless, squalid, unaspiring Irishman, fed on potatoes, living in [a] pig-stye, doting on a superstition, multiplies like rabbits or ephemera", whereas "the frugal, foreseeing, self-respecting, ambitious Scot, stern in morality, spiritual in his faith, sagacious and disciplined in his intelligence, passes his best years in struggle and in celibacy, marries late, and leaves few behind him". In order to prevent disasters, the State should exercise "a salutary but unrelenting paternal despotism, and supply the deficiency [of restraint] by vigilant and timely prohibition", as well as by raising the cultural level of the poor (Greg 1868, 361): a conclusion hardly consonant with Spencer's advocacy of unrestrained *laissez-faire*, and not exactly in tune with Malthus' political views. Yet, if the world was providentially organised in order to provide stimulus to exertion in the "struggle for life", or "race of life" (terms Greg used before reading Darwin), how could a law of nature – natural selection – generate opposite results? In an essay entitled "Malthus notwithstanding" (1872, rept. in Greg 1874a) Greg confessed that he had been trying to show that Malthus' premises were wrong. He had failed, but only until he reconsidered Spencer's law. In 1868 he had mentioned it fleetingly, but he now defined it as "a masterpiece of rigorous reasoning". As "physiological influences or laws" dispelled the Malthusian ghost, Greg restated his faith in the "wonderful" effectiveness of the *vis medicatrix naturae*. Three generations of healthy life were enough to eliminate hereditary diseases, and hygiene would restrain "our morbid appetites". Unlimited progress was possible, provided we fought against three great enemies: the allegedly perpetual struggle for existence, the multiplication of the unfit, and the advance of democracy (Greg 1874a, 12). "Providence will be vindicated from our premature misgivings when we discover that there exist natural laws, *whose operation is to modify and diminish human fecundity in proportion as mankind advances in real civilization*, in moral and intellectual development" (Greg 1874a: 75; emphasis original).

The liberal economist Walter Bagehot took it for granted that education and the "habit of using the mind" reduced reproductive power, especially in women. In man this was not so much the result of great mental activity as of strain, anxiety, nervousness and that kind of higher intellectual work which caused "a subtle and obscure pain". The "female frame" had a limited amount of force, which, if invested in some way, could not be used in another. But what about the proliferation of the lower, non-educated people, with whom so gentle and nature-given a remedy would not be equally effective? Bagehot dug up a favourite of some of Malthus' opponents, giving it a particular twist: the diminished growth of population in towns was nature's compensation for its loss of vigour. Great cities performed the function of concentrating the "weakest and least valuable members of the race", such as alcoholics and criminals and other kinds of "lower nervous organisation". They could therefore be regarded "as a huge cleansing machinery, which, no doubt, shows us a great deal that is detestable, but also takes away much of it, and prevents more coming, not only in that place but in others" (Bagehot 1978: 336).

Darwin's cousin, Francis Galton, shared Greg's concerns, but the remedy he proposed, eugenics, did not rely on nature's wisdom.[15] Nature had been doing its duty so far, although in a slow, tortuous and painful way. But civilisation was now preventing it from continuing to do so; it was time for man to do better and faster by taking his future in his own hands (Galton 1865, 1869). But if, as Galton put it, man had to redress natural selection by a rational selection, the State should intervene in some way. Karl Pearson put his "socialism" in the service of eugenics (Hale 2014). But there was something paradoxical in the whole debate: on the one hand, for the struggle for existence and natural selection to be effective in favouring the fittest, competition had to be open and unrestricted; on the other, the very same theory seemed to justify restrictions in order to steer struggle and selection back on the right track, as if the Malthusian–Darwinian theory must be vindicated against itself. To some extent, the root of the problem lay in Malthus himself. His doctrine could be read as meaning that the struggle for existence caused by the disproportion between population and resources *must be reduced* as far as possible, in order for the beneficent effects of the principle not to be overtaken by its evil effects. But what if moral restraint was pushed too far, especially in the most prudent and virtuous part of the populations? Man's efforts should be applied in two opposite directions: lessening the struggle to avoid evils, whilst keeping it sufficiently alive to be beneficial.

Darwin's own attitude towards these problems was ambivalent, if not ambiguous. In *The Descent of Man* (1871) he quoted Greg approvingly (including his comparison between the Irish and the Scots, although he softened it by omitting any mention of potatoes, pig-styes and superstition). However, he thought that sympathy for those who suffered was "the noblest part of our nature" and had evolved from the social instincts of animals. Thus, he went on to say, we should accept the undoubtedly negative fact that "the reckless, degraded, and often vicious members of society, tend to increase at a quicker rate than the provident and generally virtuous members". Darwin felt somehow reassured by statistics showing that there were "some checks to this downward tendency", as the intemperate suffered from a high mortality rate, the "extremely profligate" left few offspring, and "some elimination of the worst disposition is always in progress even in the most civilised nations":

> Malefactors are executed or imprisoned for long periods [...] Melancholic or insane persons are confined, or commit suicide. Violent and quarrelsome men often come to a bloody end. The restless and unwilling to follow a steady occupation—and this relic of barbarism is a great check to civilisation—emigrate to newly-settled countries, where they prove useful pioneers [...] Profligate women bear few children, and profligate men rarely marry; both suffer from disease.
>
> (Darwin 2004: 162–163)

Quoting the biologist Edwin Ray Lankester, he added that intemperance was "so highly destructive" as to drastically reduce the expectation of life of the intemperate with respect to that of rural labourers at the same age. Darwin relied on the statistical inquiries of the Scottish physician and Superintendent of Statistics in Scotland, James Stark, according to whom "at all ages the death-rate is higher in towns than in rural districts", as well as those "of our highest authority on such questions", the physician and medical statistician William Farr. "On the whole", Darwin wrote,

> we may conclude with Dr Farr that the lesser mortality of married than unmarried men, which seems to be a general law, "is mainly due to the

constant elimination of imperfect types, and to the skilful selection of the finest individuals out of each successive generation"; the selection relating only to the marriage state, and acting on all corporeal, intellectual and moral qualities. We may, therefore, infer that sound and good men who out of prudence remain for a time unmarried, do not suffer a high rate of mortality.

(ibid: 166)

In this way both Malthus and natural selection were vindicated. And so were "*moral* qualities".

Spencer's theory of population attracted the same Wallace who had been inspired by Malthus on his path to natural selection. Wallace's battle for land nationalisation and other social reforms were in line with his belief that evolution would, and should, culminate in some form of beings "more perfect than man" himself. Influenced by Owenism in his youth and an admirer of Spencer's *Social Statics* (Claeys 1987, 2008) Wallace found support for his social views in the American political economist and journalist Henry George, whose *Progress and Poverty* (1879) became a universal best-seller. On 9 July 1881, he sent Darwin a letter in which he recommended it in enthusiastic terms. The book contained "an elaborate discussion" of Malthus, in which

Mr. George, while admitting the main principle as self-evident and as actually operating in the case of animals and plants, denies that it ever has operated in the case of man, still less that it has any bearing whatever on the vast social and political questions which have been supported by a reference to it. [...] It is devoted mainly to a brilliant discussion and refutation of some of the most widely accepted maxims of political economy, such as the relation of wages and capital, the nature of rent and interest, the laws of distribution, etc., but all treated as parts of the main problem stated in the title-page, "An Enquiry into the causes of Industrial Depression and of Increase of Want with Increase of Wealth." It is the most startling, novel and original book of the last twenty years, and if I mistake not will in the future rank as making an advance in political and social science equal to that made by Adam Smith a century ago.

(Wallace 1916: 260)[16]

George claimed that it was social injustice, not nature, that caused destitution and misery. With the right social conditions population growth would increase the collective power of people to provide for one another. Overpopulation had nothing to do with the impoverishment of the working classes. The fundamental cause was that people were shut off from the land, that is from the main source of wealth in any society (incidentally, this was Malthus' belief, contrary to Ricardo). The only remedy was to return the land to the people, who would rent it from the State. George also proposed a single tax on that rent to simplify the burdensome tax system that plagued both the old European societies and the newer American one: all taxes on labour, industry and trade that impeded their free development should be abolished.

Wallace invoked Spencer's "remarkable essay" on population to argue that in a well-organised society, such as that described in Edward Bellamy's utopian novel *Looking Backward* (1888), there would be no Malthusian danger:

> In a state of society in which all have their faculty fully cultivated and fully exercised throughout life, a slight general diminution of fertility would at once arise, and this diminution, added to that caused by the late average period of marriage, would at once bring the rate of increase of population within manageable limits. The same general principle enables us to look forward to that distant future when the world will be fully peopled, in perfect confidence that an equilibrium between the birth and death rates will then be brought about by a combination of physical and social agencies, and the bug-bear of over-population become finally extinct.
>
> (Wallace 1890: 334–335; rept. in Wallace 1900, 1: 509–526; cf. 1913: 141–143)

As "our present phase of social development is not only extremely imperfect but vicious and rotten at the core", the development of the nervous system has been limited to a small portion of the population. In a society organised as "a great family" no positive check would be necessary. Through later marriages and less children "a system of selection will come spontaneously". "The far greater and deeper problem of the improvement of the race" will be entrusted "to the cultivated minds and pure instincts of the Women of the Future" (Wallace 1890: 330–331, 336–337). Once freed from economic and social subordination, and the need to marry "rich but ugly, defective and rotten men", women will be able to select the best individuals with whom to produce healthy offspring and to care for them properly (Wallace 1916, 2: 160–161; cf. 69, 198–199; cf. Slotten 2004: 286–287; Paul 2008).

As the new century approached, it was depopulation rather than over-population that became a source for concern in countries engaged in imperialist competition (Winter and Teitelbaum 1985). In the latter part of the nineteenth century population growth rates had not followed the Malthusian exponential curve. The birth rate had started to decline almost uninterruptedly in most Western countries from about 1870, although absolute population growth continued to be high for some time to come. In the emerging discipline of demography, Malthus' influence began to wane, for it appeared that the forerunners in reducing the number of their offspring were the upper classes of society, and not the lower classes (Soloway 1990). The decline of fertility in general, and its differential decline along social class lines in particular, gave further impulse to the eugenics movement and to the development of mathematical analysis, which would in turn contribute to the development of a new approach to Darwinian natural selection (see below).

In the meantime, *neo*-Malthusianism had developed. Many were convinced of a continuity between it and Malthus' Malthusianism, but there was a decisive difference: encouraging birth control actively disrupted the moral meaning Malthus attributed to individual, self-imposed *moral* restraint, and would have abhorred him, who denounced contraceptives as "violations of the marriage bed and improper acts to conceal the consequences of irregular connections" (Malthus 1803: 11). In his *Autobiography* ([1873], 1924: 111, 231) John Stuart Mill, "an ultra-*neo*-Malthusian" (Winch 2001: 429) who "departed from Malthus' stern *paideia*" (Walter 2020: 34), recollected:

> Malthus' population principle was quite as much a banner, and point of union among us [young men who would later be called "philosophic radicals"], as any opinion specially belonging to Bentham. This great doctrine, originally brought forward as an argument against the indefinite improvability of human affairs, we took up with ardent zeal in the contrary sense, as indicating the sole means of realizing that improvability by securing full employment at high wages to the whole labouring population through a voluntary restriction of the increase of their numbers [...] The notion that it was possible to go further than this in removing the injustice [...] involved in the fact that some are born to riches and the vast majority to poverty, I then reckoned chimerical, and only hoped that by universal education, leading to voluntary restraint of population, the portion of the poor might be made tolerable.

In 1823 Mill had been sent to prison for distributing leaflets on birth control. During the 1868 election campaign he sent a subscription to the election expenses of the social reformer and apostle of birth control Charles Bradlaugh, whom he considered "a man of ability". In 1877 Bradlaugh was taken to court on charges of obscenity for publishing a book on birth control. He wanted to subpoena Darwin and to use parts from his works in his defence. Darwin politely refused: any artificial check on the natural rate of population increase would favour immorality, destroy chastity and undermine the family; over-multiplication was useful, since it caused a struggle for existence in which the fittest survived; population increase should therefore be encouraged, being positive in the long run, in spite of its immediate negative consequences (Darwin to Bradlaugh, 6 June 1877 (DAR, 202: 32). Darwin was a Malthusian, but not a *neo*-Malthusian.

Malthus and evolutionary biologists

If we turn to the debates on biological evolution we find that the Darwin–Malthus connection was much less discussed than one could have expected. Malthus' name was hardly mentioned in the most comprehensive accounts of these debates (Romanes 1892–1897; Plate 1903; Morgan 1903; Kellogg 1907; Delage and Goldsmith 1909). Nor was there any critical discussion of the

Malthusian basis of Darwin's struggle for life in the main works of those biologists who have a reserved place in all histories of post-Darwinian biology, such
as August Weismann or Hugo de Vries.[17] The former only payed lip service to
the Malthusian inspiration in an official celebration (Seward 1909: 19). The
latter mentioned Malthus only once in his major work to say that Darwin's
natural selection, "is simply the idea of a genius and does not directly follows
from Malthus's work" (ibid: 35). Important supporters of alternative views on
evolution, such as Nägeli (1884), Cope (1887, 1896), Eimer (1890 although he
discussed the struggle for life at some length), and Osborn (1917) hardly mentioned Malthus' name at all. In his history of evolution doctrines Osborn
(1894) simply made a few references to Darwin's reading of Malthus.

Curiously, the best example of this strange lack of interest for what Malthus
really said comes from within Darwin's own circle. The botanist Joseph Dalton
Hooker, one of Darwin's closest friends, and one of the first to know about
Darwin's speculations on the "species question", wrote to his American colleague, Asa Gray, after the end of the American Civil War:

> Did you ever read that painful book, Malthus on Population? I did the
> other day, and was painfully impressed by it. I had supposed he was a sort
> of materialist, who advised the checking of the population by restrictive
> means, and was surprised to find nothing of the sort, and a rather fine
> exordium at the end on a future state and the benefits of Christianity! His
> arguments seem incontrovertible to me.
>
> (L. Huxley 1918, II: 43, where no exact date is given)

His friend's book had turned the world upside down, but Hooker either was
not bothered to read it accurately, or he cavalierly skipped over what Darwin
had said about the origins of his main idea! However, Hooker made up
immediately for lost time and improvised crude applications of "scientific
principles" to society and politics. He had a "dogma" that "Brains + Beauty =
Breeding + Wealth". The war in America, which was a form of the struggle
for existence, could bring about "the only conceivable good" of "clear[ing] off
the mass of scum under which [the nation] groaned". He also embarked on a
somewhat Malthusian prophecy on the future of America:

> You [Americans] will one day have a property smitten *residuum* that will
> yearly increase in the same ratio as wealth at the other end—a class who
> won't be educated, and who will vote for equal distribution of property
> and of all God's gifts, for no "meum" and "tuum", but for "God for us
> all", and that god their bellies. Power and wealth will lapse into the hands
> of the strong with you, and laws will keep them there.
>
> (ibid: 38–44)

When they discussed the struggle for life, most biological critics of Darwin
concentrated on its *effects* on the formation of new species. They objected that:

1) some (self)regulatory mechanism was in operation independently of struggle and selection; 2) minute, fluctuating chance variations were too little, particularly in their initial stage, to have survival value, or were obliterated by free inter-crossing. For different reasons, neither biological Darwinians (and neo-Darwinians) nor their opponents seemed much bothered by the fact that the concept of the struggle for life had been inspired by a political economist.

Malthus and Darwin in the social sciences

In the second half of the nineteenth century the debate on the extent to which the social sciences should avail themselves of biology became animated. Darwinism, or what was deemed such, was invoked not only by supporters of traditional *laissez-faire* but also by supporters of what is now referred to as "Reform Darwinism". As remarked above, "social Darwinism" is an inadequate expression, as there were many different ways in which evolution was used in the social sciences. So much so that in many cases "social Lamarckism" and "social Spencerism" would seem more appropriate terms. It was often the case that one aspect of Spencer, of Darwin, of Malthus, or of this or that Spencerian, Darwinian, Malthusian, was set against another, according to expediency. The result could be better described by the technical term "mess".

The United States offer an interesting instance of this. The Harvard philosopher and political economist Francis Bowen (who had incidentally, as a member of the U.S. Silver Commission on currency reform, written in 1877 the minority report against the restoration of the double standard and the remonetisation of silver) said in 1879 that by resurrecting Malthus' erroneous theory of population from its death-bed, Darwin had aggravated pessimism, atheism, social disaster and cruel indifference to the poor. Social processes were the opposite of natural ones. Far from adopting a socialist alternative, Bowen believed that the higher, fittest but less prolific classes should reproduce more (Hofstadter 1955). Surely this was nothing other than an invitation to undo the Malthusian message.

The sociologist Lester Frank Ward, author of the first comprehensive treatise of sociology published in the United States (1883) was a supporter of rational, planned social action to curb competitive individualism. He argued that man was the only animal to which Malthus' law did not apply (Ward 1893: 134–135). "The psychic element, the intellectual, or inventive faculty" endowed man with "the power of completely destroying the relations between the law of population and that of subsistence by regulating both". But for the barriers to "the equitable distribution of the products of thought and labor [...] there could never be any danger that population would outstrip the means of subsistence". Thanks to steam and other mechanical powers, production was now "practically unlimited", and "the power of mind [could be] exercised in rational restraint and in control of the laws of production". "The character rather than the number of offspring", that is "the quality instead of the quantity of the population" should now become the chief concern. As "intelligence [...]

exempts man from the operation of the Malthusian law", but "the natural development of the native capacity for intelligence does not keep pace with the artificial requirements of the civilized state", Ward formulated "another Malthusian law, as it were": "In the progress of civilization the capacity to acquire knowledge increases only in an arithmetical ratio or some lower ratio, the amount of knowledge necessary to be acquired increases in a geometrical or some higher ratio" (Ward 1888: 21–23).

At the other end of the spectrum we find William Graham Sumner (1913; Sumner and Keller 1927, 1: Chapter 1). An inflexible supporter of individual competition as a law of nature, he was more Malthusian than others in believing that the foundation of the wage-fund doctrine, and of society itself, lay in the relative proportions of population and available land. He argued that where people are relatively thin on the ground, the struggle for existence is less harsh, but when there is an earth hunger democracy becomes impossible. In these circumstances rivalry for leadership in the struggle against nature is inevitable and leads to the survival of the fittest, since human beings, like any other organism, are unequal. Competition is a law of nature, and economic success is a reward for ability *and* virtue. Social, economic and moral or religious reasons lay behind Sumner's (in)famous phrase "the millionaires are a product of natural selection" (Sumner 1914: 90).

For another critic of the Ricardian wage-fund doctrine, the economist Simon Nelson Patten (1894), Ward's sociology was still too biological. However, Patten was also of the opinion that Malthus' doctrine of a permanent natural rate of increase in man was rigid and abstract, and was disproved by a correct understanding of Darwinism itself: evolution implied that man's social behaviour was susceptible to change depending to circumstances (Patten 1885: 78–79). Like Ward, Patten relied on the inheritance of acquired characters as the material basis for the transmission of education and culture, and, in the last instance, progress. Faced with Weismann's denial of the inheritance of acquired characteristics, many sociologists, in the United States and in Europe, stood their ground for a long time. Patten eventually acknowledged defeat, but, as an opponent of the anti-environmentalism of eugenics, expressed his yearning for the old belief: the "social worker", he said in 1912, "thinks that his efforts to help individuals are of social importance, and hence sympathises with, and suffers from the downfall of Lamarckianism" (cit. in Stocking 1971: 255).

Malthusianism could hardly find an audience among the social scientists who criticised as "atomistic" the views of society based on competition rather than integration. Those who wanted to allow a role for both were faced with difficulties. This was already evident in Spencer, who supported extreme individualism and *laissez-faire*, whilst at the same time pushing the organic analogy to extremes (the nerves like telegraph wires, blood cells like coins …), to the delight of the supporters of social cooperation. Against social reforms from above, utopian dreamers and State interference under cover of philanthropy, he argued that societies "are not made, but grow", that is, they develop according to natural laws, and cannot, and should not, be directed from above, as their spontaneous development would in this case only be altered to the risk of regression to a more primitive condition (Spencer 1969). But, Huxley asked as early as 1873, how could one reconcile individualism and social organicism?

> Suppose that, in accordance with this [Spencer's] view, each muscle were to maintain that the nervous system had no right to interfere with its contraction, except to prevent it from hindering the contraction of another muscle; or each gland, that it had a right to secrete, so long as its secretion interfered with no other; suppose every separate cell left free to follow its own "interest," and *laissez-faire* lord of all, what would become of the body physiological?
>
> (Huxley 1893–1894, I: 271)

As Spencer was probably the most influential thinker of the second half of the century, his ambiguities were reflected in the work of those who dealt with him. Supporters of free competition as well as cooperationists, conservatives and reformers (including some anarchists), Darwinians and (neo)-Lamarckians, all found something useful in him, and something to decry.

The importance of individual competition, and of Malthusian struggle, was downplayed by those who unreservedly adopted an organic view of society. A few examples will be useful. The Estonian-born Paul Lilienfeld, who was president of the Institut International de Sociologie in 1875–1878, argued that theories of individualism *à outrance* were one-sided and basically flawed. They focused on personal interest, without considering all the "psycho-physical factors" which act simultaneously in human society and modify the operation of this or that law. The law of the tendential imbalance between population and resources, which had been "discovered by Malthus and completed [*sic*] by Ricardo's theory of rent", and which was "derived [*sic*] from the struggle for existence and the survival of the fittest", was a case in point (Lilienfeld 1896: xxxii; a statement that is a wonderful instance of "reading back" and shows that many social writers considered Malthus and Darwin as one and the same). Malthus was right in principle, but wrong in the arithmetical part of his law, since the means of subsistence can also increase geometrically, "hand in hand with population". "Higher factors", neglected by Malthus, modify the way in which the struggle for existence acts in society: inventions, scientific developments, education, morality and above all the spirit of initiative and the "energy of labour" itself. By these factors, "the means of subsistence can be increased for an indefinitely long time through labour and capital, indeed much faster than population can multiply" (Lilienfeld 1873–1879, II: 267). Blinded by individualism, like Ricardo, Malthus had oversimplified a highly complex problem. His law was basically biological, not social (ibid: 273). A genuinely social law was instead that of "social embryology", according to which societies develop like individual organisms as a coherent whole, and that of "evolution (*Entwickelung*) and regression (*Rückschritt*)". By "social" Lilienfeld meant "based on a higher biology". He filled his massive volumes with bio-medical analogies, from which he drew lessons against "social pathologies".[18]

In his *De la division du travail social* (1893) Émile Durkheim argued that, although its supporters represented it as a logical consequence of the principles of Darwinism, the theory "which makes egotism the point of departure for humanity, and altruism only a recent conquest" was false.

> In the name of the dogma of the struggle for existence and natural selection, they paint in the saddest colors this primitive humanity whose hunger and thirst, always badly satisfied, were their only passions; those sombre times when men had no other care and no other occupation than to quarrel with one another over their miserable nourishment [...] The hypotheses of Darwin [...] overlook the essential element of moral life, that is, the moderating influence that society exercises over its members, which tempers and neutralises the brutal action of the struggle for existence and selection. Whenever there are societies, there is altruism, because there is solidarity.
>
> (Durkheim 1960: 196–197)

The division of labour in society did not originate in economic or psychological factors, such as Adam Smith's doctrine that individuals tend to increase their pleasure and well-being by developing barter and exchange. It was "not only a social institution that has its source in the intelligence and will of men, but is a phenomenon of general biology whose conditions must be sought in the essential properties of organized matter" (ibid: 41; cf. Hejl 1995). Durkheim referred to some zoologists, particularly Henri Milne-Edwards, and said that Darwin's principle of the divergence of characters accounted for the fact that in areas where the conflict of individuals was more acute there was always a greater diversity in the species which inhabited that area.[19] The division of labour was, to be sure, a result of the growth of population and the struggle for existence, but "a mellowed *dénouement*".

> [It] *varies in direct ratio with the volume and density of societies* [...] Thanks to it, opponents are not obliged to fight to a finish, but can exist one beside the other. Also, in proportion to its development, it furnishes the means of maintenance and survival to a greater number of individuals who, in more homogeneous societies, would be condemned to extinction [...] The division of labour unites at the same time that it opposes; it makes the activities it differentiates converge; it brings together those it separates.
>
> (ibid: 262, 270, 276; italics are Durkheim's)

It was not competition that determined this conciliation: "The individuals among whom the struggle is waged must already be solidary and feel so. That is to say, they must belong to the same society" (ibid: 276).

Another French sociologist, René Worms, recognised that the struggle for life was "the universal law of societies, as it is the universal law of individual organisms", but added that it "has produced alternately (*tour à tour*) the differentiation and the reconciliation (*rapprochement*) of social groups". This "divergence and convergence" has transferred the struggle from the military terrain to the industrial domain, "where it is less harmful", and to the mental, "where it is beneficent". It will certainly not cease for the moment, but "it will transform itself into the most useful form for mankind" (Worms 1895: 272, 279–280). Solidarity, mercy and sympathy advance alongside civilisation and make a family of society, whose weakest members must be aided as much as possible, "until differentiation might replace competition (*concurrence*).

The English economist Alfred Marshall agreed that the division of labour had a biological foundation.[20] Yet he also believed in "the law that the struggle for existence causes those organisms to multiply which are best fitted to derive benefit from their environment", a law, he added, which required to be interpreted carefully, as "those that utilize the environment most, may turn out to be those that benefit those around them most", but this is not necessarily the case (Marshall 1895: 322–323). Malthus' rates of increase were not to be taken literally:

> What he meant, stated in modern language, was that the Law of Dimin-ishing Return, which underlies the whole of his argument, would begin to operate sharply after the produce of the island had been doubled. Doubled labour might give doubled produce: but quadrupled labour would hardly treble it: octupled labour would not quadruple it.
>
> (ibid: 258, note)

Marshall also referred to Spencer's theory that "nervous strain" could reduce, and that it was probable "that the progress of civilization will of itself hold the growth of population completely in check" (ibid: 263, note). However, Mar-shall's discussion was convoluted, as he (like many others) proved unable to distinguish between actual birth rate and "fecundity", and was unable to make up his mind as to the effects of "severe nervous strain", of "luxurious habits of living", of the "active life" of "those who make little expensive provision for the future of themselves and their families", and of the late marriages of those who "have as a class more than the average of constitutional and nervous strength" (ibid: 264).[21] In a word, he did not distinguish between biological and social factors (a common confusion until as late as the 1930s: see La Vergata 2019). Whatever the case, when he reflected on nothing less than human nature, Marshall did not miss the opportunity to make a *moral* appeal to exer-tion in Malthusian style:

> The truth seems to be that as human nature is constituted, man rapidly degenerates unless he has some hard work to do, some difficulties to overcome; and that some strenuous exertion is necessary for physical and moral health. The fullness of life lies in the development and activity of as many and as high faculties as possible [...] Although the power of sus-taining great muscular exertion seems to rest on constitutional strength and

other physical conditions, yet even it depends also on force of will, and strength of character. Energy of this kind, which may perhaps be taken to be the strength of the man, as distinguished from that of his body, is moral rather than physical; but yet it depends on the physical condition of nervous strength. This strength of the man himself, this resolution, energy and self-mastery, or in short this "vigour" is the source of all progress: it shows itself in great deeds, in great thoughts and in the capacity for true religious feeling.

(ibid: 211–212, 275)

When dealing with human nature in the light of biological evolution, social scientists were faced with further problems. What about "imitation", "suggestion", "herd instincts" and other aspects of "crowd" or "mass" psychology"? To what extent did man's animal heritage influence rational behaviour? Or were the social faculties of *homo oeconomicus* "originally derived from an antecedent economic instinct", as Lindley M. Keasbey, professor of Political Sciences at Brynmawr College, Pennsylvania, wrote in the preface to his translation of the Italian economist Achille Loria's *Economic Foundations of Society* (Loria 1899: VII)?[22] The work of such authors as Tarde, Trotter or Le Bon challenged individualistic views of society and opened a new chapter in the social sciences.

The use of biological models was opposed by those social scientists and economists who, like, for instance, Walras, Jevons and Pareto, preferred "mechanical" models (Mirowski 1989; Hodgson 1995). This was partly a consequence of the lasting influence of Newtonianism as the paradigm of science (Cohen 1994). But it was one thing to look at Newtonianism as an ideal, and another to treat sociology and economics as physical sciences. Equations and a deductive approach did not marry easily with inductions from vital statistics. Furthermore, there were important differences between an engineering- or physicist-minded approach and a purely theoretical and deductive one. Far from coinciding, quantification and mathematisation were mostly pursued in isolation from one another (Porter 1994). After the 1920s, merely mechanical analogies were increasingly abandoned for mathematical models, and mathematical formalism became dominant in the 1930s and 1940s (Ingrao and Israel 1990; Andreozzi 1998). Whatever the case, it is a fact that Malthus was ignored or criticised by many continental "mechanic" or "mathematical" economists. Léon Walras, for instance, mentioned him only once in his *Théorie mathématique de la richesse sociale* (1883), and never in *Études d'économie politique appliquée* (1898). A supporter of Georgism, he pointed out "the errors in matters of pure political theory which were typical of the English school, such as the identification of the entrepreneur with the capitalist, and the Ricardian conception of rent" (1883: 179). He did not like "the empiricism and vague phrases" (1898: 302) of that approach. In return, his approach was accused of being remote from practice and aiming at merely abstract laws of exchange, as he himself had foreseen. Capital, Walras argued, must be created by saving before it can be used to make profit. Progress is possible, even when the quantity of land does not increase, only if increase of the quantity of capitals properly said precedes and exceeds the increase in quantity of people. A progressive society is one in which "capital increases faster than population [...] Social interest requires that population should increase, but that it should be preceded by that of capital". In what could be read as an implicit rejection of the moral sermons delivered by Malthus and others, Walras added: "Work does not suffice to make products; rent from land and profit of capital are necessary" (ibid: 37, 282).

Walras' successor on the chair of Political Economy at the University of Lausanne, Vilfredo Pareto, paid more attention to Malthus (Ingrao 1991). Malthus, he wrote, did not deserve the charges levelled by "ethical sociologists" and "sentimental anti-Malthusians" (Pareto 1935: I, § 77: 40), who generally misrepresented him. However, Malthus' theories were "an instance of the errors into which one inevitably falls when theory is confused with practice, and scientific investigation with moral preaching" (Pareto 1919: Chapter 8, § 89: 401). Malthus' work was "very confused" (ibid: § 91). He deserved credit for its "scientific part", where he looked for uniformity of phenomena and showed that population would increase more than what is observed if the "generative force" was not contained by some checks. But he wanted to go one step further, by establishing a rate of population growth which was invalidated, for instance, by the fact that in the nineteenth century the English population had doubled in 54 years, whilst wealth increased even more rapidly (ibid: § 92; cf. Pareto 1896–1897, §§ 211–212). Likewise, facts did not support Malthus' contention that the checks to population are necessarily represented by moral restraint, vice or misery. The polemical part of Malthus' book, where he wanted to show that "human well-being and ill-being depend almost exclusively on the number of births, and little or nothing on the action of government or the social system", was "manifestly erroneous" (Pareto 1919: § 95: 403). In the "preceptive part" of his book, Malthus claimed that he had "discovered the panacea, that is the moral restraint", in other words, that he had "solved the social question" and "unveiled to the world the great mystery". That part could be ignored: "one further sermon, in addition to the numberless ones which have been preached to demonstrate how beneficial, beautiful and noble chastity is, is worth nothing" (ibid: § 96: 402–403).

Pareto also criticised "social Darwinism", by which he meant a sociological theory aiming "to constitute a rigidly scientific body of doctrine", but doomed to failure because "the principles on which the theoretical structure was based were too far removed from experience". This doctrine had "declined with the Darwinian biological theory in which it originated [...]. The explanations of facts that it yielded were too often merely verbal". As "every form of social organization or life [had] to be explained by its utility, [...] arbitrary and imaginary utilities were brought into play. Unwittingly, the theory was just a return to the old theory of final causes" (Pareto 1935: I, § 828: 492).[23]

Darwinism de-Malthusianised

As improved official statistics covering longer periods of time series demonstrated that the growth rates of populations were not constant, Malthus' law was increasingly relegated to the background of social and biological sciences. It remained a general reference for those who, like Karl Pearson and the so-called biometricians, pursued a mathematical approach to evolution. But after a long and tortuous debate on Mendelism this same approach eventually led to the rise of population genetics, which transformed the image of the Malthus–Darwin association. One of its leading architects, the English statistician, mathematician and biologist Ronald A. Fisher, stated in a seminal work of twentieth-century biology (more than one third of which, incidentally, was devoted to eugenic issues) that the geometrical rate of increase, "with its impressive picture of over-population, has been widely represented as a logical basis of the argument for natural selection". But to say that the increase will be in geometrical progression is "logically irrelevant". We should simply say that the production of off-spring is "excessive", and "only excessive in relation to an imaginary world, as the 'high geometrical rate of increase' is only attained by abolishing a real death rate, while retaining a real rate of reproduction". There was, Fisher added,

> something like a relic of creationist philosophy in arguing from the observation, let us say, that a cod spawns a million eggs, that *therefore* its offspring are subject to Natural Selection; and it has the disadvantage of excluding fecundity from the class of characteristics of which we may attempt to appreciate the aptitude.

It would be instructive, Fisher said, to enquire by what physiological mechanisms "a just apportionment is made between the nutriment devoted to the gonads and that devoted to the rest of the parental organism", and what circumstances "in the life-history and environment would render profitable the diversion of a greater or lesser share of the available resources towards reproduction". The fact that Darwin and Wallace were led through reading Malthus to appreciate the importance of natural selection was telling "as to the philosophy of their age", but should no longer lead to "confuse the consequences of that principle with its foundation" (Fisher 1958: 47). Fisher used the term "Malthusian parameter of population increase" for the measure of the relative growth-rate of the population, a measure that could be determined by means of the vital statistics of an organism in relation to its environment (ibid: 50).

In the meantime, the bases of population ecology had also been laid (Mitman 1992; Hagen 1992; Golley 1993). Mathematical analyses of predator–prey interactions and "biological associations" had been developed by Volterra and Lotka, the struggle for life was given a mathematical reformulation by Gause, and studies of selective pressure on populations had opened new fields of research. Just as in economics there were tensions between a statistical approach trying to reduce natural complexity to numbers and a theoretical-deductive approach, something similar happened in biology, where the demographic approach had to compete with the revitalised belief that the growth or decline of population was governed by a natural law, although not a Malthusian one. Inspired by Pearson's advocacy of a statistical view of nature, the

Johns Hopkins biologist Raymond Pearl combined a mathematical approach with laboratory studies of population sequences and cycles, to build biostatistical models. He warned that

> the solution of the problem to which Malthus addressed himself is going to come more from the intensive study of lower forms of life in the laboratory, under physically and chemically controlled conditions, than from any manipulation of never quite satisfactory demographic statistics.
>
> (1925: 5)

Pearl and his colleague Lowell J. Read had come to the conclusion that the growth rates of Western populations were not following the Malthusian exponential curve, but were instead levelling off and tended to follow an S-shaped curve. This "logistic curve" was supposed to be universally valid and based on an underlying biological mechanism, namely the inhibition of fertility by increased population density (Kingsland 1988: 189; Soloway 1990: 254). Biological populations, including human populations, had a homeostatic, that is self-regulating, propensity. From this point of view, Pearl saw the decline of population as a natural and beneficial result of urban over-crowding. His ambition was to develop a separate branch of mathematical biology, the "biology of groups" (de Gans 1999, 2002).

Since then many things have changed in both the biological and the social sciences, but this is beyond the scope of the present chapter, and the author's competence. One thing, however, is evident: "As [Darwinians] now understand the theory, selection occurs whether or not resources are scarce" (Radick 2003: 158; cf. Gayon 1998, 2003).

A very short moral of the story

Words such as "nature" and "evolution" tend to take on moral overtones, and, when discussed, to bring moral biases out into the open. Moral assumptions can also lurk behind numbers. After all, economic, social and political issues all eventually relate to those elusive things, "human behaviour" and "human nature". This is why the word "moral" has inevitably crept into this chapter. For good or bad, the Malthus–Darwin connection was also evaluated in moral terms, whether explicitly or implicitly. "Moral" proved to be the mediator between "political", "social" and "biological". It provided a common context, or, rather, a no man's land for disputes and exchanges, transferences and overlaps.

It is in the nature of ghosts that they tend to reappear. Since the 1960s, that of "population Malthus" has materialised in ecological robes in the discourse on the "population bomb", the "limits to growth", sustainability, and worldwide imbalances and inequalities in a globalised world (Mayhew 2016). But this is quite another story. One can only hope that its actors will write it without moralising nature and naturalising society, or, as old Hume put it, without subreptitiously passing from "is" to "ought".

Notes

1 I would like to express my sincere thanks to Gábor Bíró for inviting me to contribute to this volume and for his comments on an earlier draft of my chapter. I am indebted to Clare Tame for revising my English, and to the anonymous reviewer who gave a flattering evaluation of the present text and suggested some authentic improvements.

2 Geddes and Thomson (1889) had offered an evolutionary account of the development of altruism: the social struggle for life had gradually evolved into "the struggle for the life of others". Thomson (1909) argued that the ultimate meaning of the struggle for life was "endeavour after well-being". There was, then, continuity between egoism in nature and altruism in society. Cf. La Vergata 1990b, c.

3 Other occurrences of "struggle" are in vol. 2: 49, 52, 312, 322.

4 Darwin's mistake: the name of the Swiss botanist was Augustin-Pyramus de Candolle.

5 For instance, in Notebook D: 167 and Notebook E: 48–49 (Darwin 1987: 386, 409). On p. 409 Darwin goes so far as writing "the order in this perfect <uni>-world". Darwin later doubted whether it was legitimate to use "final cause". In his notes on McCulloch, he wrote: "The Final cause of innumerable eggs is explained by Malthus.—", but immediately asked: "is it anomaly in me to talk of Final causes: consider this!—consider these barren Virgins" (Darwin 1987: 637). Final causes had famously been defined "barren virgins" by Francis Bacon.

6 The title of Fichte's book was *Der geschlossene Handelsstaat* (1800). A more literal translation would be "commercial State", but the term *Handel* has a wider meaning than "trade" or "commerce".

7 There is a vast literature on Marxism and Darwinism. See, among others, Meek 1957; Dangeville 1978; Paul 1979; Naccache 1980; Christen 1981; Heyer 1982; Vidoni 1985; Pancaldi 1994; Weikart 1999; Charbit 2009; Schmidt 2014; Gehrke 2020: 198–201.

8 With the partial exception represented by the German social-democratic leader Karl Kautsky. On his oscillations on the population problem see Weikart 1999; La Vergata 2000; Gehrke 2020: 206–209.

9 On Darwinism in Russia also see Rogers 1963; Vucinich 1988; Krementsov 2010; Markov and Melnik 2020.

10 Royer argued strongly in favour of opportunities for women. On Royer see Conry 1974; Clark 1984; Fraisse 1985; Miles 1989; Molina 1992; Blanckaert 1996; Harvey 1997; Bernardini 1997.

11 Ibid.: 141. Guyot thought that Ricardo was wrong to base his theory of profits on declining wages, "for if this theory were true, profits would rise in proportion to the poverty of the labourers, and the richest manufacturers would be found in the poorest countries" (ibid.: 174).

12 In the first part of this section I will avail myself of materials used in La Vergata (2019). I am grateful to Springer Nature AG for their permission to do so.

13 Darwin complimented Spencer, but two days later he described Spencer's theory as "such dreadful hypothetical rubbish on the nature of reproduction" (Darwin 1985–, vol. 8: 106, 109–110).

14 The economist James Bonar, author of a classical study on Malthus (1895), saw an analogy between the fact that "the morally worse men" might prove "the more fit to survive in the sense that they are the best able to suck advantage from their surroundings" and the fact that "the holders of the wore [sic] coins […] get advantage over the holders of the finer under 'Gresham's law' of the currency. The worse coinage survived because it was the fitter; it was the fitter because, being the worse and yet accepted, it was the more economical" (Bonar 1893: 359).

15 The literature on eugenics is enormous. For a concise view see Larson 2010.

16 As one would have expected, T.H. Huxley (1893–1894, I: 369–382) criticised George most severely. George's ideas launched a school of thought and movement that were influential for several decades.

17 Weismann, however, sponsored the German translation (1895) of Benjamin Kidd's *Social Evolution* (1894), for which he wrote a Preface dealing with the application of Darwinism to society and where he attacked socialism.

18 On Lilienfeld and other representatives of organicism in sociology in the German-speaking world, such as Albert Schäffle, see Hutter 1994. On German debates on Malthus see Ferdinand 1999.

19 Darwin himself had been inspired by Milne-Edwards, who had in turn borrowed the phrase and the analogy from Adam Smith. Darwin's take, however, was not "merely the transfer of a concept but a reworking of its fundamental significance, and the production of a new concept at the ecological level" (Limoges 1994: 330).

20 On Marshall and biology see Levine 1983; Niman 1991; Thomas 1991; Hodgson 1993; Limoges and Ménard 1994; Schabas 1994.

21 "Nervous strain", Marshall pointed out, must not be confused with the social phenomenon of "nervousness", "which, as a rule, indicates a general deficiency of nervous strength; though sometimes it proceeds from nervous irritability or want of balance" (ibid.: note).

22 Loria was a critic of social Darwinism and supported social legislation to promote cooperation and small-scale agrarian property. He argued that Malthus' doctrine was false. Although attracted by socialism, he did not take an active part in it. His deterministic interpretation of Marxism was harshly criticised by Engels and Gramsci. See Loria 1882, 1897, 1909, 1912, and cf. Di Taranto 1995; Donnini Macciò and Romani 2020.

23 It is not easy to understand why Pareto considered social Darwinism as "a well-ordered body of doctrine" (ibid.). He must have been aware of its many and contrasting varieties, for he himself made a selection when he mentioned (approvingly) as instances of it only a couple of works which fitted his pessimistic view of society (including Georges Vacher de Lapouge, the French theorist of racial inequalities). Pareto also ventured into some awkward criticisms of Darwinism as a biological theory (ibid.: IV, § 2142: 1475). Suffice it to say that according to him Darwin "err [ed] in regarding the adaptation [to the environment] as perfect" (ibid.: III, § 1770: 1230).

References

Alexander, Denis R. and Numbers, Ronald L. (eds). 2010. *Biology and ideology from Descartes to Dawkins*. Chicago and London: University of Chicago Press.

Andreozzi, Luciano. 1998. Analogie e modelli meccanici all'alba della demografia matematica. Il caso della "logistica". *Bollettino di demografia storica* 29: 5–22.

Andrews, David. 2020. The reception of Malthus' essay on population in the United States. In Faccarello, Izumo and Morishita (eds): 53–82. doi:10.4337/9781788977579.00007.

Bagehot, Walter. 1978. Economic studies: Malthus (1880). In N. St John-Stevas (ed.), *The collected works of Walter Bagehot*, vol. 11. London: The Economist.

Bannister, Robert C. 1979. *Social Darwinism. Science and myth in Anglo-American social thought*. With a new preface. Philadelphia:Temple University Press.

Béjin, André. 1984. Du principe de population au principe de sélection: Malthus et les darwinistes sociaux. In Fauve-Chamoux (ed.): 337–347.

Bellomy, Donald C. 1984. "Social Darwinism revisited." Perspectives in American History. New Series. 1: 1-130.

Benton, Ted. 1982. Social Darwinism and socialist Darwinism in Germany: 1860 to 1900. *Rivista di filosofia*, 22–23: 79–121.

Benton, Ted. 2008. Wallace's dilemmas: the laws of nature and the human spirit. In Smith and Beccaloni (eds): 368–390.

Bernardini, Jean-Marc. 1997. *Le darwinisme social en France (1859–1918). Fascination et regret d'une idéologie*. Paris: CNRS Éditions.

Blanckaert, Claude. 1996. Royer, Clémence. In Tort (ed.), vol. 3: 3744–3749.

Bonar, James. 1893. *Philosophy and political economy*. London: Frank Cass.

Bonar, James. 1895. *Malthus and his work*. London: Macmillan.

Bowen, Francis. 1879. Malthusianism, Darwinism, and pessimism. *North American Review* 129: 447–472.

Bowler, Peter J. 1976. Malthus, Darwin, and the concept of struggle. *Journal of the History of Ideas* 37: 631–650.

Bowler, Peter J. 1990. *The invention of progress: the Victorians and the past*. Oxford: Blackwell. doi:10.1177/027046769301300346.

Browne, Janet. 1980. Darwin's botanic arithmetic and the "principle of divergence". *Journal of the History of Biology* 13: 53–89.

Browne, Janet. 1995. *Charles Darwin: voyaging*. London: Jonathan Cape.

Černyševskij, Nikolaj Gavrilovič. 1890. Origine de la théorie qui considère la "lutte pour la vie" comme chose bienfaisante. Traduit et abrégé par A. Tweritinoff. *Société nouvelle* 6 (2): 259–282.

Chamberlin, J.E. and Gilman, S.L. (eds). 1985. *Degeneration: the dark side of progress*. New York: Columbia University Press.

Charbit, Yves 1981. *Du malthusianisme au populationnisme. Les économistes français et la population, 1840–1870*. Paris: INED and Presses Universitaires de France.

Charbit, Yves 1988. Les économistes libéraux et la population (1840–1870). In J. Dupâquier (ed.), *Histoire de la population française. III. De 1789 à 1914*. Paris: Presses Universitaires de France: 467–481.

Charbit, Yves 2009. *Economic, social and demographic thought in the XIXth century: the population debate from Malthus to Marx*. Berlin: Springer. doi:10.1007/978-971-4020-9960-1.

Christen, Yves. 1981. *Le grand affrontement. Marx et Darwin*. Paris: Albin Michel.

Claeys, Gregory. 1987. *Machinery, money, and the millennium: from moral economy to socialism, 1815–1860*. Princeton, NJ: Princeton University Press.

Claeys, Gregory. 2000. The "survival of the fittest" and the origins of Social Darwinism. *Journal of the History of Ideas* 61: 223–240. doi:10.1353/jhi.2000.0014.

Claeys, Gregory. 2008. *Wallace and Owenism*. In Smith and Beccaloni (eds): 235–262.

Clark, Linda L. 1984. *Social Darwinism in France*. Tuscaloosa: University of Alabama Press.

Cohen, I. Bernard (ed.) 1994. *The natural sciences and the social sciences. Some critical and historical perspectives*. Dordrecht, Boston and London: Kluwer Academic Publishers (Boston Studies in the Philosophy of Sciences, 150). doi:10.1007/978-994-017-3391-5.

Cohen, I. Bernard. 1994. *An analysis of interactions between the natural sciences and the social sciences*. In Cohen (ed.): 1–99. doi:10.1007/978-994-017-3391-5-1.

Collini, Stephen, Winch, Donald and Burrow, John. 1983. *The noble science of politics: a study in nineteenth-century intellectual history*. Cambridge: Cambridge University Press.

Conry, Yvette. 1974. *L'introduction du darwinisme en France au XIXe siècle*. Paris: Vrin.

Conry, Yvette. 1981. Organisme et organisation: de Darwin à la génétique des populations. *Revue de Synthèse*, third series, 102: 291–391.

Conry, Yvette. 1985. Per evitare il tranello delle origini: divisione del lavoro e principio di divergenza nella teoria darwiniana dal 1839 al 1859. In Walter Tega (ed.), *L'anno di Darwin. Problemi di un centenario*, 19–35. Parma: Pratiche Editrice.

Cope, Edward D. 1887. *The origin of the fittest. Essays on evolution*. New York: Appleton.

Cope, Edward D. 1896. *The primary factors of organic evolution*. Chicago: Open Court.

Cornell, John F. 1987. God's magnificent law: the bad influence of theistic metaphysics on Darwin's estimation of natural selection. *Journal of the History of Biology* 20: 381–412. doi:10.1007/BF00139461.

Cremaschi, Sergio. 2014. *Utilitarianism and Malthus' virtue ethics*. London and New York: Routledge.

Dangeville, Roger (ed.). 1978. *Marx, Engels. Critique de Malthus*. Introduction, translation and notes by Roger Dangeville. Paris: Maspero.

DAR. Darwin Archives, Cambridge University Library, DAR. 202: 32.

Darwin, Charles. 1859. *On the origin of species by means of natural selection, or the preservation of the favoured races in the struggle for existence*. London: John Murray.

Darwin, Charles. 1985–. *The correspondence of Charles Darwin*, ed. by F. Burkhardt et al. Cambridge: Cambridge University Press.

Darwin, Charles. 1987. *Charles Darwin's notebooks, 1836–1844*, ed. by Paul H. Barrett et al. London: British Museum (Natural History); Cambridge: Cambridge University Press.

Darwin, Charles. 2004. *The descent of man and selection in relation to sex*. Rept. of 1879 edition, with an introduction by James Moore and Adrian Desmond. London: Penguin Books (1st ed. 1871).

Daston, Lorraine and Vidal, Fernando (eds). 2004. *The moral authority of nature*. Chicago and London: The University of Chicago Press.

de Gans, Henk A. 1999. *Population forecasting 1895–1945. The transition to modernity*. Dordrecht, Boston and London: Kluwer Academic Publishers. doi:10.1007/978-994-011-4766-8.

de Gans, Henk A. 2002. Law or speculation? A debate on the method of forecasting population size in the 1920s. *Population* 57 (1): 83–108. doi:10.2307/3246628.

de Vries, Hugo. 1909–1910. *The mutation theory: experiments and observations on the origin of species in the vegetable kingdom*. Chicago: Open Court (orig. *Die Mutationstheorie. Versuche und Beobachtungen über die Entstehung der Arten im Pflanzenreich*. Leipzig: Veit, 1901–1903). doi:10.5962/bhl.title.17297.

Dean, R. 1995. Owenism and the Malthusian population question, 1815–1835. *History of Political Economy* 27: 579–597. doi:10.1215/00182702-00182727-3-579.

Delage, Yves and Goldsmith, Marie. 1909. *Les theories de l'évolution*. Paris: Flammarion.

Desmond, Adrian and Moore, James. 1991. *Darwin*. London: Michael Joseph.

Di Taranto, Giuseppe. 1995. Popolazione e malthusianesimo nei dibattiti di fine secolo. *Il pensiero economico italiano* 3 (2): 167–189.

Dolan, Brian (ed.). 2000. *Malthus, medicine, and morality: "Malthusianism" after 1798*. Amsterdam: Rodopi.

Donnini Macciò, Daniela and Romani, Roberto. 2020. Malthus's Italian incarnations, 1815–1915. In Faccarello, Izumo and Morishita (eds): 236–273. doi:10.4337/9781788977579.00010.

Dugatkin, Lee Alan. 2011. *The prince of evolution. Peter Kropotkin's adventures in science and politics*. Online: CreateSpace (Amazon.com.).

Durkheim, Émile. 1960. *The division of labour in society*. Fourth printing. Glencoe, IL: The Free Press of Glencoe (orig. De la division du travail social. Étude sur l'organisation des sociétés supérieures, 1893).

Eimer, Theodor. 1890. *Organic evolution as the result of the inheritance of acquired characters according to the laws of organic growth*. Engl. transl. by J.T. Cunningham, London: Macmillan (orig. Die Entstehung der Arten auf Grund von Vererben erworbener Eigenschaften nach den Gesetzen organischen Wachsens. Jena: Fischer, 1888).

Engels, Eve Marie and Glick, Thomas (eds). 2008. *The reception of Charles Darwin in Europe*. London: Continuum.

Eversley, D.E.C. 1959. *Social theories of fertility and the Malthusian debate*. Oxford: Oxford University Press.

Faccarello, Gilbert 2020. "Enlightened Saint Malthus" or the "gloomy Protestant of dismal England"? The reception of Malthus in the French language. In Faccarello, Izumo and Morishita (eds): 83–173. doi:10.4337/9781788977579.00008.

Faccarello, Gilbert, Izumo, Masashi and Morishita, Hiromi (eds) 2020. *Malthus across nations. The reception of Thomas Robert Malthus in Europe, America and Japan*. Cheltenham and Northampton, MA: Edward Elgar Publishing. doi:10.4337/9781788977579.

Fauve-Chamoux, Antoinette (ed.). 1984. *Malthus hier et aujourd'hui* (Congrès International de Démographie Historique). Paris: Éditions du C.N.R.S.

Ferdinand, Ursula. 1999. *Das Malthusische Erbe. Entwicklungsstraenge der Bevoelkerungstheorie im 19. Jahrhundert und deren Einfluß auf die radikale Frauenbewegung in Deutschland*. Münster: LIT.

Fichman, Martin. 2001. Science in theistic contexts: a case study of Alfred Russel Wallace on human evolution. *Osiris* 16: 227–250.

Fichman, Martin. 2004. *An elusive Victorian: the evolution of Alfred Russel Wallace*. Chicago: University of Chicago Press. doi:10.7208/chicago/9780226246154.001.0001.

Fisher, Ronald Aylmer. 1958. *The genetical theory of natural selection*. Second revised edition. New York: Dover (orig. Oxford: Oxford University Press, 1930).

Fraisse, Geneviève. 1985. *Clémence Royer, philosophe et femme de science*. Paris: La Découverte.

Fuhrmann, Martin. 2002. *Volksvermehrung als Staatsaufgabe? Bevölkerungs- und Ehepolitik in der deutschen politischen und ökonomischen Theorie des 18. und 19. Jahrhunderts*. Paderborn: Schöningh.

Galton, Francis. 1865. Hereditary talent and character. *Macmillan's Magazine* 12: 157–166, 318–327.

Galton, Francis. 1869. *Hereditary genius: an inquiry into its laws and consequences*. London: Murray.

Gause, G.F. 1934. *The struggle for existence*. Baltimore: Williams and Wilkins. Rept. New York: Dover, 1971.

Gayon, Jean. 1998. *Darwinism's struggle for survival: heredity and the hypothesis of natural selection*. Cambridge: Cambridge University Press (orig. Darwin et l'après-Darwin. Une histoire de l'hypothèse de la sélection naturelle. Paris: Éditions Kimé, 1992).

Gayon, Jean. 2003. From Darwin to today in evolutionary biology. In Hodge and Radick (eds): 240–264. doi:10.1017/CCOL0521771978.011.

Geddes, Patrick and Thomson, John Arthur. 1899. *The evolution of sex*. London: W. Scott.

Gehrke, Christian 2020. *The reception of Malthus in Germany and Austria in the 19th century*. In Faccarello, Izumo and Morishita (eds): 174–235. doi:10.4337/9781788977579.00009.

George, Henry. 1879. *Progress and poverty. An inquiry into the causes of industrial depression and of increase of want with increase of wealth*. New York: Appleton.

Golley, Frank B. 1993. *A history of the ecosystem concept in ecology: more than the sum of the parts*. New Haven: Yale University Press.

Gordon, Scott 1989. Darwin and political economy: the connection reconsidered. *Journal of the History of Biology* 22: 437–459.

Gould, Stephen Jay. 1980. *The panda's thumb*. Harmondsworth: Penguin Books (first ed. 1978).

Greene, John C. 1981. *Science, ideology, and world view: essays in the history of evolutionary ideas*. Berkeley and Los Angeles: University of California Press. Greg, William Rathbone. 1843. Resources of an increasing population: emigration or manufactures. *Westminster Review* 40: 101–122.

Greg, William Rathbone. 1849. Unsound social philosophy. *Edinburgh Review* 90: 496–524.

Greg, William Rathbone. 1851a. English socialism, and communistic associations. *Edinburgh Review* 93: 1–33.

Greg, William Rathbone. 1851b. England as it is. *Edinburgh Review* 93: 305–309.

Greg, William Rathbone. 1853. Charity, noxious and beneficent. *Westminster Review* 54 (old series), 3 (new series): 62–88.

Greg, William Rathbone. 1854. The great social problem. *Edinburgh Review* 100: 163–192.

Greg, William Rathbone. 1868. On the failure of natural selection in the case of man. *Fraser's Magazine* 78: 353–362.

Greg, William Rathbone. 1874a. Malthus notwithstanding. In *Enigmas of life*. 9th ed. London: Trübner & Co. (1st ed. 1872).

Greg, William Rathbone. 1874b. *Rocks ahead; or, the warnings of Cassandra*. London: Trübner & Co.

Guyot, Yves. 1892. *Principles of social economy*. Second edition. London: Swan Sonnenschein; New York: Charles Scribner's Sons (orig. La science économique, 1881).

Hagen, Joel B. 1992. *An entangled bank: the origins of ecosystems ecology*. New Brunswick, NJ: Rutgers University Press.

Hale, Piers J. 2014. *Political descent: Malthus, mutualism and the politics of evolution in Victorian England*. Chicago: University of Chicago Press.

Hale, Piers J. 2016. Finding a place for the anti-Malthusian tradition in the Victorian evolution debates. In Mayhew (ed.): 182–207. doi:10.1017/CBO9781139939485.008.

Hankins, F.H. 1930. Does advancing civilization involve a decline in natural fertility? In *Studies in quantitative and cultural sociology. Papers presented at the twenty-fourth annual meeting of the American Sociological Society, held at Washington, DC, 27–30 December, 1929* (pp. 115–122). Publications of the American Sociological Society, Chicago: University of Chicago Press.

Hankins, F.H. 1932. Has the reproductive power of western peoples declined? In G.H. L.F. Pitt-Rivers (ed.), *Problems of population. Being the report of the proceedings of the second general assembly of the International Union for the Scientifc Investigation of Population Problems, held at the Royal Society of Arts, London, 15–18 June, 1931* (pp. 181–188). London: George Allen & Unwin. Rept. Port Washington, New York and London: Kennikat Press, 1971.

Harvey, Joy. 1997. *"Almost a man of genius." Clémence Royer, feminism, and nineteenth-century science*. New Brunswick, NJ and London: Rutgers University Press.

Harvey, Joy. 2008. Darwin in a French dress: translating, publishing and supporting Darwin in nineteenth-century France. In Engels and Glick (eds): 354–374.

Harvey-Phillips, M.B. 1984. Malthus' theodicy: the intellectual background of his contribution to political economy. *History of Political Economy* 16: 591–608.

Hawkins, Mike. 1997. *Social Darwinism in European and American thought, 1860–1945. Nature as model and nature as threat*. Cambridge: Cambridge University Press. doi:10.1017/CBO9780511558481.

Hayward, J.E.S. 1959. Solidarity: the social history of an idea in nineteenth-century France. *International Review of Social History* 4: 261–284.

Hayward, J.E.S. 1961. The official philosophy of the French Third Republic: Léon Bourgeois and solidarism. *International Review of Social History* 6: 19–48.

Hejl, Peter M. 1995. The importance of the concepts of "organism" and "evolution" in Émile Durkheim's division of social labor and the influence of Herbert Spencer. In Maasen, S., Mendelsohn, E. and Weingart, P. (eds), 155–191. *Biology as society, society as biology: metaphors*. Sociology of the Sciences (A Yearbook – 1994), vol. 18. Dordrecht: Kluwer. doi:10.1007/978-994-011-0673-3_8.

Herbert, Sandra. 1971. Darwin, Malthus, and selection. *Journal of the History of Biology* 4: 209–217.

Herbert, Sandra. 1977. The place of man in the development of Darwin's theory of transmutation. Part II. *Journal of the History of Biology* 10: 155–227.

Heyer, Paul. 1982. *Nature, human nature and society: Marx, Darwin, biology and the human sciences*. London: Greenwood Press.

Hodge, Jonathan and Radick, Gregory (eds). 2003. *The Cambridge companion to Darwin*. Cambridge: Cambridge University Press.

Hodgson, Geoffrey M. 1993. The Mecca of Alfred Marshall. *The Economic Journal* 103: 406–415. doi:10.2307/2234779.

Hodgson, Geoffrey M. 1995. Biological and physical metaphors in economics. In Maasen, S., Mendelsohn, E. and Weingart, P. (eds), 339–356. *Biology as society, society as biology: metaphors*. Sociology of the Sciences (A Yearbook – 1994), vol. 18. Dordrecht: Kluwer. doi:10.1007/978-994-011-0673-3_14.

Hofstadter, Richard. 1955. *Social Darwinism in American thought*. Revised edition. Boston: The Beacon Press (first ed. 1944).

Hull, David L. (ed.). 1973. *Darwin and his critics: the reception of Darwin's theory of evolution by the scientific community*. Cambridge, MA: Harvard University Press.

Hutter, Michael. 1994. Organism as a metaphor in German economic thought. In Mirowski (ed.): 289–321. doi:10.1017/CBO9780511572128.011.

Huxley, Leonard (ed.). 1918. *The life and letters of Sir Joseph Dalton Hooker*. London: Murray.

Huxley, Thomas Henry. 1863. *On our knowledge of the causes of the phenomena of organic nature. Being six lectures to working men, delivered at the Museum of Practical Geology*. London: Robert Hardwicke. Rept. as The Origin of Species; or, The Causes of the Phenomena of Organic Nature *in Huxley*, 1893–1894, vol. 2.

Huxley, Thomas Henry. 1893–1894. *Collected essays*. London: Macmillan.

Ingrao, Bruna. 1991. L'analogia meccanica nel pensiero di Pareto. In Giovanni Busino (ed.), *Pareto oggi*. Bologna: Il Mulino.

Ingrao, Bruna and Israel, Giorgio. 1990. *The invisible hand. Economic equilibrium in the history of science*. Cambridge, MA: MIT Press (orig. La mano invisibile: l'equilibrio economico nella storia della scienza. Roma-Bari: Laterza, 1987).Ipsen, Carl. 1996. *Dictating demography: the problem of population in Fascist Italy*. Cambridge: Cambridge University Press. doi:10.1017/CBO9780511581953.

Isemburg, Teresa. 1977. Il dibattito su Malthus e sulla popolazione nell'Italia di fine '800. *Studi storici* 18: 41–67.

Jones, Greta. 1980. *Social Darwinism in English thought. The interaction between biological and social theory*. Brighton: The Harvester Press; Atlantic Highlands, NJ: Humanities Press.

Kellogg, Vernon Lyman. 1907. *Darwinism to-day: A discussion of present-day scientific selection theories, together with a brief account of the principal other proposed auxiliary and alternative theories of species-formation*. New York: Henry Holt and Co.

Keynes, John Maynard. 1933. *Essays in biography*. London: Macmillan.

Keynes, John Maynard. 2004. The end of laissez-faire (1926). In *The end of laissez-faire. The economic consequences of the peace*. Amherst, NY: Prometheus.

Kingsland, Sharon. 1985. *Modeling nature. Episodes in the history of populational ecology*. Chicago: University of Chicago Press.

Kingsland, Sharon. 1988. Evolution and debates over human progress from Darwin to socio- biology. *Population and Development Review* 14: 167–198.

Kohn, David (ed.). 1980. Theories to work by: rejected theories, reproduction, and Darwin's path to natural selection. *Studies in the History of Biology* 4: 67–170.

Kohn, David (ed.). 1985. *The Darwinian heritage. A centennial appraisal*. Princeton, NJ: Princeton University Press; Wellington: Nova Pacifica. Kohn, David. 1985. Darwin's principle of divergence as internal dialogue. In Kohn (ed.): 245–257.

Kostitzin, V.A. 1934. *Biologie mathématique*. Paris: Armand Colin.

Krementsov, Nikolai. 2010. Darwinism, Marxism, and genetics in the Soviet Union. In Alexander and Numbers (eds): 215–246. doi:10.7208/chicago/9780226608426.003.0010.

Kropotkin, Pëtr Alekseevič. 1902. *Mutual aid: a factor of evolution*. London: Heinemann.

La Vergata, Antonello. 1982. Biologia, scienze umane e "darwinismo sociale". Considerazioni contro una categoria storiografica dannosa. *Intersezioni* 2 (1): 77–97.

La Vergata, Antonello. 1985. Images of Darwin. A historiographic overview. In Kohn, David (ed.). The Darwinian heritage. A centennial appraisal. Princeton: Princeton University Press; Wellington: Nova Pacifica, pp. 901-972.

La Vergata, Antonello. 1990a. Il lamarckismo fra riduzionismo biologico e migliorismo sociale. *Intersezioni* 10 (3): 495–516. La Vergata, Antonello. 1990b. *Nonostante Malthus, Fecondità, popolazioni e armonia della natura: 1700–1900*. Turin: Bollati Boringhieri.

La Vergata, Antonello. 1990c. *L'equilibrio e la guerra della natura. Dalla teologia naturale al Darwinismo*. Naples: Morano.

La Vergata, Antonello. 1992. Les bases biologiques de la solidarité. In Tort (ed.): 55–87.

La Vergata, Antonello. 2000. Biology and sociology of fertility. Reactions to the Malthusian threat, 1798–1933. In Dolan (ed.): 189–222. doi:10.1163/9789004333338_010.

La Vergata, Antonello. 2019. Food, nerves, and fertility. Variations on the moral economy of the body, 1700–1920. *History and Philosophy of the Life Sciences* 41. doi:10.1007/s40656-40019-0272-z.

Lanessan, Jean-Louisde. 1881. *Étude sur la doctrine de Darwin: la lutte pour l'existence et l'"association pour la lutte"*. Paris: O. Doin.

Lanessan, Jean-Louisde. 1903. *La lutte por l'existence et l'évolution des sociétés*. Paris: Alcan.

Larson, Edward J. 2010. Biology and the emergence of the Anglo-American eugenics movement. In Alexander and Numbers (eds): 165–191. doi:10.7208/9780226608426–008.

LeMahieu, D.L. 1979. Malthus and the theology of scarcity. *Journal of the History of Ideas* 40: 467–474.

Levine, A.L. 1983. Marshall's principles and the "biological viewpoint". *Manchester School* 53: 276–293.

Lilienfeld, Paulvon (Pavel Fëdorovič Lilienfeld Toal'). 1873–1879. *Gedanken über die Sozialwissenschaft der Zukunft*. Mitau: E. Behre's Verlag (vols 1–4); Hamburg: Gebrüder Behre's Verlag – Mitau: E. Behre's Verlag (vol. 5).

Lilienfeld, Paulvon (Pavel Fëdorovič Lilienfeld Toal'). 1896. *La Pathologie sociale*. Paris: Giard et Brière.

Lilienfeld, Paulvon (Pavel Fëdorovič Lilienfeld Toal'). 1898. *Zur Vertheidigung der organischen Methode in der Soziologie*. Berlin: Reimer.

Limoges, Camille. 1994. Milne-Edwards, Darwin, Durkheim and the division of labour: a case study in reciprocal conceptual exchanges between the social and the natural sciences. In Cohen (ed.): 317–343. doi:10.1007/978-994-017-3391-5_10.

Limoges, Camille and Ménard, Claude. 1994. Organization and the division of labor: biological metaphors at work in Alfred Marshall's Principles of Economics. In Mirowski (ed.): 336–359. Loria, Achille. 1882. *La legge di popolazione e il sistema sociale.* Siena: Lazzeri.

Loria, Achille. 1897. La vecchia e la nuova fase nella teoria della popolazione. In *Verso la giustizia sociale (idee, battaglie ed apostoli).* Milan: SEI: 343–353.

Loria, Achille. 1899. *Economic foundations of society.* Transl. from the French edition of 1893 by Lindley M. Keasbey. London: Swan Sonnenschein; New York: Charles Scribner's Sons (orig. Le basi economiche della costituzione sociale. Turin. 1886).

Loria, Achille. 1909. *Malthus.* Rome: Formiggini.

Loria, Achille. 1912. *La dernière évolution de la théorie de l'évolution.* Paris: Giard et Brière.

Lotka, Alfred James. 1925. *Elements of physical biology.* Baltimore: Williams and Wilkins. Rept. as Elements of mathematical biology. New York: Dover, 1956.

Maccabelli, Terenzio. 2008. Social anthropology in economic literature at the end of the nineteenth century: eugenic and racist explanations of inequality. *American Journal of Economics and Sociology* 67 (3): 483–527. doi:10.1111/j.1536–7150.2008.00584.x.

Malthus, Thomas Robert. 1803. *An essay on the principle of population; or, A view of its past and present effects on human happiness; with an enquiry into our prospects respecting the future removal or mitigation of the evils which it occasions.* Second edition. London: for J. Johnson by T. Bensley.

Malthus, Thomas Robert. 1826. *An essay on the principle of population; or, A view of its past and present effects on human happiness; with an enquiry into our prospects respecting the future removal or mitigation of the evils which it occasions.* Sixth edition. In E.A. Wrigley and D. Souden (eds), *The works of Thomas Robert Malthus,* vol. 2. London: William Pickering.

Malthus, Thomas Robert. 1976. *An essay on the principle of population and A summary view of the principle of population.* Edited with an introduction by Anthony Flew. Harmonsdworth: Penguin Books.

Mantovani, Claudia. 2004. *Rigenerare la società. L'eugenetica in Italia dalle origini ottocentesche agli anni Trenta.* Soveria Mannelli: Rubbettino.

Markov, Maxim and Melnik, Denis. 2020. The reception of Malthus in Russia. In Faccarello, Izumo and Morishita (eds): 359–399. doi:10.4337/9781788977579.00013.

Marshall, Alfred. 1895. *Principles of economics.* Third Edition. London: Macmillan (first ed. 1890).

MEGA. Marx, Karl and Engels, Friedrich. 1927–. *Gesamtausgabe.* Moscow, Berlin and Amsterdam: Internationales Marx-Engels-Stiftung.

MEW. Marx, Karl and Engels, Friedrich. 1956–. *Werke.* Berlin: Dietz Verlag, Rosa-Luxemburg-Stiftung.

Mayhew, Robert (ed.). 2014. *Malthus: the life and legacies of an untimely prophet.* Cambridge, MA: Harvard University Press. doi:10.4159/harvard.9780674419407.

Mayhew, Robert (ed.). 2016. *New perspectives on Malthus.* Cambridge: Cambridge University Press. doi:10.1017/CBO9781139939485. Mayr, Ernst. 1988. *Towards a philosophy of biology. Observations of an evolutionist.* Cambridge, MA and London: Harvard University Press.

McAtee, W.L. 1936. The Malthusian principle in nature. *Scientific Monthly* 42: 444–456.

McCulloch, John. 1837. *Proofs and illustrations of the attributes of God.* London: Duncan.

McKinney, H.L. 1972. *Wallace and natural selection.* New Haven: Yale University Press.

McLaren, Angus. 1983. *Sexuality and the social order: the debate over the fertility of women and workers in France, 1770–1920.* New York: Holmes and Meyer.

Meek, Ronald (ed.). 1953. *Marx and Engels on Malthus.* London: Lawrence and Wishart.

Miles, Sara Joan. 1989. Clémence Royer et De l'Origine des espèces. Traductrice ou traîtresse? *Revue de synthèse* 4 (1) (January–March): 61–83.

Mill, John Stuart. 1924. *Autobiography of John Stuart Mill, published for the first time without alterations or omissions from the original manuscript in the possession of Columbia University,* with a preface by John Jacob Coss. New York: Columbia University Press.

Mirowski, Philip (ed.). 1989. *More heat than light. Economics as social physics, physics as nature's economics.* Cambridge: Cambridge University Press. doi:10.1017/CBO9780511559990.

Mirowski, Philip (ed.). 1994. *Natural images in economic thought: "markets read in tooth and claw".* Cambridge: Cambridge University Press. doi:10.1017/CBO9780511572128.

Mitman, Gregg. 1992. *The state of nature. Ecology, community, and American social thought, 1900–1950.* Chicago: University of Chicago Press.

Molina, Gérard. 1992. Le savant et ses interprètes. In Tort (ed.): 362–386.

Molinari, Gustave. 1880. *L'évolution économique du dix-neuvième siècle. Théorie du progrès.* Paris: Reinwald.

Molinari, Gustave. 1901. *Les problèmes du XXe siècle.* Paris: Guillaumin.

Molinari, Gustave. 1908. *L'économie de l'histoire. Théorie de l'évolution.* Paris: Alcan.

Moore, James. 1997. Wallace's Malthusian moment: the common context revisited. In *Victorian science in context,* ed. Bernard Lightman, 290–311. Chicago: University of Chicago Press. doi:10.7208/9780226481104–016.

Morgan, Thomas Hunt. 1903. *Evolution and adaptation.* New York and London: Macmillan.

Naccache, Bernard. 1980. *Marx critique de Darwin.* Paris: Vrin.

Nägeli, Carl Wilhelmvon. Zusammenfassung. 1884. *Mechanisch-physiologische Theorie der Abstammungslehre.* Munich: Druck und Verlag von R. Oldenbourg (Engl. transl. by V.A. Clark and F.A. Waugh, A Mechanico-physiological Theory of Organic Evolution. Summary. Chicago: Open Court, 1898).

Nietzsche, Friedrich. 2001. *The gay science.* English translation by Josefine Nauckhoff, ed. by Bernard Williams. Cambridge: Cambridge University Press (originally *Die fröhliche Wissenschaft,* 1882).

Nietzsche, Friedrich. 2002. *Beyond good and evil.* English translation by Judith Norman, ed. by Rolf-Peter Horstmann and Judith Norman. Cambridge: Cambridge University Press (originally *Jenseits vom Gute und Böse,* 1886).

Nietzsche, Friedrich. 2005. *Twilight of the idols.* English translation by Judith Norman. In *The Anti-Christ. Ecce Homo. Twilight of the idols,* ed. by Aaron Ridley and Judith Norman. Cambridge: Cambridge University Press (originally *Götzen-Dämmerung,* 1888).

Niman, Neil B. 1991. Biological analogies in Marshall's Work. *Journal of the History of Economic Thought* 13 (1): 19–36. doi:10.1017/S1053837200003370.

Osborn, Henry F. 1894. *From the Greeks to Darwin. An outline of the development of the evolution idea.* New York and London: Macmillan.

Osborn, Henry F. 1917. *The origin and evolution of life. On the theory of action and reaction of energy.* New York: Scribner.

Ospovat, Dov. 1981. *The development of Darwin's theory: natural history, natural theology, natural selection, 1838–1859.* Cambridge: Cambridge University Press.

Paley, William. 1802. *Natural theology: or, evidences of the existence and attributes of the Deity, collected from the appearances of nature.* London: printed for R. Faulder by Wilks and Taylor.

Pancaldi, Giuliano. 1994. *The technology of nature: Marx's thoughts on Darwin.* In Cohen (ed.): 257–274. doi:10.1007/978-994-017-3391-5_7.

Pareto, Vilfredo. 1896–1897. *Cours d'économie politique.* Lausanne: Rouge. Two vols.

Pareto, Vilfredo. 1916. *Trattato di sociologia generale.* Florence: Barbèra. Two vols.

Pareto, Vilfredo. 1919. *Manuale di economia politica, con una introduzione alla scienza sociale.* Milano: Società Editrice Libraria (first ed. 1906).

Pareto, Vilfredo. 1923. *Trattato di sociologia generale.* Second edition. Florence: Barbèra. Three vols.

Pareto, Vilfredo. 1935. *The mind and society.* New York: Harcourt, Brace and Co. (English transl. of Pareto 1923). Four vols.

Patten, Simon Nelson. 1885. *The premises of political economy. Being a re-examination of certain fundamental principles of economic science.* Philadelphia: J.B. Lippincott & Co.

Patten, Simon Nelson. 1894. The failure of biologic sociology. *Annals of the American Academy of Political and Social Science* 4: 919–947.

Paul, Diane B. 1979. Marxism, Darwinism, and the theory of two sciences. *Marxist Perspectives* 2: 116–143.

Paul, Diane B. 2008. Wallace, women, and eugenics. In Smith and Beccaloni (eds): 263–278.

Paul, Diane B. and Beattie, John. 2007. Discarding dichotomies: Sam Schweber and Darwin studies. In Gavroglu, Costas and Renn, Jürgen (eds), *Positioning the history of science.* Dordrecht: Springer (Boston Studies in Philosophy of Science, 248). doi:10.1007/1-4020-5420-5423_21.

Pearce, T. 2010. "A great complication of circumstances" – Darwin and the economy of nature. *Journal of the History of Biology* 43: 493–528. doi:10.1007/s10739-10009-9205-0.

Pearl, Raymond. 1922. *The biology of death.* Philadelphia and London: J.B. Lippincott.

Pearl, Raymond. 1925. *The biology of population growth.* New York: Knopf.

Peel, J.D.Y. 1971. *Herbert Spencer: the evolution of a sociologist.* New York: Basic Books.

Persell, Stuart M. 1999. *Neo-Lamarckism and the evolution controversy in France, 1870–1920.* Lewiston, Queenston and Lampeter: Edwin Mellen Press.

Pick, D. 1989. *Faces of degeneration. A European disorder, c. 1848–c. 1918.* Cambridge: Cambridge University Press.

Plate, Ludwig. 1903. *Über die Bedeutung des Darwin'schen Selectionsprincips und Probleme der Artbildung.* Leipzig: Engelmann.

Pogliano, Claudio. 1983. L'enigma demologico. Natalità, popolazione, socialismo (1880–1900). *Schema* 8: 7–42.

Pogliano, Claudio. 1984. Scienza e stirpe: eugenica in Italia (1912–1939). *Passato e presente* 2 (5): 61–97.

Porter, Theodore M. 1994. Rigor and practicality: rival ideals of quantification in nineteenth-century economics. In Mirowski (ed.): 128–170. doi:10.1017/CBO9780511572128.006.

Pullen, J.M. 1981. Malthus's theological ideas and their influence on his principle of population. *History of Political Economy* 13: 39–54.

Quinet, Edgar. 1869–1870. *La Création.* Paris: Hachette.

Raby, Peter. 2001. *Alfred Russel Wallace. A life.* London: Chatto & Windus; Princeton, NJ: Princeton University Press. doi:10.2307/j.ctv17db3ct.

Radick, Gregory. (2003). Is the theory of natural selection independent of its history? In Hodge and Radick (eds): 143–167. doi:10.1017/CCOL0521771978.007.

Richards, Robert J. 1987. *Darwin and the emergence of evolutionary theories of mind and behavior*. Chicago and London: University of Chicago Press.

Rogers, James Allen. 1963. The Russian populist's response to Darwin. *Slavic Review* 22: 456–468.

Romanes, George John. 1892–1897. Darwin and after Darwin: An exposition of the Darwinian theory and a discussion of post-Darwinian questions. London: Longmans.

Ronsin, Francis. 1980. *La grève des ventres. Propagande néo-malthusienne et baisse de la natalité en France (XIXe–XXe siècles)*. Paris: Aubier Montaigne.

Royer, Clémence. 1862. Translator's Preface. In Charles Darwin, *De l'origine ds espèces, ou des lois du progress chez les êtres organisés*. Paris: Guillaumin et Cie.

Royer, Clémence. 1870. *Origine de l'homme et des sociétés*. Paris: Guillaumin. Rept. Paris: Jean-Michel Place, 1990.

Rupp-Eisenreich, Britta. 1992. Le darwinisme social en Allemagne. In Tort (ed.): 169–236.

Ruse, Michael. 2010. Evolution and the idea of social progress. In Alexander and Numbers (eds): 247–275. doi:10.7208/9780226608426–011.

Santurri, Edmund N. 1982. Theodicy and social policy in Malthus' thought. *Journal of the History of Ideas* 43: 315–350.

Schabas, Margaret. 1994. The greyhound and the mastiff: Darwinian themes in Mill and Marshall. In Mirowski (ed.): 322–335. doi:10.1017/CBO9780511572128.012.

Schabas, Margaret. 2005. *The natural origins of economics*. Chicago: University of Chicago Press. doi:10.7208/chicago/9780226735719.001.0001.

Schäffle, Albert. 1875–1878. *Bau und Leben des socialen Körpers. Encyclopädischer Entwurf einer realen Anatomie, Physiologie und Psychologie der menschlichen Gesellschaft mit besonderer Rücksicht auf die Volkswirtschaft als socialen Stoffwechsel*. Tübingen: Verlag der H. Laupp'schen Buchhandlung.

Scheler, Max. 1915. *Der Genius des Krieges und der Deutsche Krieg*. Leipzig: Verlag der weißen Bücher.

Schmidt, Alfred. 2014. *The Concept of Nature in Marx*. London: Verso (orig. Der Begriff der Natur in der Lehre von Marx. Frankfurt a.M.: Europäische Verlagsanstalt, 1962).

Schweber, Silvan S. 1977. The origin of the *Origin* revisited. *Journal of the History of Biology* 10: 229–316.

Schweber, Silvan S. 1978. The genesis of natural selection – 1838: some further insights. *BioScience* 28: 321–326.

Schweber, Silvan S. 1979. The young Darwin. *Journal of the History of Biology* 12: 175–192.

Schweber, Silvan S. 1980. Darwin and the political economists: divergence of character. *Journal of the History of Biology* 13: 195–289.

Schweber, Silvan S. 1983. Facteurs idéologiques et intellectuels dans la genèse de la théorie de la selection naturelle. In *De Darwin au darwinisme: science et idéologie*, ed. Yvette Conry, 123–142. Paris: Vrin.

Schweber, Silvan S. 1985. The wider British context of Darwin's theorizing. In Kohn (ed.): 35–69.

Schweber, Silvan S. 1994. Darwin and the agronomists: an influence of political economy on scientific thought. In Cohen (ed.): 305–316. doi:10.1007/978-994-017-3391-5_9.

Semmel, Bernard. 1960. *Imperialism and social reform. English social-imperial thought, 1895–1914*. London: Allen & Unwin.

Seward, A.C. (ed.). 1909. *Darwin and modern science: essays in commemoration of the birth of Charles Darwin and of the fiftieth anniversary of the publication of the Origin of Species*. Cambridge: Cambridge University Press (digital rept. 2009).

Shanahan, Timothy. 2004. *The evolution of Darwinism. Selection, adaptation, and progress in evolutionary biology*. Cambridge: Cambridge University Press. doi:10.1017/CBO9780511616686.

Shermer, Michael. 2002. *In Darwin's shadow. The life and science of Alfred Russel Wallace. A biographical study on the psychology of history*. Oxford: Oxford University Press.

Slotten, Ross A. 2004. *The heretic in Darwin's court: the life of Alfred Russel Wallace*. New York: Columbia University Press.

Smith, Charles H. 1992. Alfred Russel Wallace on spiritualism, man, and evolution: an analytical essay. Torrington, CT (revised 1999). https://people.wku.edu/charles.smith/essays/ARWPAMPH.htm.

Smith, Charles H. 2003a. Wallace's "second moment": intelligent conviction and the course of human evolution. http://people.wku.edu/charles.smith/essays/WALLMO.htm.

Smith, Charles H. 2003b. Alfred Russel Wallace: evolution of an evolutionist. https://people.wku.edu/charles.smith/wallace/chsarw4.htm.

Smith, Charles H. 2004a. Wallace's unfinished business. *Complexity* 10: 25–32.

Smith, Charles H. 2004b. Alfred Russel Wallace on man: a famous "change of mind" – or not? *History and Philosophy of the Life Sciences* 26: 257–270. Smith, Charles H. 2008. Wallace, spiritualism, and beyond: "change," or "no change"? In Smith and Beccaloni (eds): 391–424.

Smith, Charles H. and Beccaloni, George (eds). 2008. *Natural selection and beyond. The intellectual legacy of Alfred Russel Wallace*. Oxford: Oxford University Press.

Smith, Kenneth. 2013. *The Malthusian controversy*. London: Routledge. (1st ed. 1951). doi:10.4324/9781315019239.

Soloway, Richard A. 1990. *Demography and degeneration. Eugenics and the declining birth rate in twentieth century Britain*. Chapel Hill and London: The North Carolina University Press.

Spencer, Herbert. 1852. A theory of population, deduced from the general law of animal fertility. *Westminster Review* 57 (old series), 16 (new series): 468–501.

Spencer, Herbert. 1969. *The Social Organism* (1860). Rept. in The Man Versus *the State. With Four Essays on Politics and Society*, edited with an introduction by Donald G. MacRae, 195–233. Harmondsworth: Penguin Books.

Spengler, Owald. 1918–1923. *Der Untergang des Abendlandes. Umrisse einer Morphologie der Weltgeschichte*. Munich: C.A. Beck'sche Verlagsbuchhandlung.

Stack, David A. 2003. *The first Darwinian Left: A study in the relation of classes in Victorian society*. Oxford: Clarendon Press.

Stack, David A. 2008. Out of "the limbo of 'Unpracticable Politics'": the origins and essence of Wallace's advocacy of land nationalization. In Smith and Beccaloni (eds): 305–319.

Stebbins, R.E. 1972. France. In *The comparative reception of Darwinism*, ed. Thomas F. Glick, 117–167. Austin and London: University of Texas Press.

Stocking, George W.Jr. 1971. *Race, culture and evolution. Essays in the history of anthropology*. New York: Free Press; London: Collier Macmillan (orig. 1968).Sumner, William Graham. 1913. *Earth hunger and other essays*. New Haven: Yale University Press.

Sumner, William Graham. 1914. *The challenge of facts and other essays*. New Haven: Yale University Press.

Sumner, William Graham and Keller, Albert Galloway. 1927. *The science of society*. New Haven: Yale University Press.

Tammone, William. 1995. Competition, the division of labor, and Darwin's principle of divergence. *Journal of the History of Biology* 28: 109–121. doi:10.1007/BF01061248.

Tapinos, Georges Photios. 1999. Paul Leroy-Beaulieu et la question de la population. L'impératif démographique, limite du libéralisme économique. *Population* 54 (1): 103–124.

Tarde, Gabriel. 1898. *Etudes de psychologie sociale*. Paris: Giard et Brière.

Thomas, Brinley. 1991. Alfred Marshall on economic biology, *Review of Political Economy* 3 (1): 1–14.

Thomson, John Arthur. 1909. *Darwinism and human life. The South African Lectures for 1909*. London: Andrew Melrose.

Todes, Daniel P. 1989. *Darwin without Malthus. The struggle for existence in Russian evolutionary thought*. New York and Oxford: Oxford University Press.

Tort, Patrick (ed.). 1992. *Darwinisme et société*. Paris: Presses Universitaires de France.

Tort, Patrick (ed.). 1996. *Dictionnaire du darwinisme et de l'évolution*. Paris: Presses Universitaires de France.

Tort, Patrick (ed.). 2008. The interminable decline of Lamarckism in France. In Engels and Glick (eds): 329–353.

Venturi, Franco. 1972. *Il populismo russo*. Turin: Einaudi (first ed. 1952).

Vidoni, Ferdinando. 1985. *Natura e storia. Marx ed Engels interpreti del darwinismo*. Bari: Dedalo.

Volterra, Vito. 1931. *Leçons sur la théorie mathématique de la lutte pour la vie*, drafted by M. Brelot. Paris: Gauthier-Villars et Cie.

Volterra, Vito and D'Ancona, Umberto. 1935. *Les associations biologiques*. Paris: Hermann. Vorzimmer, Peter J. 1969. Darwin, Malthus, and the theory of natural selection. *Journal of the History of Biology* 30: 527–542.

Vucinich, Alexander. 1988. *Darwin in Russian thought*. Berkeley: University of California Press.

Wallace, Alfred Russel. 1890. Human Selection. *Fortnightly Review* 54 (old series), 48 (new series): 334–335. Rept. in Wallace 1900, 1: 509–526.

Wallace, Alfred Russel. 1900. *Studies scientific and social*. London: Macmillan.

Wallace, Alfred Russel. 1913. *Social environment and moral progress*. London: Cassell.

Wallace, Alfred Russel. 1916. *Letters and reminiscences*, ed. by James Marchant. London: Cassel.

Walras, Léon. 1883. *Théorie mathématique de la richesse sociale*. Lausanne: Corbaz.

Walras, Léon. 1898. *Études d'économie politique appliquée (Théorie de la production de la richesse sociale)*. Lausanne: Corbaz.

Walras, Léon. 1954. *Elements of pure economy, or the theory of social wealth*. Published for the American Economic Society and the Royal Economic Society. Homewood, IL: Richard D. Irwin (orig. *Éléments d'économie politique pure, ou théorie de la richesse sociale*. Lausanne: Corbaz, 1874).

Walter, Ryan. 2020. Malthus's principle of population in Britain: restatement and antiquation. In Faccarello, Izumo and Morishita (eds): 18–52. doi:10.4337/9781788977579.00006.

Ward, Lester Frank. 1883. *Dynamic sociology*. New York: D. Appleton & Co.

Ward, Lester Frank. 1888. Discussion. In James C. Welling. The law of Malthus. *American Anthropologist* 1(1): 21–23.

Ward, Lester Frank. 1893. *The psychic factors of civilization*. Boston: Ginn & Co.

Waterman, A.M.C. 1983. Malthus as a theologian: the "First Essay" and the relation between political economy and Christian theology. In J. Dupâquier, Fauve-Chamoux, Antoinette and E. Grebenik (eds), *Malthus past and present*, 195–209. London: Academic Press.

Waterman, A.M.C. 1991. *Revolution, economics and religion: Christian political economy, 1798–1833*. Cambridge: Cambridge University Press.

Weikart, Richard. 1993. The origins of Social Darwinism in Germany, 1859–1895. *Journal of the History of Ideas* 54: 469–488. doi:10.2307/2710024.

Weikart, Richard. 1999. *Socialist Darwinism. Evolution in German socialist thought from Marx to Bernstein*. San Francisco, London and Bethesda: International Scholar Publications.

Weindlig, Paul. 1991. *Darwinism and social Darwinism in imperial Germany: the contribution of the cell biologist Oskar Hertwig (1849–1922)*. Stuttgart: Gustav Fischer Verlag.

Weindling, Paul. 1989. *Health, race and German politics between national unification and Nazism, 1870–1945*. Cambridge: Cambridge University Press.

Weingart, Peter, Kroll, Jürgen and Bayertz, Kurt. 1988. *Rasse, Blut und Gene. Geschichte der Eugenik und Rassenhygiene in Deutschland*. Frankfurt a.M.: Suhrkamp.

Wigand, Albert. 1874–1877. *Der Darwinismus und die Naturforschung Newtons und Cuviers. Beiträge zur Methodik der Naturforschung und zur Speciesfrage*. Braunschweig: Vieweg und Sohn.

Winch, Donald. 1993. Robert Malthus: Christian moral scientist, arch-demoralizer, or implicit secular utilitarian? *Utilitas* 5: 239–245. doi:10.1017/S0953820800005781.

Winch, Donald. 1996. *Riches and poverty: an intellectual history of political economy in Britain, 1750–1834*. Cambridge: Cambridge University Press.

Winch, Donald. 2001. Darwin fallen among political economists. *Proceedings of the American Philosophical Society* 145: 415–437.

Winch, Donald. 2009. *Wealth and life. Essays on the intellectual history of political economy in Britain, 1848–1914*. Cambridge: Cambridge University Press.

Winter, Jay M. and Teitelbaum, Michael S. 1985. *The fear of population decline*. New York: Academic Press.

Worms, René. 1895. *Organisme et société*. Paris: Giard et Brière.

Worms, René. 1910. *Les principes biologiques de l'action sociale*, Paris: Giard et Brière.

Wrigley, E.A. 1988. Malthus on the prospects of the labouring poor. *Historical Journal* 31: 613–629.

Young, Brian. 2000. Malthus among the theologians. In Dolan (ed.): 93–113. doi:10.1163/9789004333338_006.

Young, Robert M. 1969. Malthus and the evolutionists: the common context of biological and social theory. *Past and Present* 43: 109–145. Rept. in Young 1985b.

Young, Robert M. 1985a. Darwinism is social. In Kohn (ed.): 609–639.

Young, Robert M. 1985b. *Darwin's Metaphor*. Cambridge: Cambridge University Press.

Young, Robert M. 2000. Malthus on man – in animals no moral restraint. In Dolan (ed.): 93–114.

Yule, G. Udny, 1925. The growth of population and the factors which control it. *Journal of the Royal Statistical Society* 88: 1–58.

5   J.S. Mill's understanding of the "organic" nature of socialism

Helen McCabe

Despite some recent challenges,[1] the "received" view of John Stuart Mill is that he was a "classical" liberal, and an advocate of "classical" *laissez-faire* economics. It may well, therefore, come as a surprise that Mill described himself – and Harriet Taylor – as being "under the general designation of Socialists" by the mid-to-late 1840s (Mill 1981: 239).[2] That is, even before they[3] started work on the *Principles of Political Economy*, often viewed as a textbook of classical economics, they viewed their ideas as a "qualified Socialism", influenced by – but not identical with – the so-called "utopian" socialists, particularly William Thompson (and Anna Wheeler), Henri de Saint-Simon and his followers, and – by the end of the decade – Charles Fourier and his followers (especially Victor Considerant), and Louis Blanc (Mill and Taylor 1965: 202–14). A little later, they were also influenced by the ideas of consumer co-operators (for instance, the Rochdale Pioneers), and the experience of producer co-operators, particularly in France after 1848 (Mill and Taylor 1965: 775–94).

In contrast to what we might now understand by the term, Mill (and Taylor) saw socialism as involving the communal ownership of property, and of labour being organised "on the common account", with labour organised by leaders democratically elected by the community "and voluntarily obeyed by them", and with "the division of the produce" of their combined labour being "a public act" done in accordance with some principle of justice "conformable to the ideas of justice or policy prevailing in the community" (ibid: 202). They preferred a decentralised form (as did Fourier, Considerant, Thompson, Owen, Blanc and other co-operators) and had many concerns about more centralised forms (such as Saint-Simonism or what we now identify as Marxism), particularly where they might be instituted by violent and sudden means (ibid: 210–11; Mill 1967c: 737–49). They viewed socialism as a plausible outcome of contemporary trends they observed, particularly a movement led by the working classes themselves away from relations of protection (by employers and aristocrats) and deference (from workers) to independence and – as co-operative socialist George Jacob Holyoake put it – "self help by the people" (Mill and Taylor 1965: 758–65; Holyoake 1882).[4] As Joseph Persky has recently expertly outlined, Mill – rooted as he was in Ricardian economic theory – also saw socialism as the likely outcome of economic forces such as the tendency of the rate of profit towards zero and the onset of the

DOI: 10.4324/9781003138655-5

"stationary state" (Persky 2016: 81–8; Mill and Taylor 1965: 752–7). Mill and Taylor also viewed socialism as the probable outcome of discernible movements in human history between "organic" and "critical" ages (Mill 1981: 171–5). In addition, Mill offered an account rooted in human psychology and the slow impact on it of socialisation in human societies which makes socialism a natural, perhaps even inevitable, outcome of human progress (Mill 1985a: 227, 231–3). Relatedly, Mill and Taylor regarded socialism as a *desirable* "ultimate result of human progress" (Mill and Taylor 1965: xcv). They also believed their preferred form of it to be feasible, with some core elements of it (such as co-operation) being "available as a present resource" to willing volunteers (Mill and Taylor 1965: 775–94; Mill 1967c: 750).[5]

This view of socialism was only possible – for Mill at least – because he adopted a more expansive view of possible social reform. He adopted, from Taylor and from the Saint-Simonians, both the view of history just described, and the idea that the "laws of production" were "fixed" in the same way as other laws of nature (like the law of gravity) but that the "laws of distribution" were malleable, human constructs which, although they also had predictable consequences, could be changed, making social systems liable to questions of justice in ways which were denied by some of his fellow political economists (and also in ways which are simply inappropriate to consider for physical laws like gravity) (Mill 1981: 255–7). To give one example: a rising population rate will, *ceteris paribus*, result in starvation – but population rates are within human control, susceptible to change from a variety of causes including improved education, increased female independence, different religious teachings, and altered economic conditions (Mill and Taylor 1965: 765–6). Combined, these ideas revealed to Mill that his father and Jeremy Bentham's preferred reforms were not the "*dernier mot* of social improvement" (Mill 1981: 175), and suggested that something more just, more equitable, more fraternal, more "organic" would replace the current "critical age" – that is, that the future would, probably, be socialist and, moreover, that this would be a good thing for humanity.

In this chapter I explore these ideas in more detail. I first consider the implications of Mill's view of history for his economics and how he saw economic institutions and change affecting the creation of "organic" and "critical" ages. Second, I turn to Mill's view of the laws of production and distribution, and their impact on his political economy, particularly in bringing a "human" element into his economic theory.

Organic and critical ages – and socialism as the final organic age

Mill was brought up to be a standard-bearer for the "philosophical-radicalism" of his father (James Mill) and Bentham (Persky 2016: 1–88). He lost his unreflective faith in these ideas during his famous "crisis" in the winter of 1826/7 (Mill 1981: 137–91). The following years found him piecing together a much less partisan political philosophy. Alongside re-committing to some previously held beliefs, but in a more authentic, reflective manner, this involved absorbing new ideas from a variety of places. Two key sources for these new ideas were Gustave d'Eichthal, a young Saint-Simonian whom Mill met in 1828 (Mill 1963: 26), and Harriet Taylor, a fellow radical, feminist and reformer, whom Mill met in 1830 (Mill 1981: 193).

D'Eichthal is important for introducing Mill both to the ideas of Saint-Simon and his followers, and to those of Auguste Comte (then also identifying himself as a Saint-Simonian) (Mill 1963: 26; Mill 1981: 173). Mill says that "[t]he writers by whom, more than any others, a new mode of political thinking was brought home to me" were the Saint-Simonians (Mill 1981: 171). He was "greatly struck with the connected view which they for the first time presented to me, of the natural order of human progress; and especially with their division of all history into organic periods and critical periods" (ibid).

Organic periods are those in which

> mankind accept with firm conviction some positive creed, claiming jurisdiction over all their actions, and containing more or less of truth and adaptation to the needs of humanity. Under its influence they make all the progress compatible with the creed, and finally outgrow it.

What follows is a critical period, "in which mankind lose their old convictions without acquiring any new ones, of a general or authoritative character, except the conviction that the old ones are false". An example of an organic age is Medieval Christendom, with the Reformation being the corresponding critical age. Mill notes that these ideas "were the general property of Europe", but he felt they had "never been so completely systematised" as by the Saint-Simonians, "nor the distinguishing characteristics of a critical period so powerfully set forth" (ibid). Their characterisation of "the peculiarities of an era of transition of opinion", enabled Mill to never again "mistake the moral and intellectual characteristics of such an era, for the normal attributes of humanity" (ibid: 173). He adds:

> I looked forward, through the present age of loud disputes but generally weak convictions, to a future which shall unite the best qualities of the critical with the best qualities of the organic periods: unchecked liberty of thought, unbounded freedom of individual action in all modes not hurtful to others;[6] but also, convictions as to what is right and wrong, useful and pernicious, deeply engraven on the feelings by early education and general unanimity of sentiment, and so firmly grounded in reason and the true exigencies of life, that they shall not, like all former and present creeds, religious, ethical, and political, require to be periodically thrown off and replaced by others.
>
> (Mill 1981: 173)

It is that future which Mill (and Taylor) would eventually come to see as best achieved via their preferred form of socialism.

This view of history is not referenced explicitly in Mill's economic writings, but it underpins much of his critical commentary on contemporary society in such works, as well as his views regarding feasible and desirable futures.[7] Mill saw economic structures and relations as important parts of our life-long education, and thus playing a vital role in either hindering or encouraging "general unanimity of sentiment". Similarly, he recognised that political economy was key to properly understanding "the true exigencies of life". He viewed political economy as being part of *politics* (Mill 1984: 245), and noticed that "creeds" of political economy had been "thrown off" in critical periods just as much as religious or ethical creeds, and political hierarchies. That is, the critical period in which he lived was still dismantling and rejecting feudalism – and that involved core changes to economic structures (for instance, the movement away from serfdom and relations of dependence and service to wage-labour and the increasing independence of working people).

We might think that capitalism is compatible with Mill's view of an "organic" age. Under capitalism "mankind accept with firm convictions some positive creed" which is at least sufficiently adapted to the needs of humanity that it has not been "thrown off", be that neoliberalism or social-democracy. Certainly Mill identified his *own* age as a critical one, still busily rejecting the "organic age" which existed before the Reformation, and not yet acquiring new "authoritative" views, apart from a general renunciation of what had gone before. But his own age was not yet fully formed "capitalism". Or, from a Marxist perspective, perhaps Mill was merely not prescient enough in noticing he no longer lived in a critical age, but a new organic one of capitalism.[8]

Moreover, Mill emphasised "unchecked liberty of thought" and "unbounded freedom of action" as key elements in a future age which combines the "best" elements of critical and organic ages. These are generally associated more with capitalism than with socialism – though this association may neither be entirely correct, nor necessary. Certainly, in *Principles* Mill stressed the importance of individuality, and the freedom necessary to develop it, when discussing the desirability of communism (Mill and Taylor 1965: 209) Although identifying a great deal of unfreedom in contemporary society, Mill was sceptical that small-scale, self-sufficient communities where everything was owned communally, where labour was done on the common account, and where the product of that labour was distributed in strictly equal portions,[9] would secure this vital "mainspring of mental and moral progress" (Mill and Taylor 1965: 209). This has been taken by some commentators on Mill's socialism as support for capitalism, and as undermining – even over-riding – Mill's claim to have been "under the general designation of socialist" in his *Autobiography* (Schapiro 1943; Hainds 1946; Fredman and Gordon 1967; Losman 1971; Thomas 1985; Kurer 1992; Winch 2009). Though we should note that Mill said such concerns, like others, were "vastly exaggerated" (Mill and Taylor 1965: 209).

It is not, then, impossible to imagine an "organic" capitalist age. However, Mill's preferred organic age was *not* capitalist, but a form of (non-communistic) socialism. He describes his (and Taylor's) position as follows:

While we repudiated with the greatest energy that tyranny of society over the individual which most Socialistic systems are supposed to involve, we yet looked forward to a time when society will no longer be divided into the idle and the industrious; when the rule that they who do not work shall not eat, will be applied not to paupers only, but impartially to all; when the division of the produce of labour, instead of depending ... on the accident of birth, will be made by concert, on an acknowledged principle of justice; and when it will no longer either be, or be thought to be, impossible for human beings to exert themselves strenuously in procuring benefits which are not to be exclusively their own, but to be shared with the society they belong to. The social problem of the future we considered to be, how to unite the greatest individual liberty of action, with a common ownership in the raw material of the globe, and an equal participation of all in the benefits of combined labour.

(Mill 1981: 239)

This involves "critical" aspects of individual liberty (of action and thought), but also an "organic", over-arching "positive creed" (we might nowadays use the term "ideology"), which provides a justification for a classless society where all who are able work (unless – as Mill puts it elsewhere – they have "earned rest by previous toil" [Mill and Taylor 1965: 758]); where labour is done on the common, rather than individual, account, and the "produce" of it is distributed according to a generally accepted principle of justice (e.g. equal shares, or "from each according to their capacity, to each according to their need"); where there is (at least) communal ownership of land and natural resources; and where people work (and live) as equals.

Some of this might be achievable under a very-reformed system of individual property, perhaps akin to modern ideas of a "property-owning democracy".[10] That is, we might imagine a society where land and natural resources are communally owned (probably by the state), but where people retain the right to own capital (not just articles of consumption) individually; where the "acknowledged principle of justice" on which distribution is based would be that which Mill thought the only justification of private property, securing for the labourer the fruits of his or her own labour, with some sort of fair proportionality between effort and reward (Mill and Taylor 1965: 208); and where everyone works in profit-sharing businesses. In such a society, the "idle rich" would no longer be able to own land (which Mill saw as being the root cause of many rich people's ability to live a life without labouring), and large individual personal fortunes might be tempered both by profit-sharing and also by Mill's other proposals for limiting inheritance to a "moderate independence" (ibid: 887), which are in line with the foundational principle of justice for private property – that people's remuneration or wealth ought to be directly linked to, and proportional to, their effort (ibid: 208).

However, such a system of individual property would not *really* achieve the "equal participation of all in the benefits of combined labour", because profit-sharing is *not* an equal, but instead still very hierarchical, relationship. Moreover, in such a world human beings would *not* "exert themselves strenuously in procuring benefits which are not to be exclusively their own", for the very point of profit-sharing, individual property, and linking remuneration with effort is that people are motivated to work for *their own* benefit. Similarly, although we might think that even modern capitalist societies have "an acknowledged principle of justice" which is always implicitly referred to in questions around, for instance, welfare systems or unemployment benefits (and which underpins ideas about the "deserving poor", for instance), it is hard to see any capitalist society's division of the "produce of labour" being "made in concert", because so much is deliberately left to the "hidden hand" of the market.

From what Mill writes elsewhere, it is clear that among the "convictions as to what is right and wrong, useful and pernicious" he had in mind as forming an important part of the "positive creed" of a future organic age was seeing working as being motivated by a concern for the good of others, not merely oneself. Indeed, Mill says he "entirely subscribe[d]" to an

> idea of M. Comte, which has great beauty and grandeur in it ... that every person who lives by any useful work, should be habituated to regard himself not as an individual working for his private benefit, but as a public functionary; and his wages ... not as the remuneration or purchase money of his labour, which should be given freely, but as the provision made by society to enable him to carry it on, and to replace the materials and products which have been consumed in the process[11] ... What M. Comte really means is that we should regard working for the benefit of others as a good in itself; that we should desire it for its own sake, and not for the sake of remuneration, which cannot justly be claimed for doing what we like: that the proper return for a service to society is the gratitude of society: and that the moral claim of any one in regard to the provision of his personal wants, is not a question of *quid pro quo* in respect to his co-operation, but of how much the circumstances of society permit to be assigned to him, consistently with the just claim of others.
>
> (Mill 1985b: 340–1)

This "creed" is obviously incompatible with the underlying principles of capitalism. To make the point even more plainly, Mill adds "[t]he rough method of settling the labourer's share of the produce, the competition of the market, may represent a practical necessity, but certainly not a moral ideal" (ibid: 341).

That is, individual property, wage labour, and an underlying principle of justice linking remuneration and effort may be a "positive creed" which is adapted to the current "exigencies of human life". It may even contain some "truth": it is more fair that remuneration is proportional to effort rather than that there is an "inverse ratio" such that "the largest portion" of the produce of labour goes to "those who have never worked at all ... and so on in a decreasing scale, the remuneration dwindling as the work grows harder and more disagreeable, until the most fatiguing and exhausting bodily labour cannot count with certainty on being able to earn even the necessaries of life" (Mill and Taylor 1965: 207). It is, however, even *more* just (on Mill's view) that we contribute according to capacity, and distribute according to need (ibid: 203). This distributive principle, though, however true and however much it meets the needs of humanity, is not "adapted" to them in one crucial sense: human beings are not (yet) capable of adopting it as a foundational principle of justice. Where "higher" principles of justice like it (and like equal shares, which Mill viewed as inferior to Blanc's idea) were adopted in France in 1848, people were happy to "take" but not to "give" (ibid: 782). What worked better was "allowing everyone a fixed minimum, sufficient for subsistence" and then "apportion[ing] all further remuneration according to the work done" (ibid) – a sort of hybrid between meeting needs and harnessing self-interest.[12]

Mill's view of organic and critical ages is concerned with ideational "creeds" rather than material conditions: there have been organic, and also critical, ages at all stages of economic development. These terms are descriptive, though they also help explain the process and the observable pattern of historical change. Mill notes that in organic ages "mankind ... make all the progress compatible with the creed, and finally outgrow it" (Mill 1981: 171). This "progress" is not solely intellectual or in terms of ideas. Mill certainly has in mind increases in knowledge (from abstract theory through to applied sciences), but he also has in mind social, political and economic "progress". For instance, in explaining why he did not support a "paternalist" view of the "the probable futurity of the labouring classes" as a good society, Mill acknowledges that "in an age of lawless violence and insecurity ... in which life is beset with dangers and sufferings at every step ... a generous giving of protection, and a grateful receiving of it, are the strongest ties which connect human beings" (Mill and Taylor 1965: 760). However, "these virtues and sentiments ... belong emphatically to a rude and imperfect state of the social union". Nowadays, "human beings, of ordinary strength and courage" have no need to "glow with warmest gratitude and devotion in return for protection" (ibid).

> The laws protect them ... No man or woman who either possesses or is able to earn an independent livelihood, requires any other protection than that which the law could and ought to give. This being the case, it argues great ignorance of human nature to continue taking for granted that relations founded on protection must always subsist, and not to see that the assumption of the part of a protector, and of the power which belongs to it, without any of the necessities which justify it, must engender feelings opposite to loyalty.
>
> (ibid: 761)[13]

On the one hand, of course, this is an account which is firmly concerned with what Karl Marx called the "superstructure" – laws, sentiments, ideology. And Marxists might criticise Mill for being too concerned with how ideology changes, and not with the underlying changes in the relations of the factors of production. But what I want to emphasise is that, even here, Mill (and Taylor) are evidently not ignorant of, nor ignoring, economic and material factors. These are key to ensuring "security", because they are foundational to, and necessary for, men and women being able "to earn an independent livelihood", and it is *this* ability which fundamentally undermines the need for, and the "virtue" of, relations of protection and dependence. Of course, on Mill and Taylor's account, we need not only the kind of economic arrangements and technology which allow *everyone* [14] to earn an "independent" living (i.e. not one rooted in, for instance, feudal service) but a system of law which protects *everyone* (not just the rich). That is, we need to move not only from feudalism to a market economy, but from the limited protections of – say – Magna Carta (which only applied to the barons who had enough power to wrest such protections from the King), to laws which recognise the fully equal rights of every person before the law (i.e. the Human Rights Act). Importantly, though, Mill sees economic and political "movement" as having an interactive relationship.

Similarly, in the passage on Comte's view of labour quoted above, Mill notes that it is only in a modern market economy where "every one in fact works much more for others than for himself, since his productions are to be consumed by others" that we can realise the "moral ideal" of labour.[15] However, he notes that this economic fact (relying on the underlying relation of the factors of production) could produce both a "right" and a "wrong" view of labour. Comte thought that labourers' "thoughts and imagination should adapt themselves to the real state of the fact" of their work, and they would see the "true" reality – and moral ideal – of labour. But, Mill says,

> [t]he practical problem … is not quite so simple, for a strong sense that he is working for others may lead to nothing better than feeling himself necessary to them, and instead of freely giving his commodity, may only encourage him to put a high price upon it.
>
> (ibid: 340)

Economic facts – that is – are not enough: we also need moral education, and economic realities will not necessarily lead us to the "right" moral conclusions.

In Marxist terms, then, the "superstructure" and underlying relations of the factors of production interact, but are also in many ways independent of each other.[16] "Progress" in *both* under the overarching ideology of an "organic" age eventually makes that age untenable, and a critical age begins. Importantly, for understanding Mill (and Taylor's) economic thought, "progress" in terms of greater combination and also specialisation of labour in a market economy, along with seismic changes in political and religious beliefs, meant "the poor had come out of leading strings, and cannot any longer be governed or treated like children" (Mill and Taylor 1965: 763). The facts of new relations of production, combined with working people's access to education (through schools, and also through widely circulating newspapers) meant Mill could not think "that they will be permanently contended with the condition of labouring for wages as their ultimate status", but would demand at least profit-sharing, and increasingly move away from reliance on capitalists, and assert their independence in co-operatives (ibid: 766–9) – that is, in socialism.

These historical and socio-economic trends, then, led Mill to expect something like socialism would form the next organic age. He also had normative reasons for desiring that it would, concerning justice, equality, individuality, and also reasons we might broadly call concerned with "fraternity",[17] and which are linked to his utilitarianism.

Mill expressed a desire that "the influences which form moral character" should ensure that "the feeling of unity with our fellow creatures shall be ... as deeply rooted in our character, and to our consciences as completely a part of our nature, as the horror of crime is in an ordinarily well-brought up young person" today (Mill 1985a: 227). This would allow people to act to achieve the greatest happiness of the greatest number without external coercion, but only from internal promptings, making it feel entirely "natural", just like – for most people – not murdering someone feels today. Acting to achieve the greatest happiness of the greatest number is, for Mill, *the* overarching moral goal, and test of "right" action. It is easier to achieve when we feel "in unity" with our fellow-creatures than when we feel opposed, or indifferent, to them.

Mill – brought up as an "associationist" – thought a great deal of human psychology was malleable, for instance our motivations and our conscience. But he thought some things were firmly grounded in our "nature", most obviously seeking pleasure and avoiding pain. He also thought that

> the social feelings of mankind; the desire to be in unity with our fellow creatures ... is ... a powerful principle in human nature, and happily one of those which tend to become stronger, even without express inculcation, from the influences of advancing civilisation.
>
> (Mill 1985a: 231)

Economic practices play a role in creating both external and internal "sanctions", which – in turn – shape our individual consciences, though – as Mill notes in relation to Comte – economic realities are not sufficient to give people the "right" moral ideas. Similarly, "advancing civilisation" has an economic element – not least increasingly "combined" labour, which forms the preconditions for Comte's (and Mill's) view of labour, and the "moral" view of working. "[S]avage independence" as depicted in Hobbes' "state of nature" famously makes "combination", trust, "social feeling", "unity" and "civilisation" impossible (ibid).[18] Great "nation-builders" like Akbar or Charlemagne help forge the necessary basic social bonds, acting like Leviathans in overcoming the rational bases for "savage independence" (Mill and Taylor 1977: 234). This achieved, though, Mill tells an *economic* story about increasing "combination" of labour, and thus of people in *Principles* (Mill and Taylor 1965: 116–30), and a more psychological and ethical story in *Utilitarianism*, as well as a political story about socialisation through increasing participation in "the public" sphere, where citizens are forced to "weigh interests not [their] own" and "apply principles and maxims which have for their reason of existence the common good" in *Considerations on Representative Government* (Mill 1977: 412).[19]

Indeed, given Mill's association with "classical" political economists like David Ricardo and Adam Smith, it is worth noting the sub-heading in Chapter 8 of Book 1 of *Principles* "Combination of labour a principal cause of superior productiveness" and his emphasis that "[o]f this great aid to production, a single department, known by the name of Division of Labour, has engaged a large share of the attention of political economists ... to the exclusion of other cases and exemplifications of the same comprehensive law" (Mill and Taylor 1965: 116).[20] "Simple co-operation ... is the first step in social improvement" (ibid: 117).[21] Division of labour, and specialisation, relies on "Complex Co-operation", "the combination of several labourers to help one another by a division of operations" (ibid). Complex co-operation happens almost unconsciously, at least on the part of the workers involved, because the whole of modern society is a vast complex of co-operation (ibid: 118). And when it *is* so, the conditions are such that the "moral" view of labour may be realised – not spontaneously, through mere knowledge of the economic facts – but through a combination of those facts and ethical education. Co-operation is a rational "next step" in the combination of labour; it helps workers to a desirable kind of solidarity or fraternity (or at least, it does when it is living up to its own principles);[22] and – ultimately – it better-enables people to take the "moral" view of their mutual dependence, both through further highlighting that interdependence, *and* by encouraging a more "moral" view of economic interaction.

Socialism is discussed in *Principles* as a set of different economic arrangements, but Mill was also well aware that socialism had more normative elements, emphasising mutuality, equality, fraternity, emancipation and justice. Moreover, Mill shared many of these same concerns. In *Principles* we see him engaging seriously with socialist ideas of private property and distributive justice, and endorsing them as "higher" than those which purportedly underpin individual property, and *much* "higher" than those which *actually* underpinned contemporary capitalism (Mill and Taylor 1965: 201–18, 758). This is echoed in the *Autobiography*, as are his concerns about class-division and social disharmony (Mill 1981: 239–41). In his 1845 piece, *The Claims of Labour*, he decries the "widening breach between those who toil and those who live on the produce of former toil", and says the underlying "principle" of his "Utopia", on which he "place[d his] ... chief hope for healing" that breach, was "raising the labourer from a receiver of hire – a mere bought instrument in the work of production, having no residuary interest in the work itself – to the position of being, in some sort, a partner in it" (Mill 1967a: 382). Similarly, in *Principles* he says:

> I confess I am not charmed with the ideal of life held out by those who think that the normal state of human beings is that of struggling to get on;

that the trampling, crushing, elbowing and treading on each other's heels, which form the existing type of social life, are the most desirable lot of human kind, or anything but the disagreeable symptoms of one of the phases of industrial progress.

(Mill and Taylor: 1965: 754)

His (and Taylor's) description of "a transformation" of the economy "which ... would be the nearest approach to social justice, and the most beneficial ordering of industrial affairs for the universal good, which it is possible at present to foresee" involves working people founding producer- and consumer co-operatives in order to slowly, organically and peacefully ensure the "existing accumulations of capital ... by a kind of spontaneous process, become in the end the joint property of all who participate in their productive employment" (ibid: 793–4). This involves the voluntary actions of capitalists following their own self-interested pursuit of profits, not just the actions of some enlightened employers adopting profit-sharing for normative reasons (ibid). It *also* involves the deliberate action of working people, not only pursuing their self-interest, but self-consciously determining to "work for one another" and seeking to free themselves from the "tax" or "heavy tribute" put on them by capitalists and thereby overcome – without violence – the contemporary antagonistic and exploitative relationship between employers and employed (ibid: 775). Indeed, the word "socialism" was invented to contrast it with "individualism", and Mill (despite championing individuality) notes that, "Socialism, as long as it attacks the existing individualism, is easily triumphant" (Mill 1967d: 444).

Mill does not offer an account of *why* his preferred form of socialism would be an organic age, not needing to be "thrown off" as all others have – moreover, he leaves open the possibility of further reforms which we are not yet capable of imagining (Mill 1981: 173). His is not, for instance, a dialectical story. However, we can see how Mill might have thought that a society which achieved justice *and* "the free development of individuality" (Mill and Taylor 1977: 261); which combined toleration with mutual respect and kindness; which had achieved a stationary state in which no one experienced privation, and no one was motivated to try to exploit their fellow citizens for their private advantage; which had universally adopted both a secular "religion" supporting utilitarian principles and positivist principles regarding knowledge-creation which would lead to wider and wider general acceptance of an increasing number of "truths" which *really were* true; which had eradicated divisions (and power-imbalances resulting in exploitation and oppression) based on class, race and sex/gender; and in which there was at least some recognition of environmental concerns such that they would act as a curb to production, human habitation and cultivation would be one in which there was no further need for the "throwing off" of this creed.[23] It would be *already* well-adapted to the "true exigencies of human life", *and* flexible enough to adapt organically to any future "truths" and events.

Of course, this is an optimistic view – perhaps even (with its underlying faith not only in positivism but in the idea that many truths were *already* incontrovertibly known) arrogant. But given that this *is* how Mill saw socialism, we can see why he might think it would be a "final" organic age.

In this section I have sought to show how Mill's view of history as moving between "organic" and "critical" ages intertwined with his economics, because he saw economics as playing an important role in this "progress", in both the stability and the eventual instability of "organic" ages. This is a key "human" element of his economics, which takes seriously real – and changing – human attitudes, and considers the impact of prevailing ideologies on economics (and of economics on prevailing ideologies). Moreover, Mill sees motivations of human nature, as well as economic rationales, as providing explanations of key changes in economic structures (for instance, combination of labour). Further, he emphasises that there is a "moral" element of economic relationships, because they are between humans, most clearly exemplified in his discussion of the "moral" view of labour.

Socialism, for Mill, was expected as the future organic age *both* because of economic changes and innovations *and* because it encapsulated many desirable normative concepts (such as harmony, egalitarianism and justice) he thought had their root in human nature and could be seen coming to greater and greater importance and feasibility throughout human history. His account, then, emphasises core human elements of economics and progress in political economy. This is rooted in Mill's reading of the Saint-Simonians, but he made it very much his own.

The laws of production and distribution

The second area in which Mill emphasised the "human" element in economics was his (in)famous distinction between the laws of production and distribution. Mill recalls that interaction with the Saint-Simonians taught him "a new mode" of thinking, of which one fundamental element was this distinction (Mill 1981: 71, 175). Mill said "the common run of political economists" "confuse ... together, under the designation of economic laws, which they deem incapable of being defeated or modified by human effort" the "laws" of production and distribution (ibid: 255). To this view he now vehemently dissented, going so far as to criticise Harriet Martineau (and her fellow "classical" political economists) for assuming that the current economic model is "as little under human control as the division of day and night" (Mill 1967b: 227).

The laws of production, Mill asserted, are indeed "dependent on the properties of objects", and thus cannot be changed, bent or transgressed (Mill 1981: 255). (There is a famous adage to this effect, that the world cannot be fed from a single plant pot.) However, the modes of distribution "subject to certain conditions, depend on human will". This means that distributive outcomes can be "modified by human effort", and are liable to be evaluated not only on the grounds of efficiency but also of justice. Mill felt many political economists were guilty of ascribing the same necessity to things dependent on the unchangeable conditions of our earthly existence, and to those which, being but necessary consequences of particular social arrangements are merely coextensive with these.

(ibid)

This leads them to assume that "the shares which fall, in the division of the produce, to labourers, capitalists, and landlords" are "an inherent necessity, against which no human means can avail" (ibid: 257).

He describes *Principles* as having

yielded to none of its predecessors in aiming at the scientific appreciation of the action of these causes, under the conditions which they presuppose: but it set the example of not treating those conditions as final. The economic generalisations which depend, not on necessities of nature but on those combined with the existing arrangements of society, it deals with only as provisional, and as liable to be much altered by the progress of social improvement.

Recognising his debt to the Saint-Simonians, Mill adds this idea was "made a living principle pervading and animating the book by my wife's promptings" (ibid). One obvious element of this is *Principles'* structure. Book I (Production) is concerned with explaining the social-scientific "laws" of this element of political economy. Book II (Distribution) takes seriously questions about *possible* modes of distribution, and the predictable, unavoidable outcomes which arise from them (Mill and Taylor 1965: 245–51, 210–14). Book IV (Influence of the Progress of Society on Production and Distribution) is concerned with exploring the impact of different "arrangements of society" on economic questions, such as the impact of "the progress of industry and population on values and prices" (Chapter 2), "the tendency of profits to a minimum" (Chapter 4), or "the probable futurity of the labouring classes" (Chapter 7). Book V (On the Influence of Government) considers the influence of government in general, but mainly on a modern industrial society, and the consequences of some potential changes in policy over, for instance, tax (Chapters 3, 4, 5 and 6), and "laisser-faire" (sic) (Chapters 8, 9, 10 and 11). It is most obviously concerned with the ways in which human decision-making and action shapes economic outcomes (and the extent to which it cannot), because governments are made up of humans; and were increasingly responsive to public opinion throughout the period in which Mill (and Taylor) was writing and revising *Principles* – in particular, public opinion which insisted that governments respond to questions about justice (and just distributions of wealth). Mill did not think that the demand for fairer distribution of wealth could be met with responses which tried to pretend distribution was out of the government's hand – indeed, out of human control. There might be economic "facts" (to do with production, and the interaction between production and feasible modes of distribution) which meant the current, very unfair, distribution was the best possible – but working people (in particular) deserved an explanation of that fact, and it had to be given in such a way that they would see it was true and not merely a self-protective tissue of lies (ibid: 763).

Principles, even in its structure, then, encapsulates Mill's thinking that, although there were certain "necessary consequences of particular social arrangements" which *were* "coextensive" with any set of social arrangements, these social arrangements themselves were a matter of human choice and construction, and capable of change by human endeavour. We see this very clearly in his discussion of private property regimes in Book II, and in his discussion of "the probable futurity of the labouring population" and the impact of government action (in Books IV and V respectively).

In these chapters, for instance, it is clear that capitalism necessitates a certain division of the means of production and the product of labour between labourers, capitalists and landlords. Similarly, feudalism necessitates a particular division between landowners, freemen and serfs. However, these two divisions are very different, arising from the differences in the systems themselves. Moreover, *both* systems are human constructions, and change as a result of human endeavour. Thus, contemporary capitalism was not "fixed" but capable of being improved.

Mill's view of the difference between the laws of production and distribution has been much criticised, but it is both plausible and consistent.[24] His brief account in the *Autobiography* can appear to imply that laws of production are completely immutable, and laws of distribution entirely malleable, but this was not his actual position. He did not think the laws of production and distribution were entirely independent of each other, and he did not think that *all* distributive outcomes were *simply* a matter of human choice.

What Mill *did* think was that, within any society, however it determines distribution, the laws of production are dependent on physical facts such as fecundity; distance to markets; condition of infrastructure; levels of technical advance in, for instance, tools; climate (and ability to mitigate its effects); and natural resources like water and minerals. But advances in "human" elements like skill, craft and knowledge also affect production. Scientific knowledge can improve agricultural practice and thus the fecundity of a particular piece of land, though it cannot exceed *some* physical limit. Improvements in transport can create demand and increase production – but not infinitely. Technical advances in machinery can greatly increase production – but, again, not infinitely as eventually production will outstrip demand (even with human-invented mechanisms for manipulating demand like advertising, built-in obsolescence and fashion).

Similarly, "[g]iven certain institutions and customs, wages, profits, and rent [i.e. distributions of wealth] will be determined by certain causes" which are also predictable and determined (Mill 1981: 255–7). But these causes are themselves the outcome of social arrangements, and these are human constructions, and can be changed by human effort (ibid; Mill 1974: 918). That is, the distributions under feudalism are predictable once we understand its economic structure, and so are distributions under capitalism or even socialism: but which social structure we live under is at least partly a human choice, though also constrained by "laws of production" – for instance, socialism is only really "available as a present resource" (Mill 1967c: 750) at an advanced stage of "complex cooperation" of labour, which in itself relies on other important factors of production (and advances in those factors, themselves influenced by "human" elements such as education, knowledge and motivation).

In this way, the laws of production and distribution are inter-related: our "modes of production" are in some sense dependent on previous distributions (e.g. of ownership rights over, and profits arising from, land, capital and labour), and the social system we have which "gives" our current laws of distribution depends on what was produced in the past, and how.[25] But what Mill wanted to emphasise was that distributive outcomes are, to some extent at least, dependent on human choice, because the social systems with which they are "coextensive" are a matter of human construction, and *are* capable of being changed through conscious human action.

This view of production and distribution marks a radical break with the earlier traditions of political economy in which Mill had been raised. His sensitivity to the relationship between economics and society more widely – to changing ideas, religion, politics and even psychology – also mark a difference to the often criticised view of "*homo economicus*" (though more modern economists might merely say this is because Mill's economics is not far-advanced enough!). His view, however, raises interesting questions about feasibility and "availability"[26] when it comes to economic systems. Mill was adamant that we should not take the status quo as "fixed and unchangeable", but he was concerned that facts (economic, and also historical, social, political, psychological and other) as well as normative considerations needed to be taken into account when planning reform.

Combined with his new view of history, and identification of his own period as a "critical age" which would eventually be replaced by a new "organic age", these ideas about the different "nature" of the laws of production and distribution allowed Mill to reject his father's (and Bentham's) preferred reforms as the "*dernier mot* of social improvement" and to see that much more was possible. It is true that Mill thought political economists would have to consider regimes of individual property for a long time to come, as communal schemes may not (as yet) be feasible – but it is also true that he advocated feasible and "available" advances in the organisation of labour (and production) around co-operation that would begin an "organic" transition to socialism (Mill and Taylor 1965: 214, 793–4).

Conclusion

Mill's introduction to Saint-Simonian thought led to two fundamental shifts in his economic thinking. One regards the movement of human history. This both opened up broader horizons for social, political and economic reform beyond what he had previously thought possible, and impacted his thinking about the history – and possible future – of economic arrangements. Mill's theory of history has an important place for ideas and "human" elements such as ethics, psychology, religion, political organisations and what we might broadly think of as "ideology", and a more materialist account of changing relations between key factors of production (and distributions of resources, and thus power, between different groups of people).

The second element regards key differences in the laws of production and of distribution. This also allowed Mill to see that much more was possible in terms of social reform, and also to explain what limits there might be (in terms of feasibility and "availability") for certain reforms, and why. The complex inter-relation between "physical" or "natural" and "human" influences means Mill did not draw a stark and complete distinction between the nature of these laws, but he did think that patterns of distribution (e.g. property rights) were not "immutable", and that – particularly where they created disutility and injus-tice – society had a duty to ensure they were indeed the best possible (i.e. most desirable, feasible and available) arrangements.

Mill credited the Saint-Simonians (and particularly his close friend, d'Eich-thal) with introducing him to these ideas, but also emphasised his co-author and (future) wife's role in making these ideas "living truths". In particular, he was keen to give due credit for her important role in the way these ideas influenced the *Principles* both in terms of its structure and its content.

When *Principles* was first published, Mill wanted to formally credit Taylor's role in the book, but eventually only included the planned dedication in a few "presentation" copies (Mill 1981: 257).[27] Over the years, her role has been down-played, even denied, in the main by those who wish to explain away Mill's socialism by putting it down to his inability to resist her.[28] These claims are unwarranted.[29] However, the fact that *Principles* was co-authored adds a final "human" quality to Mill's economics via the mode in which his most famous, and impactful, economic treatise came into being. *Principles* was a "labour of love" in more than one way. For twenty years after they met, Mill and Taylor's relationship was limited to friendship and co-authoring, even though it was evident to them, and to Taylor's husband, that they craved a much closer union (which they finally achieved in 1851). Many, though by no means all, of their joint work concerned political economy, and we ought to recognise this in re-assessing Taylor's place in the historical canon. Moreover, their discussions over drafting and editing *Principles* formed a key part of their relationship.

Moving away from the personal, Mill notes that the "abstract and purely scientific" part of *Principles* came from him, but the "properly human element came from her" (Mill 1981: 257). Taylor was, Mill says, more "courageous and farsighted" than he would have been without her. However, Mill also thought that because "[h]er mind invested all ideas in a concrete shape, and formed to itself a conception of how they would actually work", she kept his feet on the ground and prevented him from being "really visionary" (ibid). That is, Taylor was willing to countenance radical ideas such as the abolition of the regime of individual property and its replacement by socialist ideas of communal property; but she was also highly alert to questions of feasibility and availability concerning any proposed reforms. She was, then, alert to questions of human possibility, as well as to questions of human need, and this capacity infuses *Principles* and others of Mill's economic works.

Their combined approach, then, incorporates "human" elements in economic thought through – put most simply – appreciating that real human beings create economies and act within economic structures. Indeed, Mill defined Political Economy as the study of "the sources and conditions of wealth and material prosperity for aggregate bodies of human beings" offering "important lessons ... for the guidance of life, and for the estimation of laws and institutions", emphasising the importance of "knowing all it can teach in order to have true views of the course of human affairs, or form plans for their improvement which will stand actual trial" (Mill 1984: 245). These "bodies" operate within a natural world which can be affected in myriad ways by human beings, but which is not entirely malleable. In the end, matter cannot be created nor destroyed; gravity cannot be denied; or the second law of thermodynamics be reversed. Mill's contemporaries tried to deny the insights of political economy as "unfeeling" because it "recognises unpleasant facts". Mill retorted:

> For my part, the most unfeeling thing I know of is the law of gravitation: it breaks the neck of the best and most amiable person without scruple, if he forgets for a single moment to give heed to it ... My advice ... is to study the great writers on Political Economy, and hold firmly by whatever in them you find true: and depend upon it that if you are not selfish or hard-hearted already, Political Economy will not make you so.
>
> (ibid)

He was, of course, *also* very invested in a "moral" education which would make it harder and harder for anyone to be "selfish or hard-hearted", and his belief in what such moral improvement, alongside technological advance, could achieve led him to embrace socialism as not only desirable, but feasible – even probable. His criterion of "desirable" was based on a rounded view of human happiness, not just maximising profit, productivity or production.[30] As a utilitarian, this concept of *human* happiness, and a dedication to maximising it, guided his thinking on political economy. He recognised there were "fixed" laws and tendencies which could be studied like those of any science – but he emphasised that these laws did not determine *everything* about human society and human happiness (just as the laws of gravity do not), and we could use our knowledge and understanding of political economy to vastly improve not only our own happiness but that of everyone in the world, and of future generations to come. He saw this happy society being best achieved in a socialist future where all who are able will work; where the produce of that work will be distributed in accordance with agreed principles of justice; and where people will be motivated to work for the benefit of the whole of society, not just themselves (Mill 1981: 239). He and Taylor saw great potential for achieving this through producer- and consumer-co-operatives, which were themselves the outcome of millennia of human history and slow progress towards combined labour and "generous" understandings of justice and the nature of human interdependence in a modern economy (ibid; Mill and Taylor 1965: 793–4).

Notes

1 E.g. from Bruce Baum, Wendy Sarvasy, Oskar Kurer, Gregory Claeys, Jonathan Riley and William Stafford.
2 For a detailed exploration of this claim, see McCabe 2021.
3 I will deal with Taylor's role in *Principles of Political Economy* below, but it is important to note that Mill says this was the first of his works in which she played a "conspicuous" co-authoring role. Mill 1981: 255.
4 Both a peaceful transition to a decentralised form of socialism and a more violent transition to a centralised version seemed *possible*, particularly given the intransigence of many governments which prompted frustrated workers to feel violence was their only means of enacting change. Mill warned against such desperate action as undermining the socialists' over-arching goals in *Chapters*, as well as preferring a decentralised, more plural version of socialism for other reasons connected to individuality. For more on this, see McCabe 2021: 93–136, 197–238.
5 For more on "desirable", "feasible" and "available" as I use them here, see McCabe 2019: 291–309.
6 It is interesting to note that this passage contains a version of the harm principle, and to speculate whether Mill really *did* think that at the time, or whether this is him interpolating backwards his later views as published in *Liberty*.
7 Mill's initial enthusiasm for Saint-Simonism also waned over the 1840s, in part as he came to be more familiar with more attractive, and more feasible, forms of socialism, such as Fourierism. However, Mill's description of his position in the 1830s chimes very strongly with his later works, such as *Liberty, Principles, Utilitarianism, Considerations of Representative Government* and the *Three Essays on Religion*. Mill 1981: 173.
8 Here, some differences in formative experiences may play a part: Mill was 42 in 1848, Marx 30. Bruce Kinzer notes that Mill's formative life-experience of industry was based in London (and to a lesser extent, Paris) which, Kinzer argues, remained mainly artisanal (Kinzer 2000: 27–54), and Mill grew up knowing many artisans, friends of his father, such as Francis Place the radical leather-breeches maker. Marx, on the other hand, benefitted greatly from Friedrich Engels' first-hand knowledge of the new industrial organisation (such as large factories) and the processes of "proletarianisation" being pioneered in Manchester (among other experiences). But this may well underplay Mill's knowledge of industrialisation in both the UK and France (even if this knowledge was not first-hand).
9 Which is how they defined communism – see Mill and Taylor 1965: 201–9.
10 For more on which, see McCabe 2021.
11 There are evident links here to Saint-Simonism and their idea of a centrally managed economy in which all are "salaried" employees, giving and receiving according to their capacities. Mill did not endorse fully centralised or "planned" economies, for a variety of reasons. He also endorsed as a "still higher" principle of justice than this (or equal shares) Blanc's idea of "from each according to their capacities, to each according to their needs" (Mill and Taylor 1965: 203, Mill 1985a: 244).

12 With interesting links to Fourier's ideas – for more on which, see McCabe 2018: 35–61.
13 Mill and Taylor rightly note that the law does not *actually* always give the protection it ought to give – particularly to women, but I have trimmed this as not being relevant to the point at hand.
14 And that it is *everyone* – men *and* women – is very important. Mill and Taylor also both evidently thought that there would need to be important economic changes and ideational/ideological ones before we could achieve female equality, as well.
15 Mill 1985b: 340–41.
16 This is one reason I disagree with Persky when he argues that Mill had a materialist conception of history, though I agree Mill was by no means purely an idealist (in Marxist/Hegelian terms). For more on this, see McCabe 2020a.
17 For an in-depth discussion of which, see McCabe 2021.
18 Mill appears to have seen Hobbes' state of nature as more than a thought experiment, citing it – for instance – as a strong reason to avoid revolution in Mill 1967c: 749.
19 This is one reason representative democracy is both the only fit form of government for Mill's Britain and not, he thinks, a fit form of government for all countries at all times, including contemporaneously.
20 Indeed, Mill evidently thought that the advantages of the "higher degrees" of the division of labour could be (and had been) overstated – ibid: 122–30.
21 The words are Wakefield's, whom Mill is favourably quoting.
22 Mill was very critical of co-operatives which started hiring other employees as wage-labourers, as undermining the "moral" element of co-operation, which was its greatest asset (privately owned firms still being likely, in Mill's view, to be more efficient and productive) – ibid: 783. See also Mill 1988: 6–9.
23 For more on these elements of Mill's socialism, see McCabe 2021.
24 Smith 1985: 267–84; Marx 1973: 676; Cohen 1978: 108–11; and most recently Persky 2016: 157–60.
25 See also Ryan 1974: 164–5.
26 For more on the terms I am using see McCabe 2020a.
27 Mill says it was Taylor's dislike of publicity which made them decide on this course of action. Jo-Ellen Jacobs instead suggests that it was in response to pressure from Taylor's husband, because Taylor wrote to her husband only ten days before publication expressing herself still undecided about its inclusion but concluded "on the whole I am inclined to think it desirable", to which her husband replied expressing his "surprise", and adding "[c]onsideration made me decidedly think ... that all dedications are in bad taste, & that under our circumstances the proposed one would evince ... a want of taste & tact which I could not have believed possible" (Jacobs 1998: 291, 472).
28 For instance, Winch 2009: 50–4; Robbins 1952: 142, Robbins 1967: xxxix; Von Mises 1978: 195; Hayek 1942: xxx; Légé 2008: 199, 202; Rees 1985: 7; Schwartz 1972: 190–2; Levy 1981: 279; Ekelund and Tollison 1976: 215. This view is also somewhat supported by Elijah Millgram's assertion that Taylor declared the outcomes, and Mill "made up" arguments to prove them (Millgram 2019: 3–78, 132).
29 For more on this, see McCabe 2020b: 197–234.
30 See Mill and Taylor 1965: 754–6.

References

Cohen, G.A. 1978. *Karl Marx's Theory of History: A Defence*. Oxford. Clarendon Press.
Ekelund, Robert B. and Robert D. Tollison. 1976. "The New Political Economy of J. S. Mill: The Means to Social Justice", *The Canadian Journal of Economics* 9 (2): 213–231.

Fredman, L.E. and B.L.J. Gordon. 1967. "John Stuart Mill and Socialism", *Mill Newsletter* 3 (1): 3–7.

Hainds, J.R. 1946. "John Stuart Mill and the Saint-Simonians", *Journal of the History of Ideas* 7 (1): 103–112.

Hayek, Friedrich. 1942. "J.S. Mill at Twenty-Five", in J.S. Mill, *The Spirit of the Age*. Chicago. University of Chicago Press.

Holyoake, George Jacob. 1882. *Self-Help by the People: Thirty-Three Years of Co-operation in Rochdale*. London. Trübener & Co.

Jacobs, Jo-Ellen. 1998. *The Complete Works of Harriet Taylor Mill*. Bloomington and Indianapolis. Indiana University Press.

Kinzer, Bruce. 2000. "J.S. Mill and London", *Nineteenth-Century Prose* 47 (1): 27–54.

Kurer, Oskar. 1992. "J.S. Mill and Utopian Socialism", *The Economic Record* 68 (202): 222–232.

Légé, Phillippe. 2008. "Hayek's Readings of Mill", *Journal of the History of Economic Thought* 30 (2): 199–215. doi:10.1017/S1042771608000185.

Levy, Michael B. 1981. "Mill's Stationary State & the Transcendence of Liberalism", *Polity* 14 (2): 273–293.

Losman, Donald L. 1971. "J.S. Mill on Alternative Economic Systems", *American Journal of Economics and Sociology* 30 (1): 84–104.

Marx, Karl. 1973. *Grundrisse*, translated by Martin Nicolaus. Harmondsworth: Penguin.

McCabe, Helen. 2018. "John Stuart Mill and Fourierism: 'Association', 'Friendly Rivalry' and Distributive Justice", *Global Intellectual History* 4 (1): 35–61. doi:10.1080/23801883.2018.1435983.

McCabe, Helen. 2019. "'Navigating by the North Star': The Role of the 'Ideal' in J.S. Mill's View of 'Utopian' Schemes and the Possibilities of Social Transformation", *Utilitas* 31 (3): 291–309. doi:10.1017/S0953820819000074.

McCabe, Helen. 2020a. "Mill's 'Modern' Radicalism Re-Examined: Joseph Persky's *The Political Economy of Progress*", *Utilitas* 32 (2): 147–164. doi:10.1017/S0953820819000244.

McCabe, Helen. 2020b. "Harriet Taylor and the Development of John Stuart Mill's Socialism", *Nineteenth-Century Prose* 47 (1): 197–234.

McCabe, Helen. 2021. *John Stuart Mill, Socialist*. Montreal and Kingston. McGill-Queens University Press.

Mill, John Stuart. 1963. Letter 24, to Gustave d'Eichthal, 11 March 1829. *Collected Works of J.S. Mill* XII, edited by Francis E. Mineka. Toronto. University of Toronto Press.

Mill, John Stuart. 1967a. *The Claims of Labour. Collected Works of J.S. Mill* IV, edited by John Robson. Toronto. University of Toronto Press.

Mill, John Stuart. 1967b. Miss Martineau's Summary of Political Economy. *Collected Works of J.S. Mill* IV, edited by John Robson. Toronto. University of Toronto Press.

Mill, John Stuart. 1967c. *Chapters on Socialism. Collected Works of J.S. Mill* V, edited by John Robson. Toronto. University of Toronto Press.

Mill, John Stuart. 1967d. *Newman's Political Economy. Collected Works of J.S. Mill* V, edited by John Robson. Toronto. University of Toronto Press.

Mill, John Stuart. 1974. *A System of Logic. Collected Works of J.S. Mill* VII and VIII, edited by John Robson. Toronto. University of Toronto Press.

Mill, John Stuart. 1977. *Considerations of Representative Government. Collected Works of J.S. Mill* XIX, edited by John Robson. Toronto. University of Toronto Press.

Mill, John Stuart. 1981. *Autobiography. Collected Works of J.S. Mill* I, edited by John Robson. Toronto. University of Toronto Press.

Mill, John Stuart. 1984. *Inaugural Address Delivered to the University of St. Andrews. Collected Works of J.S. Mill* XXI, edited by John Robson. Toronto. University of Toronto Press.

Mill, John Stuart. 1985a. *Utilitarianism. Collected Works of J.S. Mill* X, edited by F.E.L. Priestley. Toronto. University of Toronto Press.

Mill, John Stuart. 1985b. *Auguste Comte and Positivism. Collected Works of J.S. Mill* X, edited by F.E.L. Priestley. Toronto. University of Toronto Press. Mill, John Stuart. 1988. *Cooperation. Collected Works of J.S. Mill* XXVIII, edited by John Robson. Toronto. University of Toronto Press.

Mill, John Stuart and Taylor, Harriet. 1965. *Principles of Political Economy. Collected Works of J.S. Mill* II and III, edited by F.E.L Priestly and John Robson. Toronto. University of Toronto Press.

Mill, John Stuart and Taylor, Harriet. 1977. *Liberty. Collected Works of J.S. Mill* XVIII, edited by John Robson. Toronto. University of Toronto Press.

Millgram, Elijah. 2019. *John Stuart Mill and the Meaning of Life*. Oxford. Oxford University Press.

Persky, Joseph. 2016. *The Political Economy of Progress*. Oxford. Oxford University Press.

Rees, J.C. 1985. *John Stuart Mill's On Liberty*. Oxford. Clarendon Press.

Robbins, Lionel. 1952. *The Theory of Economic Policy in English Classical Political Economy*. London. Macmillan.

Robbins, Lionel. 1967. "Introduction", *Collected Works of J.S. Mill* IV, edited by John Robson. Toronto. University of Toronto Press. Ryan, Alan. 1974. *J.S. Mill*. London. Routledge.

Schapiro, Salwyn J. 1943. "John Stuart Mill: Pioneer of Democratic Liberalism in England", *Journal of the History of Ideas* 4 (2): 127–160.

Schwartz, Pedro. 1972. *The New Political Economy of J.S. Mill*. London: Weidenfeld and Nicholson for the London School of Economics.

Smith, Vardaman R. 1985. "John Stuart Mill's Famous Distinction between Production and Distribution", *Economics and Philosophy* 1 (2): 267–284. doi:10.1017/S0266267100002492.

Taylor, Harriet. 1998. *Complete Works of Harriet Taylor Mill*, edited by Jo-Ellen Jacobs. Bloomington. University of Indiana State Press.

Thomas, William. 1985. *Mill*. Oxford. Oxford University Press.

Von Mises, Ludwig. 1978. *Liberalism: A Socio-Economic Exposition*. Mission, KA. Sheed, Andrews and McMeel.

Winch, Donald. 2009. *Wealth and Life: Essays on the Intellectual History of Political Economy in Britain, 1848–1914*. Cambridge. Cambridge University Press.

6 The concept of organic growth in Marshall's work

Neil B. Niman

Marshall's commitment to Economic Biology goes beyond a few references here and there to Darwinian ideas. It reflects a scientific tradition that began with the formation of the Statistical Section of the British Association for the Advancement of Science (more commonly known as Section F), the debates that followed the publication of Lyell's *Principles of Geology* (1830), the Analytical Machine of Charles Babbage (1837), and the subsequent development of Darwin's *On the Origin of Species* (1859). The importance of biology to Marshall transcends the basic shift from statics to dynamics that took place in nineteenth century science. Instead, it highlights the important distinction made at the time between organic growth and the natural progression of matter.

The Victorian era was a period of tremendous intellectual upheaval as religion was vying to maintain its place within the context of potentially conflicting theories of science, economics, and society. Christianity competed with Agnosticism, the Uniformitarian Geology of Lyell was challenged by the Physics of Thomson and the Darwinian Theory of Natural Selection found itself serving as the foundation for not only a theory of biological change, but also a theory of social progress. The attempt to understand the existing social order among competing views came to a head during the 1860s in what has become known as the Age of the Earth debates. The debate had profound meaning with respect to the existence of God, the role of religion, and the social order.

If we are to take Marshall at his word that "the substance of economic thought cannot well be to any extent the work of any one man: it is the product of the age" (Whitaker 1996: 80–81), then it would seem that one of the most important debates of his time (Age of the Earth) would have an important impact on the development of his thought. However, when Groenewegen (1995) writes about the "fighting sixties" and Cook (2009) pays homage to the "rounded globe of knowledge," there is little mention of important thinkers such as Charles Lyell, Charles Babbage, William Thomson, and Henry Charles Fleeming Jenkin who shaped to a large extent a great debate over whether the earth was old enough to permit theories of evolution like those expounded by Darwin, Spencer, and Lamarck.

Modern interpretations of Marshall have focused on his early philosophical writings, interest in psychology, and fascination with Hegel (Raffaelli 2003;

DOI: 10.4324/9781003138655-6

Cook 2009; Caldari 2015; Bankovsky 2019). However, even a cursory reading of Marshall's *Principles of Economics* reveals a large number of references to biological analogies, strong emphasis on the concept of organic growth, and the repeated invocation of evolution as a proxy for change. While such references have been dismissed by Mirowski (1989) and minimized by Groenewegen (1995), Marshall had ample opportunity to purge the *Principles* of such references over the thirty year period that he honed eight successive editions of his greatest work.

Rather than returning to the discussion of whether Marshall's belief that the "Mecca of the economist is Economic Biology" represents a poor understanding of biology (Moss 1982) or as a proxy for physics (Mirowski 1984), we will explore the extent to which these references reflect a broader understanding of the times in which he lived. In doing so, we will be following in the footsteps of Viner (1941) who sought to link what was "in the air" at the time with the economics of Marshall. By taking such an approach, we can gain a better understanding of why the concept of Economic Biology served as the metaphor for both a methodological approach that relied on a clear understanding of the facts and an ideological framework grounded in the promise of economic and social progress.

Viewed from this lens, it becomes possible to explore whether Marshall's use of biological analogies offers insights for today's economy. Just as time played a crucial role in the Age of the Earth debates, the same holds true in Marshall's thinking. His analysis begins with statics, flows into dynamics, and ends with the concept of organic growth. Understanding the role that each slice of time plays in the development of a more complete understanding of the economy is just as valid today as it was during the Victorian era. Through such a lens, it becomes possible to understand how new technologies such as machine learning and 3D printing are forming the foundation for the organic growth that is revolutionizing the modern economy.

The Victorian landscape

Marshall's *Principles of Economics* is in part a work of economic history, an excursion into economic analysis, a set of proscriptions for accomplishing good, and a reflection on the influence of biology and the various theories of evolution. For Marshall, who was concerned with integrating the many in the one and the one in the many, success could only be achieved by integrating these various threads into a coherent whole. As Marshall describes his own intellectual journey:

> And then I grew to think that the substance of economic thought cannot well be to any extent the work of any one man: it is the product of the age. ... And so I began to look for Adam Smith's originality more in the general conspectus which he presented than in particular doctrines. And as regards this, the more I knew of him, the more I worshipped him. It was

his balance, his sense of proportion, his power of seeing the many in the one and the one in the many, his skill in using analysis to interpret history and history to correct his analysis (especially as regards the causes that govern human nature, but also in other matters), that seem to mark him out as unique; very much as similar qualities have more recently given a similar position to Darwin.

(Whitaker 1996: 80–81)

To get a sense of the age in which Marshall lived, in contrast to the views of Marshall (Groenewegen 1995; Cook 2009) that look at the social and political influences that affected Alfred Marshall post-graduation from Cambridge University, we will explore instead his days leading up to the completion his degree in mathematics as second wrangler. It was a time of tremendous advance with the discovery of the laws of thermodynamics and the ascension of physics as a scientific discipline independent of mathematics.

It is important to recognize that under the tutelage of his coach Edward Routh, Marshall's education included

both the preeminence of such established mixed-mathematical topics as optics, hydrostatics, hydrodynamics, elastic solid theory, wave theory, astronomy, celestial mechanics, and the shape of the earth, and the continuing practice of teaching mathematical methods in close association with their physical application.

(Warwick 2003: 240)

Given that the problems found on the Tripos were based in part on current research undertaken by the Cambridge faithful, it would then make sense that one of the physical applications appearing on the exam would reflect the work of William Thomson, one of the two most outstanding mathematical physicists (along with James Clerk Maxwell) produced by Cambridge in the mid-nineteenth century.

The young Marshall, therefore, would have had a front row seat for the Age of the Earth debates that pitted the laws of physics against the biological theories of evolution; a debate with consequences that extended far beyond the borders of science and math. However, to understand the debates, it is important to acknowledge the importance of Lyell's *Principles of Geology* and the significant questions that it raised relative to notions of continuity over time.[1] Yet, even with all of that, we will begin with the formation of the Statistical Society which promoted a way of thinking about social science that parallels developments in the natural sciences to gain a full understanding of the impact of the age in which Marshall cut his intellectual teeth.

The Statistical Movement

The Statistical Movement was established in the 1830s as an intellectual force designed to investigate the condition of the poor in an effort to promote social reform. In order to accomplish a reform agenda, early members sought to create a unified theoretical social science based on the collection of social data. Beginning with the formation of Section F in the British Association for the Advancement of Science and the Statistical Society of London by Richard Jones, the cause soon expanded to include the likes of T.R. Malthus, Charles Babbage, Adolphe Quetelet, and William Whewell.[2]

Concern for the poor was not the only common interest uniting the early leaders of the Statistical Movement. A general disdain for the deductive method employed by Ricardo and his followers also bound the members of the group together. As noted by Lawrence Goldman:

> To Jones, who, with Babbage, played the most active organizational role in the first months of the movement, the object of a statistical society was to "widen" the approach to the study of society; to achieve generalizations founded on empirical data; indeed, to apply in practical analyses the alternative methodology developed in his correspondence and publications though the previous decade.
>
> (Goldman 1983: 599)[3]

This led to the construction of an alternate approach that did not result in the abandonment of theory, but rather in a theory that seeks an *understanding of the world as it is and not as it was imagined*. When Marshall writes of Richard Jones' influence, he quotes from an address given by Jones in 1833 that highlights the methodological approach adopted by Jones and his compatriots. As Marshall quoted from Jones:

> We must get comprehensive views of facts, that we may arrive at principles that are truly comprehensive. If we take a different method, if we snatch at general principles, and content ourselves with confined observations, two things will happen to us. First, what we shall call general principles, will be found to have no generality; we shall set out with declaring propositions to be universally true which, at every stop of our further progress, we shall be obliged to confess are frequently false; and secondly we shall miss a mass of useful knowledge, which those who advance to principles by a comprehensive observation of facts necessarily meet with on the road.
>
> (Marshall 1897: 296)[4]

Thus, it should not be surprising that Marshall praises Richard Jones whose "influence, though little heard of in the outside world, largely dominated the minds of those Englishmen who came to the serious study of economics after his work had been published by Dr Whewell in 1859" (Marshall 1897: 296). Solving the problems of the poor while adopting a better understanding of the world as we know it was a lifelong pursuit for Marshall and forms the foundation for his closing paragraph in an address delivered when he took up the position of Professor of Political Economy at Cambridge.[5]

Lyell's *Principles of Geology*

Interest in the facts, the world as we know it, saw a parallel development in the work of Charles Lyell's *Principles of Geology*. Lyell's book was one of the most important contributions during the nineteenth century and had far reaching consequences. It was here that Lyell introduced his Uniformity Principle which set the stage for the subsequent development of Darwin's Theory of Evolution and the ensuing debates about the coexistence of science and religion. The Uniformity Principle was based on an actualist methodology that was grounded in the belief that current observations about the present state of affairs can be used to explain past changes. This led to the conclusion that change is something that occurs slowly over vast periods of time. To reinforce the concept that change is slow and gradual, Lyell adopted a steady-state cosmology designed to combat the catastrophe theorists who contended that change occurs abruptly. This steady-state cosmology offered the alternative view that the earth should be treated as a self-regulating system. Within such a self-regulating system, any short-term changes exist as fluctuations around some mean. Permanent changes could only occur over great periods of time with gradual shifts in the mean.

Lyell's Uniformity Principle introduced the concepts of unlimited time and slow gradual change which had a large impact on Darwin's early publications in geology and the subsequent development of his theory of evolution. It was only later in terms of organic life that Darwin split from his old friend and adopted the idea of change away from some mean, albeit within the context of a natural order and not as the result of a benevolent hand. Darwin observed during his travels the great diversity that existed within a species and postulated that these differences were the result of changes that occurred over large periods of time. Those changes that were best adapted to a particular environment (which varied from location to location) were selected for survival and accounted for the differences he observed between similar species in differing environments.[6] The net result was a theory of descent through modification that could once and for all put to rest the notion that the earth was created in six days and therefore species remain invariant to change over time.[7]

Outside of geology, Lyell's Uniformity Principle found support in the writings of Charles Babbage (Lucasian Professor of Mathematics at Cambridge University). In his 1832 book, *On the Economy of Machinery and Manufacturers*, Babbage attempted to create a universal theory connecting those laws that govern nature and the "domestic economy of the factory" (Hyman 1982: 140). This led him to look not only at the mechanics of a particular production process, but also the organizational structure that directed the various activities of workers and machines.[8] Babbage's work in economics and the development of his analytical engine caught the attention of Marshall (Niman 2008) and played an important role in the development of Marshall's volume on *Industry and Trade* (1919).

The vision of a natural economy based on the division of labor and encapsulated in the science of his calculating engine led Babbage to write his own (and unsolicited) Bridgewater Treatise in 1837.[9] Once again challenging the existing orthodoxy through his writings, Babbage advocated the position that there exists a single set of unifying principles that govern both what exists in nature and what has been created by human beings. Rather than changes in natural law being the result of heavenly intervention, they were instead the product of a set of instructions programmed into the natural order at the time of creation. Just as his calculating engine could be programmed to generate random numbers, changes in natural phenomena could be explained not in terms of miracles, but rather as the result of some initial design that could be explained through mathematical principles (Dolan 1998: 314). As a result, Babbage's work provided a strong foundation for the propagation of Charles Lyell's Uniformity Principle that extended well beyond the natural sciences.

This had important implications for the development of Marshall's thought. In the case of organic life, Marshall chose Darwin's theory of evolution by means of natural selection rather than the static notion that individual species, not subject to change, are created by a higher being. While in the case of inorganic matter, Marshall's work is consistent with the steady state of Lyell's more static theory of geology instead of the dynamic progression of matter found in the work of physicists like William Thomson. In this way, Marshall, like Darwin and Babbage, found a set of unifying principles that enabled the laws governing organic and inorganic matter to coexist under the same "roof."

From this perspective, Marshall's Principles can be seen as incorporating a single line of development in the conception of science (rather than adopting and discarding concepts in a piecemeal fashion), thereby affirming Marshall's adherence to his *Principle of Continuity* (Marshall 1961: Preface to 1st edition).[10] Thus it should come as no surprise that Marshall selected the motto "Natura non facit Saltum" (Nature does not make a leap) for the title page that appeared in the first edition in 1890 and was kept there through the thirty year span of eight editions of his work.[11] For Alfred Marshall, who believed that the "main concern of economics is thus with human beings who are impelled, for good and evil, to change and progress" (1961: XV), biology provided a foundation for the subsequent development of his economic theory.

The Age of the Earth debates

The discovery of the laws of thermodynamics brought forward a different conception of the "natural economy." Work and waste emerged as the two dynamic forces propelling the Victorian economy. Work was defined as productive activity that creates economic value. Waste on the other hand, was conceived in terms of missed opportunity, wear and tear, and the inefficient use of materials and processes. For Norton Wise, this economic metaphor became the underlying foundation for the development of William Thomson's construction of modern physics. As a result, "the dynamics of work became classical field theory and classical mechanics" while "The dynamics of waste became classical thermodynamics" (Wise 1990: 251).

It was the use of precise calculations based on the laws of physics that William Thomson (Lord Kelvin) used to contend that the age of the earth was much shorter than what had been postulated by Lyell and Darwin. Backing his conclusions with all of the power of numbers and calculations, "Geologists as well as physicists now felt obliged to heed his arguments and few felt capable of withstanding them. It was only the beginning; in less than a decade, Lyell's unlimited ages had contracted into the finite limits set by Kelvin's physics" (Burchfield 1974: 309).[12] This placed Darwin's theory of natural selection in a precarious position.[13] According to Thomson's calculations, the age of the earth was much shorter than what was required by Darwin to explain the slow process of natural selection.[14]

Sharing the same basic approach as his close friend and colleague, H.C. Fleeming Jenkin (1867) in his famous review of the fourth edition of Darwin's *On the Origin of Species*, Thomson attacked the Uniformity Principle and ultimately the lynchpin of natural selection – the notion of unlimited time – using the newly formulated laws of thermodynamics. He argued that in a finite world heated by a finite sun, the available store of energy must be limited. He then went on to describe how, according to the second law of thermodynamics, every energy transformation dissipates a part of that energy, thereby rendering it useless for further transformations. The conclusion he reached was that uniformity cannot be a law of nature and that current geological forces must be less powerful than they were in the past.[15]

All of this came together in what Norton Wise characterizes as an "economy of nature" that was steeped in a static balancing approach that led to a stable natural state (Wise 1989a: 269). However, the 1830s and 40s saw many important technological developments that questioned the concept of a stationary state. The steam engine emerged as a driving force capable of changing the existing balance. The steam engine itself does not change with the exception of wearing out over time as friction takes its toll. Rather, the engine works within certain technical limitations that determine speed or load and the tracks which define the path forward. It is not changes in the engine itself that promotes growth, but rather the impact that the engine has on the expansion of the division of labor. By making markets more accessible, the engine is able to expand the division of labor and hence promote economic growth through increases in scale and scope (Chandler 1977).

With the very visible wealth created by such technological advances, evolution as a form of progressive change supplanted the notion of balance as the dominant point of view. For Wise, this transition is best seen in the work of Charles Babbage where: "The engine metaphor now extends from the literal steam engine setting machinery in motion, to capital as the engine of labour, to the machine economy as a social engine, to scientific knowledge as an engine of practical action" (Wise 1989b: 414).

Organic growth

While the physics of William Thomson contributed to the shift away from static balancing toward dynamic change, it becomes difficult to accept the

Mirowski (1989) view that the incursion of the "proto-energetics" metaphor became the foundation for all of the physical, natural, and social sciences. After all, a large schism emerged between the physicists who utilized physical principles and mathematics to assert that the earth is not old enough for the process of natural selection to have worked its "wonders," and the Evolutionists (in the Darwinian sense) who needed time to be unlimited in order for their theory to play itself out. The question of time was of fundamental importance when it came to explaining the diversity found in nature and whether or not individual species change over time. Acceptance of the physicist's position meant the abandonment for all intents and purposes of the notion of natural selection, while the rejection of the physicist's argument preserved the core of the Darwinian framework.

For Marshall, economic biology provides an alternate view of nature capable of serving both as the basis for the mechanical analogies best seen in Book Five of Marshall's *Principles* and his less fully developed notion of organic growth. The market as a self-regulating system experiences fluctuations in the short run around some equilibrium point (the first element of Lyell's Uniformity Principle). Changes in market equilibrium occur gradually as the short run turns into the long run when all inputs become variable for the firm. Adjustments over the long run are gradual and reflect changes in the capital/labor ratio as firms are allowed to vary the size of the plant. Implicit in this discussion is the notion that the product remains unchanged as time moves from the short run to the long run. This replicates the second element of the Uniformity Principle; that once created species do not change. However, as we continue to expand our view of time, the products themselves change as one age (large span of time) gives way to the next.

Developing such an understanding places us in a better position to evaluate what Marshall meant when he wrote: "But biological conceptions are more complex than those of mechanics; a volume on Foundations must therefore give a relatively large place to mechanical analogies" (1961: xiv). Mechanical principles are simpler because they are based on uniform principles. The world gets more complicated (just as it did with the emergence of the theory of evolution) when individuals or groups within uniform laws and principles are allowed to progress and develop. Thus, Marshall draws the distinction between the "normal conditions of life in the modern age" and the more organic concept of change from one age to the next. What Marshall is doing in Book Five is holding progress in some sense constant (ceteris paribus) so that he can address issues specific to the "modern age," while hinting in various places in Book Four and Appendix A and B that from a more organic perspective, life has changed tremendously between the various "Ages."

What Marshall means by organic growth is perhaps best encapsulated in the following passage found in his essay on "Biological and Mechanical Analogies":

> But the catastrophes of mechanics are caused by changes in the quantity and not in the character of the forces at work: whereas in life their

character changes also. "Progress" or "evolution," industrial and social, is not mere increase and decrease. It is organic growth, chastened and confined and occasionally reversed by the decay of innumerable factors, each of which influences and is influenced by those around it; and every such mutual influence varies with the stages which the respective factors have already reached in their growth. ... In the earlier stages of economics, we think of demand and supply as crude forces pressing against one another, and tending towards a mechanical equilibrium; but in the later stages, the balance or equilibrium is conceived not as between crude mechanical forces, but as between the organic forces of life and decay.

(1898: 317–318)

This passage introduces the notion of organic growth as something distinct from the statics and dynamics that were associated with a more mechanistic view of society that was often based upon the concept of the machine as the inert creation of living intelligence (Peel 1971: 166). Drawing such a distinction was commonplace in the early development of nineteenth century sociology, and in the case of Herbert Spencer, the acceptance of the organic analogy led to the rejection of the machine as the appropriate metaphor for society.

When Marshall proceeds to the next step where he describes organic growth, he uses the example of the healthy boy to illustrate exactly what he means:

The healthy boy grows stronger every year; but with early manhood there is some loss of agility; the zenith of his power is reached perhaps at twenty-five for such a game as racquets. For other corporeal activities the zenith comes at thirty or later. For some kinds of mental work it comes rather late; for statesmanship, for instance, it comes very late. In each case the forces of life preponderate at first; then those of crystallization and decay attain equal terms, and there is balance or equilibrium; afterwards decay predominates.

(1898: 318)

In contrast to the one-dimensional nature of the steam engine, the healthy boy's life cannot be characterized by a single monotonic function. What is different is that as the healthy boy grows and matures, some of his capabilities may decline, but others take its place with the passing of time. Thus, the level of activity may stay constant during the life of the healthy boy, while the nature of those activities changes in different, and in some cases, unexpected ways.[16] As the steam engine designed for a single task begins to age, it produces less and less power as parts wear out. This stands in marked contrast to the healthy boy, who responds to declining physical abilities by substituting mental activities that grow and develop as he ages. Thus, for the healthy *(hu)man*, the level of contribution may stay the same or even increase as statesmanlike conduct is substituted for physical acuteness.

This is nothing more than another application of Babbage's famous principle governing the division of labor. Marshall quotes Babbage when he writes:

> As Babbage pointed out, in a large factory "the master manufacturer by dividing the work to be executed into different processes, each requiring different degrees of skill or force, can purchase exactly that precise quantity of both which is necessary for each process; whereas if the whole work were executed by one workman that person must possess skill to perform the most difficult and sufficient strength to execute the most laborious of the operations into which work is divided."
>
> (Marshall 1961: 264–265)

Just as work can be divided in the factory, one's life can be divided into various tasks or experiences. Because of such a division, the individual can choose a particular course of action that makes sense given their physical and mental prowess at a particular age, but as their abilities change over time, they can substitute alternative interests that more closely match their current strengths.[17]

The metaphor of the healthy boy illustrates that economic agents are not defined in terms of what they do, but rather, *who they are at any given time.*[18] Whether a student, statesman, or entrepreneur, the healthy boy who eventually grows to become a healthy (hu)man takes on many different roles over his lifetime. As a result, when Marshall discusses equilibrium within a particular industry, the firm must not be confused with the product that it produces. Just as the healthy boy starts off playing an exceptional game of racquets and later engages in different activities, the firm may begin by producing a particular product and then shift to something different as the competitive conditions of an industry change.

Thus, while an industry is defined in terms of a particular product (e.g., the game of racquets), the firm exists independently of the products it produces and hence can apply resources to new endeavors when it discovers that it can no longer successfully compete in a particular industry. Therefore, it is not death giving way to new life that leads to progress (Loasby 1990: 123), but rather the substitution of one activity for another as the competences of the firm change over time. While the concept of mortality may apply to an industry (buggy whips giving way to gasoline for powering horseless carriages), the lesson of the healthy boy teaches us that attributes or competences such as proficiency in the game of racquets decay as the source of that competence (physical strength) robs the healthy boy of his prowess.

Similarly, the firm as distinct from the product that is produced may begin with one set of competences that provides it with success, only to discover later that what brought early success in a particular industry, is no longer a source for competitive advantage. However, the loss of a competitive advantage does not necessarily lead to the mortality of the firm. As long as new competences can be developed or acquired, the firm may regain a position of strength within an existing industry or develop an entirely new one as it struggles to survive (Niman 2004).[19]

Modern interpretations of Marshall conceive the firm as nothing more than a production function. The firm itself is thought to be synonymous with the product it produces and without the existence of the entrepreneur, there is nothing to push change in the short run and therefore nothing to be selected as competition drives all firms and the products they produce to a homogenous offering of sameness (Niman 1991b). However, an important prerequisite for evolution by means of natural selection is the existence of diversity where some characteristics are better suited for survival than others. In nature, the goal is not to be like everyone else, but rather to be sufficiently different that it becomes possible to achieve a superior outcome and hence be more likely selected for survival. The avoidance of conflict can be just as powerful as possessing superior strength or other qualities that would lead to success in a head to head competitive struggle (Niman 2000).

Social progress

While the example of the healthy boy provides us with an understanding of how diversity may exist within a population at a moment in time, it also can serve as a broader metaphor for change over multiple generations. For Marshall, what drives the individual is the belief that "A man can have no stronger stimulus to energy and enterprise than the hope of rising in life, and leaving his family to start from a higher round of the social ladder than that on which he began" (1961: 228).

The ability to rise in life depends in part on "the 'vigour' of a man which depends upon his moral strength, energy and self-mastery" (1961: 194) and on the help of the community as a whole. Marshall believed that human beings have a tribal sense of duty that "gradually grows into a noble patriotism" predicated on the desire to help others and in so doing, makes the tribe or the race stronger. As a result, those races best suited for survival are ones where "the individual is most energetic in performing varied services for the society without the prompting of direct gain to himself" (1961: 243).[20]

These ideas of community in the context of selection are consistent with the views expressed by Darwin in *The Descent of Man*. Darwin used the idea of community to explain how moral advance would give one tribe a competitive advantage over another and hence be selected for survival (Kingsland 1988).[21] As a result, moral advance becomes a positive and progressive element as part of the theory of human evolution.[22]

However moral advance can only take place if the human race is allowed to change; just as the healthy boy matures in response to his age and level of experience. Yet if life is the result of Divine intervention, and species are fixed within some predefined order, then it is difficult to imagine how moral advance can ultimately transport humanity to a higher plane of existence. Thus, for Marshall, evolution by means of natural selection plays a significant role because it provides the means to achieve his desired ends. To reach his goal of tying economics to social progress, he needs a theory of evolution where economic agents have the capacity to be selected and such a selection process requires that diversity must exist within the population in question.

We can now more clearly understand the importance of the Statistical Movement and disdain for deductive reasoning. Progress for Marshall entails embracing the diversity that exists in the world in which he lived so that he could use that diversity as an engine for social change. If the economy consists of nothing more than representative agents, then it becomes challenging at best to describe how change emerges. Without such change, the ills that plague society will continue to persist, and social progress becomes nothing more than the wishful thinking of a utopian dreamer.

A modern interpretation

Organic processes are inherently complex and can be extremely messy. Change may occur from a selection process or as the result of random drift. It can be initiated in a multitude of ways that may appear to be continuous at the macro level, but subject to disruptions at the micro level. We can use a simple example to illustrate this point.

Imagine returning to your childhood where you are sitting in your dentist's chair for a cleaning and examination. The dentist notes that your permanent teeth are crooked and if you do nothing to straighten them, you will have serious issues when you reach adulthood. The dentist refers you to an orthodontist. The orthodontist constructs a treatment plan that places metal bands and wires on your teeth. After multiple visits and tightening of the wires, your teeth are brought into alignment.

The orthodontist is a clear example of how an expansion in the division of labor can lead to a superior outcome. At the most basic level, the orthodontist is the equivalent of a production function that employs specialized knowledge along with a technology (braces) to produce straight teeth. Since the specific knowledge is embodied within a person and that person is limited to a geographical place, location represents a natural barrier to entry. The amount of profit the orthodontist earns depends on how many others are located within the same region. If we assume that all locations are equally desirable, then we would likely see that over time, orthodontists will move to those locations where the largest profits are earned. This would continue until the point is reached where all orthodontists in every region are earning the same economic profit. At this point, the story ends.

This is what Marshall meant by simpler representations that take on the form of a static analysis. There is a single type of firm (orthodontist) using a single technology (braces) to produce straight teeth. However, a more robust analysis would include other agents, products, processes, and business models. How might we explain this?

The primary barrier to entry that enables an orthodontist to earn positive economic profits (at least in the short run) is location. A national market does not exist when the knowledge of how to produce straight teeth is embodied in a human being and that person is tied to a specific place and time. Competition however knows no insurmountable barrier and the desire to earn above normal profits will batter away at that barrier until it is gone. This might take the form of an alternate product that uses a technology that diminishes the importance of the orthodontist and hence the barrier that makes above normal profits possible.

The introduction of aligners offers a competing process and product capable of challenging braces and the orthodontist. These thermoplastic aligners are created using a series of molds that represent a progressive straightening of the teeth. The beginning of this process begins with either an epoxy mold or 3D scan of the patient's teeth. The physical mold or digital file is transmitted to a lab where a CAD model is created that maps out progressive changes in the alignment of teeth and the series of molds/aligners that will need to be manufactured to generate the desired results.

What makes the entry of aligners possible is the introduction of a knowledge platform that exists independently of the orthodontist. Aligners are crafted by a licensed technician and overseen by a licensed professional who can effectively be located anywhere. Gone are the brackets and wires that must be physically manipulated to achieve the result of straighter teeth. As a result, a successful outcome relies less on the judgment of a particular professional and more on the knowledge embedded in the technician and the tools she uses to create the desired result.

Shifting a portion of the knowledge required from a local professional to a knowledge platform enables the cost of this knowledge to be spread over a larger number of patients and reduces the time that must be spent managing the treatment (no physical manipulation of wires). All of this contributes to a reduction in the cost of treatment, thereby making teeth straightening services available to a larger portion of the population. In addition, with no brackets to fall off or wires to break, there are lower maintenance costs, and it becomes easier to maintain oral health during treatment as there are no wires or brackets interfering with the cleaning of teeth. Perhaps of greatest significance, the use of aligners eliminates the stigma associated with very visible braces and this has the effect of expanding the market. Adults who do not wish to look like children feel more comfortable using the aligner product to straighten teeth that were not corrected during childhood.

By adopting a broader lens that disassociates an outcome from a particular firm or process, we can add a more realistic understanding of what is happening in the marketplace. The outcome is straight teeth and now we have two products (braces and aligners) and two processes that can be used to generate the desired result. Adding a level of complexity (multiple products and processes) permits a greater understanding of what drives change within a particular industry. What Marshall would identify as dynamics.

However, there is at least one additional chapter to the story. We have defined the industry in terms of an outcome – straight teeth – acknowledge that there are at least two products that might accomplish that goal, and recognize that each product embodies knowledge differently in the processes that are adopted to generate the desired outcome. At this point, it is important to note that products, processes, and economic agents for that matter are organized by what we will call a business model. The business model determines which inputs will be selected and combined to create a product and how entry will be gained within a particular segment of the market. The development of new business models affords the potential of adding even more complexity to the analysis. This additional level of complexity is consistent with what Marshall called organic growth.

Organic growth represents the continued development of not only innovative technologies, but also new business models. One new business model is the elimination of the dentist/orthodontist's office entirely. An example of this would be the Smile Direct Club. The Smile Direct Club closely follows the aligner product/process with a big difference. It cuts out the local professional entirely. The treatment plan and regular checkups are all performed remotely. As a result, the location barrier is eliminated completely.

The direct-to-consumer approach creates even greater economies of scale that enable companies like Smile Direct Club to offer their services at a significant discount. The substantial reduction in price and increase in convenience generates an even larger increase in the size of the market.

However, it is important to note that the introduction of new technologies such as 3D printing is making additional business models possible. Where a company like Smile Direct Club is reducing the need for the local dentist/orthodontist's office, these new technologies are empowering dentists/orthodontists to fight back by giving them the tools needed to eliminate the central laboratory and provide for their patients' needs onsite.

In this scenario, the dentist who is taking the lead in maintaining good oral health might identify the need for straighter teeth. Rather than sending an impression or 3D scan to a lab, the dentist might have the requisite software and 3D printer in the office where they can design a treatment plan, print the molds, and manufacture the aligners that will be used to create a new "smile" for the patient. As a result, it becomes possible for the dentist/orthodontist to now manage all stages of the straightening process. Technology in this instance takes what had previously resided in the knowledge platform embodied in a remote lab/technician and instead embeds it in a platform where scale is no longer required for a local professional to be price competitive in the business of straightening teeth.

What is important to understand is that while all of this adds complexity to the analysis, what has not changed is competition as the driving force for change. As knowledge shifts within an industry, new opportunities emerge as the products, processes, or business models that define an industry evolve. An organic approach begins with a desired outcome, and then looks at the growth and development of the various factors that contribute to an equilibrium that itself changes over time. In the long run, those unique combinations that best achieve the desired outcome will come to dominate; albeit not in the same way as things started.

While there are multiple products, processes, agents, and business models working simultaneously at a snapshot in time, there is order to the dynamics underlying organic change. The outcome of interest in our example is straight teeth. The analysis begins with the dentist. It is the quest for a superior outcome that leads to expansion in the division of labor that embeds specialized knowledge in the orthodontist who comes to dominate the industry. The above normal profits earned by the orthodontist creates an incentive for additional innovation. Further advances in the industry leads to the creation of aligners.

The development of aligners poses a competitive challenge to the orthodontist as knowledge becomes embodied in a technology platform rather than a human being. By embedding the specialized knowledge of the orthodontist into a technology platform, it becomes possible to conceive of new business models capable of challenging the old. As the technology platform becomes more robust, it may reach the point where it no longer makes sense for the orthodontist to remain in the teeth straightening business and the economies of scale associated with a Smile Direct Club cease to be a source of competitive advantage. Thus, in the long run, rather than becoming the victim of creative destruction (Schumpeter 1962) or disruptive innovation (Christensen et al. 2015), the dentist, in combination with advanced software and 3D printers, resumes a dominant position with respect to teeth straightening. Rather than disrupting the dentist, technological innovation eventually strengthens the position of the dentist.

At a macro level, the process underlying organic growth is a simple one. Competition expands the knowledge base. Increases in knowledge lead to the development of new competences. New competences create superior outcomes.

It is at the micro level that we see multiple pathways adding complexity to our analysis.[23] It is at the micro level where we might see the potential for disruptive innovation or creative destruction generating new opportunities depending on how technology changes, knowledge diffuses, and the division of labor expands.

Concluding remarks

It was the "death of Adam" that emerged from the Age of Earth (and other) debates that freed Marshall to pursue his goal of developing a conception of the economy that saves humanity from depredation. Gone was the perfect world of the Garden of Eden where human beings, through their free choice of will, were destined to do nothing more than temporarily disturb a pre-existing harmony created by the omnipotent hands of a higher being. In its place was a conception of life within the cosmos that permitted change in not only biological and social relationships, but in the cosmos itself.

However, as Thomson (2005) points out, the natural theology of Victorian figures such as William Paley was not only used to preserve the preeminent position of a higher being but was also used to keep the existing social order in check. As he notes:

> If change was possible, either driven by chance or (perhaps especially) if it was driven wholly or in part through human volition, if the *status quo* was not naturally law-given, then men and women might aspire to and actually change their station, as in the despised philosophies of Rousseau and Tom Paine.
>
> (Thomson 2005: 257)

This is precisely what Marshall wanted to see happen: that individuals change for the better and in turn, create a better society. Thus, his conception of the social fabric is not one that is ordained by natural law, but rather, is better characterized by his conception of Economic Freedom where modern industrial life is represented by certain fundamental characteristics. These include: "a certain independence and habit of choosing one's own course for oneself, a self-reliance; a deliberation and yet a promptness of choice and judgment, and a habit of forecasting the future and of shaping one's course with respect to distant aims" (Marshall 1961: 4). These characteristics are based on the premise that human beings must not only be free to choose, but the corresponding social fabric and ideological superstructure that coexists with them must be a product of those choices and hence change as well over time. This can only occur if human beings and the society in which they live are allowed to change and are not the first and final cause of an omnipotent being content to see the future remain the same as the past.

It was the adoption of Lyell's Uniformity Principle and Darwin's Theory of Evolution and not the physics of notables like Lord Kelvin that enabled Marshall to contend that his thought reflected a continuous lineage. A continuous line of thought that offered a big enough tent to incorporate statics, dynamics, and organic growth. An approach to economics that celebrates diversity, embraces change, and optimistically looks toward the emergence of superior outcomes.

Notes

1 Rashid (1981) notes that "Economists have generally ignored this period of interaction between economics and geology. It has been too easy to move from Newton to Darwin without the earthy interlude." The reason for this he suggests is: "In recent years it has become quite fashionable to compare the history of economics with the recent views of the history of science put forth successively by Thomas Kuhn and Imre Lakatos. Such comparisons, however, face the danger of considering economics too much from the viewpoint of subjects which have been most studied by historians of science, chiefly physics and astronomy" (Rashid 1981: 726).

2 Marshall noted that "the sheaf of corn which the Statistical Society has chosen as its emblem is a broad one" (1885b: 177) capable of supporting multiple facts at a single time. This is important because "Facts are the bricks out of which reason builds the edifice of knowledge" (1885b: 179), and mathematical approaches should not be

adopted at the expense of a broad understanding of the facts. A point that is reinforced in a 1901 letter to Bowley commenting on the publication of his book on statistics. Marshall writes "having now brought out this great and successful book, is it not time to make some further study of the broader relations between economic facts: to leave mathematics behind for a little on one side; and join more heartily in the quest for 'the One in the Many, the Many in the One?'" (Pigou 1966: 421).

3   This can also explain in part, Marshall's interest in the writings of Auguste Comte and Herbert Spencer who were interested in constructing a universal social science. Such aspirations would have placed them in accord with the broader goals of the Statistical Movement to create a holistic account of society.

4   This quote represents one of several that could have been selected to illustrate Marshall's views with respect to his methodological position. A position that is summed up by Coase in the following manner: "Marshall's general position was that, at any given time, in some parts of economics more induction was required and in other parts more deduction but that, in general, more inductive work calls for more deductive work and *vice versa*" (1975: 27).

5   "It will be my most cherished ambition, my highest endeavour, to do what with my poor ability and my limited strength I may, to increase the numbers of those, whom Cambridge, the great mother of strong men, sends out into the world with cool heads but warm hearts, willing to give some at least of their best powers to grappling with the social suffering around them; resolved not to rest content till they have done what in them lies to discover how far it is possible to open up to all the material means of a refined and noble life" (Marshall 1885a: 174).

6   It is therefore somewhat curious that when Sylvan Schweber seeks to identify the source of Darwin's conception of the division of labor – a cornerstone essential to his understanding of the amount of speciation that exists in different habitats – he points to the French Zoologist Henri Milne-Edwards and not Charles Babbage. We know that the Darwin family owned and had read Babbage's influential book on *The Economy of Machinery* because it was mentioned by Charles' sister Susan in a letter during his voyage on the *Beagle* (Burkhardt and Smith 1985: 257). But more importantly, Darwin and Babbage were good friends. As Darwin acknowledges in his autobiography, "I used to call pretty often on Babbage and regularly attended his famous evening parties. He was always worth listening to, but he was a disappointed and discontented man; and his expression was often or generally morose" (Barlow 1958: 108). Hence if Darwin was to learn about the division of labor, particularly in terms of a universal law that could be applied to the physical, social, and biological sciences, who better to learn from than Charles Babbage?

7   If the principle of the division of labor was learned from Babbage, why then does Darwin cite Milne-Edwards in his published work? Schweber (1980) suggests that Darwin cited Milne-Edwards rather than an economist because of politics: "But Darwin was also sensitive to the constraints put on the development of biology as a scientific discipline by his society. Biology, like every other science, was not to be tainted with political ideology – at least not consciously or overtly. I believe this to be one of the reasons Milne-Edwards proves so attractive to Darwin. He could metamorphose Milne-Edwards' division of physiological labor into the physiological division of labor, ascribe this principle to a great zoologist and theoretician of biology, and never have to refer to political economy" (Schweber 1980: 212–213). However, if Darwin was motivated by the desire to avoid the "taint" of political ideology, than it would seem only reasonable that he would want to distance himself as far as possible from Charles Babbage. As described by Hyman, "Babbage became a militant reformer, founding scientific societies, launching the 'decline of science' campaign, the scientific counterpart to the struggle for the first reform bill, and participating, both as campaign organizer and candidate, in liberal and radical politics" (1982: 2). This political theme continues when it comes to Babbage's

Economy of Manufactures where it served as part of the campaign for the new reformed Parliament and in more general terms, to "secure the reorganization of British industry and commerce on a scientific basis" (Hyman 1982: 111).

8 As Schumpeter notes about Babbage: "His chief merit was that he combined a command of simple but sound economic theory with a thorough first-hand knowledge of industrial technology and of the business processes relevant thereto. This almost unique combination of acquirements enabled him to provide not only a large quantity of well-known facts but also, unlike other writers who did the same thing, interpretations" (1954: 541 n. 1). These interpretations did not go unnoticed by Marshall who quoted Babbage's famous principle with respect to the division of labor (1961: 264–265), made reference to Babbage's example of the production of the horn (1961: 278 n. 2) in order to illustrate large scale production, and also, indirectly, through his contention that organization should become a factor of production (1961: 138–139) on par with labor and capital.

9 While there is no evidence that Marshall read Babbage's Bridgewater Treatise, we do know that he read Babbage's autobiography. In his autobiography, Babbage restates his Theory of Miracles; a theory that played an important role in reshaping Lyell's geology from what had been a travelogue to a more general theory. Babbage praises his own Theory of Miracles with the following comment: "The explanation which I gave of the nature of miracles in 'the Ninth Bridgewater Treatise,' published in May, 1837, has now stood the test of more than a quarter of a century, during which it has been examined by some of the deepest thinkers in many countries. Its adoption by those writers who have referred to it has, as far as my information goes, been unanimous" (Babbage 1864: 440).

10 The importance of Marshall's *Principle of Continuity* is discussed at length in Boland (1992). However, rather than adopting the position that "biology is an intermediate stage on a continuum between inexact, subjective historical studies at the one extreme and precise, objective physics at the other extreme" (Boland 1992: 40–41), an alternate view is being advanced. The position advanced here is Economic Biology serves as an intermediate stage on a continuum where inorganic matter changes, but life created by a higher being does not, and the view that matter does not change while life itself evolves slowly over time. Economic Biology as an intermediate stage, adopts the view that markets fairly quickly reach an equilibrium and hence do not change all that much, while those who utilize markets experience fundamental changes over longer periods of time.

11 The significance of this phrase has been discussed in detail in Fishburn (2004).

12 This in part helps to explain why William Thomson found himself in the position where it was "impossible to conceive either the beginning or the continuance of life without a creating an overruling power" (Smith and Wise 1989: 636). This was because "unlike God, man could not 'miraculously' create energy; but like god, man could, by his will, direct energy in its course, and so employ available energy to his own account and to his material benefit through machines" (Smith and Wise 1989: 615). Thus, Thomson adopted the position that those "laws" that govern the origin of the species are distinct and separate from those laws that govern matter.

13 For someone like Marshall who found Darwin's theory of evolution to be exciting because of its progressive element, the view expounded by physicists such as Jenkins and Thomson would have been considerably less appealing because of its pessimism toward the future. Using the laws of thermodynamics, Thomson argued that eventually the hot earth would cool down over a definite period of time. Without some compensating factor (such as radioactivity discovered in the early twentieth century), the earth would eventually cool to the point where it could no longer sustain life, as we know it. It is therefore difficult to imagine the Alfred Marshall who looks forward to the expansion of economic chivalry in an evolving economy, eagerly embracing a view of the world that ends in such a dismal note.

14 Reluctant to pursue the same route as Wallace (the co-founder of the theory of natural selection) by modifying the theory to fit in a shorter time period, Darwin was unable to mount an adequate defense, or construct suitable amendments to preserve the tenets of his theory. As described by Burchfield, Darwin's "theory of natural selection had been born in the confidence of almost unlimited time, and compromise as he must, he could not shake the fear that too little time would strangle it" (1974: 318).

15 In part, as a result of the Age of the Earth debates, the latter part of the nineteenth century became a period where there was general acceptance of the concept of evolution, but the mechanism that drives the process (selection) was met by a great deal of skepticism. In fact, Darwinism was in such disarray, that by the turn of the century, it was one step away from extinction. As Peter Bowler described it: "From the high point of the 1870s and 1880s, when 'Darwinism' had become virtually synonymous with evolution itself, the selection theory had slipped in popularity to such an extent that by 1900 its opponents were convinced it would never recover. Evolution itself remained unquestioned, but an increasing number of biologists preferred mechanisms other than selection to explain *how* it occurred" (1989: 246).

16 As Marshall reminds us "while wants are the rulers of life among the lower animals, it is to changes in the forms of efforts and activities that we must turn when in search for the keynotes of the history of mankind" (1961: 85).

17 Based on this belief, Marshall breaks rank with Adam Smith and the traditional perspective that the division of labor predicated on the pursuit of self-interest not only adds to the national dividend but also ensures the "survival of the fittest." Marshall expressed the view that this doctrine of natural organization while containing more truth than any other, had found its benefits exaggerated. In his criticism of this perspective in Appendix B of the *Principles*, Marshall contended that the main problem was that Smith and his followers argued as "though man's character and efficiency were to be regarded as a fixed quantity" (1961: 764). Yet for Marshall, survival of the fittest depended in large part on changes in character.

18 Marshall's discussion of the healthy boy mirrors his discussion of the dynamic changes that occur in an industry as we think beyond the stationary state in Book Five chapter five of his *Principles of Economics*. Just as the concept of the representative firm would come in to play as a useful device for holding this dynamic constant in order to understand how an equilibrium price emerges in the market, a similar representative moment in the life of the healthy boy could be employed to understand how a similar equilibrium position would emerge.

19 In Niman (2004), changing competences provide the source for variation that drives the process of evolution within an economy. As the firm develops new competences in order to stay competitive, these new ideas, technologies, and innovations are added to the social knowledge base. The social knowledge base provides the foundation for the formation of new firms along an evolutionary process.

20 In a letter to Benjamin Kidd referring to the fourth edition of the *Principles* and dated May 27, 1902, Marshall articulates what Darwinism means to him: "For as to Darwin, he seems to me to have done, what you seem to hold he has not done, emphasize the dominance of sacrifice for future generations as an or even *the* essential element of progress. Thus the brief hint as to my ethical position given in Book IV Ch. VIII of my Principles seemed to me to [be] mere Darwinism. (I have not developed this hint anywhere in print; though I talk about the matter more or less in lectures; & there is another touch to 'the moralist' on p. 787 of my Principles)" (Whitaker 1996: 385).

21 In doing so, Marshall is able to accomplish something that had not been done by those progressive members at the early stage of the Statistical Movement: he is able to draw a link between poverty and the rise of the factory system. Thus, he was able to go beyond the work of the early members of the Statistical Movement who

disassociated the problems of poverty from the economic requirements of modern production, thereby severing the connections "between industrialization and its social effects" (Berg 1980: 314).

22 This may explain in part, Marshall's adoration for the work of Herbert Spencer. Spencer was a generalist who might have made even Adam Smith's interests look narrow. Cutting his intellectual teeth as a young man with Lyell's *Principles of Geology*, Spencer went on to broaden his interests into nearly every field of inquiry. However, most importantly, from the perspective of Marshall, Spencer helps Marshall in making the transition from an individual interested in psychology in order to try and understand how we can know what it is that we know, to a broader social perspective where characteristics are inherited by entire races rather than by individuals (Wilson 1999: 157).

23 Thinking about evolution as occurring over multiple levels is discussed in Niman (1994).

References

Babbage, Charles. 1841. *On the Economy of Machinery and Manufactures*, 4th Edition. London: Charles Knight & C. Ludgate.

Babbage, Charles. 1864 (1968). *Passages from the Life of a Philosopher*. London: Dawsons of Pall Mall.

Backhouse, Roger. 2006. Sidgwick, Marshall and the Cambridge School of Economics, *History of Political Economy*, 38 (spring): 15–44. doi:10.1215/00182702-00182738-1-15.

Bankovsky, Miriam. 2019. Alfred Marshall's Household Economics: The Role of the Family in Cultivating an Ethical Capitalism. *Cambridge Journal of Economics*, 43: 249–267. doi:10.1093/cje/bey003.

Barlow, Nora. 1958. *The Autobiography of Charles Darwin*. New York: W.W. Norton.

Barrett, Paul H., Gautrey, Peter J., Herbert, Sandra, Kohn, David and Smith, Sydney. 1987. *Charles Darwin's Notebooks, 1836–1844*. Ithaca: Cornell University Press.

Berg, Maxine. 1980. *The Machinery Question and the Making of Political Economy 1815–1848*. Cambridge: Cambridge University Press.

Boland, Lawrence. 1992. *The Principles of Economics: Some Lies My Teachers Told Me*. London: Routledge.

Bowler, Peter J. 1989. *Evolution: The History of an Idea*, Revised Edition. Berkeley: University of California Press.

Burchfield, Joe D. 1974. Darwin and the Dilemma of Geological Time. *ISIS*, 65: 301–321.

Burkhardt, Frederick and Smith, Sydney. 1985. *The Correspondence of Charles Darwin*, Volume 1. Cambridge: Cambridge University Press.

Burkhardt, Frederick and Smith, Sydney. 1988. *The Correspondence of Charles Darwin*, Volume 4. Cambridge: Cambridge University Press.

Caldari, Katia. 2015. Marshall and Complexity: A Necessary Balance between Process and Order. *Cambridge Journal of Economics*, 3: 1071–1085. doi:10.1093/cje/bev032.

Cannon, Walter F. 1960. The Uniformitarian–Catastrophist Debate. *ISIS*, 51: 38–55.

Chandler, Alfred D. 1977. *The Visible Hand: The Managerial Revolution in American Business*. Cambridge, MA: Belknap Press.

Checkland, S.G. 1959. Growth and Progress: The Nineteenth Century View in Britain. *Economic History Review*, 12 (1): 49–62.

Coase, R.H. 1975. Marshall on Method. *Journal of Law and Economics*, 18 (1): 25–31.

Cook, Simon J. 2005. A Wrangling Machine. *History of Political Economy*, 37 (4): 659–709. doi:10.1215/00182702-00182737-4-689.

Cook, Simon J. 2007. Marshall and Babbage. Published in Raffaelli, Tiziano, Becattini, Giacomo, and Dardi, Marco (eds.), *The Elgar Companion to Alfred Marshall*. Brookfield: Edward Elgar.

Cook, Simon J. 2009. *The Intellectual Foundations of Alfred Marshall's Economic Science: A Rounded Globe of Knowledge*. Cambridge: Cambridge University Press. doi:10.1017/CBO9780511596728.

Christensen, Clayton M., Raynor, Michael E. and McDonald, Rory. 2015. What Is Disruptive Innovation? *Harvard Business Review*, December: 2–11.

Desmond, Adrian and Moore, James. 1991. *Darwin*. New York: Warner Books.

Dolan, Brian P. 1998. Representing Novelty: Charles Babbage, Charles Lyell, and Experiments in Early Victorian Geology. *History of Science*, 36: 299–327. doi:10.1177/007327539803600303.

Fishburn, Geoffrey. 2004. Natura non facit saltum in Alfred Marshall (and Charles Darwin). *History of Economics Review*, 40 (1): 59–68. doi:10.1080/18386318.2004.11681190.

Fleeming Jenkin, H.C. 1867. The Origin of the Species. *North British Review*, 46: 276–318.

Goldman, Lawrence. 1983. The Origins of British "Social Science": Political Economy, Natural Science and Statistics. *The Historical Journal*, 26 (3): 587–616.

Greene, John C. 1996. *The Death of Adam: Evolution and Its Impact on Western Thought*. Ames: Iowa State University Press.

Greene, Mott T. 1982. *Geology in the Nineteenth Century*. Ithaca: Cornell University Press.

Groenewegen, Peter. 1995. *A Soaring Eagle: Alfred Marshall 1842–1924*. Brookfield: Edward Elgar.

Groenewegen, Peter. 2001. The Evolutionary Economics of Alfred Marshall: An Overview. In Laurent, John and Nightingale, John (eds.) *Darwinism and Evolutionary Economics*. Northampton: Edward Elgar.

Hodgson, Geoffrey M. 1993. The Mecca of Alfred Marshall. *Economic Journal*, 103: 406–415. doi:10.2307/2234779.

Hyman, Anthony. 1982. *Charles Babbage*. Princeton: Princeton University Press.

Kingsland, Sharon. 1988. Evolution and Debates over Human Progress from Darwin to Sociobiology. *Population and Development Review* 14 (supplement): 167–198.

Lyell, Charles. 1830–33. *Principles of Geology*. Reprinted by University Chicago Press, Chicago, 1990.

Loasby, Brian J. 1990. Firms, Markets, and the Principle of Continuity. In Whitaker, John K. (ed.). *Centenary Essays on Alfred Marshall*. Cambridge: Cambridge University Press.

Marshall, Alfred. 1885a. *The Present Position of Economics*. Reprinted in Pigou, A.C. (ed.), *Memorials of Alfred Marshall*, New York: Augustus M. Kelley, pp. 152–174, 1966.

Marshall, Alfred. 1885b. *The Graphic Method of Statistics*. Reprinted in Pigou, A.C. (ed.), *Memorials of Alfred Marshall*, New York: Augustus M. Kelley, pp. 175–187, 1966.

Marshall, Alfred. 1897. *The Old Generation of Economists and the New*. Reprinted in Pigou, A.C. (ed.), *Memorials of Alfred Marshall*, New York: Augustus M. Kelley, pp. 295–311, 1966.

Marshall, Alfred. 1898. *Mechanical and Biological Analogies in Economics*. Reprinted in Pigou, A.C. (ed.), *Memorials of Alfred Marshall*, New York: Augustus M. Kelley, pp. 312–318, 1966.

Marshall, Alfred. 1907. *Social Possibilities of Economic Chivalry*. Reprinted in Pigou, A.C. (ed.), *Memorials of Alfred Marshall*, New York: Augustus M. Kelley, pp. 323–346, 1966.

Marshall, Alfred. 1961. *Principles of Economics*, 9th Edition. London: Macmillan.

Marshall, Alfred. 1919. *Industry and Trade*. London: Macmillan.

Mirowski, Philip. 1984. Physics and the "Marginalist" Revolution. Cambridge Journal of Economics, 8: 361–379.

Mirowski, Philip. 1989. *More Heat than Light: Economics as Social Physics: Physics as Nature's Economics*. Cambridge: Cambridge University Press. doi:10.1017/CBO9780511559990.

Moss, Laurence. 1982. Biological Theory and Technological Entrepreneurship in Marshall's Writings. *Eastern Economic Journal*, 8 (1): 3–13.

Niman, Neil B. 1991a. Biological Analogies in Marshall's Work. *Journal of the History of Economic Thought*, 13: 19–36. doi:10.1017/S1053837200003370.

Niman, Neil B. 1991b. The Entrepreneurial Function in the Theory of the Firm. *Scottish Journal of Political Economy*, 38 (2): 162–176. doi:10.1111/j.1467–9485.1991.tb00308.x.

Niman, Neil B. 1994. The Role of Biological Analogies in the Theory of the Firm. In Mirowski, Philip (ed.), *Natural Images in Economic Thought: Markets Read in Tooth and Claw*. Cambridge: Cambridge University Press. doi:10.1017/S1053837200003370.

Niman, Neil B. 2000. Competition and Economic Progress. *Journal of Bioeconomics*, 2 (3): 221–231. doi:10.1023/A:1012220127250.

Niman, Neil B. 2004. The Evolutionary Firm and Cournot's Dilemma. *Cambridge Journal of Economics*, 28 (4): 273–290. doi:10.1093/cje/28.2.273.

Niman, Neil B. 2008. Charles Babbage's Influence on the Development of Alfred Marshall's Theory of the Firm. *Journal of the History of Economic Thought*, 30(4): 479–490.

Peel, Y.D.L. 1971. *Herbert Spencer: The Evolution of a Sociologist*. New York: Basic Books.

Pigou, Arthur Cecil (ed.). 1966. *Memorials of Alfred Marshall*, New York: Augustus M. Kelley.

Raffaelli, Tiziano. 2003. *Marshall's Evolutionary Economics*. London: Routledge.

Rashid, Salim. 1979. Richard Jones and Baconian Historicism at Cambridge. *Journal of Economic Issues*, 13 (1): 159–173.

Rashid, Salim. 1981. Political Economy and Geology in the Early Nineteenth Century: Similarities and Contrasts. *History of Political Economy*, 13 (4): 726–743.

Schumpeter, Joseph A. 1954. *History of Economic Thought*, Oxford: Oxford University Press.

Schumpeter, Joseph A. 1962. *Capitalism, Socialism, and Democracy*, 3rd Edition. New York: Harper & Row.

Schweber, Silvan S. 1980. Darwin and the Political Economists: Divergence of Character. *Journal of the History of Biology*, 13: 195–289.

Schweber, Silvan S. 1985. The Wider British Context in Darwin's Theorizing. In Kohn, David (ed.), *The Darwinian Heritage*. Princeton: Princeton University Press.

Smith, Crosbie and Norton Wise, M. 1989. *Energy and Empire: A Biographical Study of Lord Kelvin*. Cambridge: Cambridge University Press.

Thomson, Keith. 2005. *Before Darwin: Reconciling God and Nature*. New Haven: Yale University Press.

Thomson, William. 1862. On the Age of the Sun's Heat. *Macmillan's Magazine*, 5: 288–393.

Thomson, William. 1863. On the Secular Cooling of the Earth. *Philosophical Magazine*, 25: 1–14.

Thomson, William. 1868. On Geological Time. Reprinted in: *Popular Lectures and Addresses*, Vol. II, London: Macmillian, pp. 10–72.

Turner, Frank Miller. 1974. *Between Science and Religion: The Reaction to Scientific Naturalism in Late Victorian England*. New Haven: Yale University Press.

Viner, Jacob. 1941. Marshall's Economics, in Relation to the Man and to His Times. *The American Economic Review*, 31 (2): 223–235.

Warwick, Andrew 2003. *Masters of Theory: Cambridge and the Rise of Mathematical Physics*. Chicago: University of Chicago Press. doi:10.7208/chicago/9780226873763.001.0001.

Whitaker, John K. (ed.). 1996. *The Correspondence of Alfred Marshall Economist, Volume Two: At the Summit, 1891–1902*, Cambridge: Cambridge University Press.

Wilson, A.N. 1999. *God's Funeral*. New York: W.W. Norton.

Wise, M. Norton. 1989a. Work and Waste: Political Economy and Natural Philosophy in Nineteenth Century Britain (I). *History of Science*, 27: 263–301. doi:10.1177/007327538902700302.

Wise, M. Norton. 1989b. Work and Waste: Political Economy and Natural Philosophy in Nineteenth Century Britain (II). *History of Science*, 27: 391–441. doi:10.1177/007327538902700403.

Wise, M. Norton. 1990. Work and Waste: Political Economy and Natural Philosophy in Nineteenth Century Britain (III). *History of Science*, 28: 221–261. doi:10.1177/007327539002800301.

Wool, David. 2001. Charles Lyell – "the Father of Geology" – as a Forerunner of Modern Ecology. *OIKOS*, 94: 385–391.

7 The role of Keynes's idea of "organic unity" in his "general theory" of capitalism[1]

Ted Winslow

The General Theory of Employment, Interest and Money is not a general theory in the sense usually assumed. It is a general theory of capitalism identified with the expression of what Keynes, in "My Early Beliefs," claims are "insane and irrational springs of wickedness in most men" (X 447)[2] in the historically and culturally specific form of irrational "money-motives" (IX 293). This much more limited sense of "general" is connected to a change in Keynes's understanding of the subject matter of economics as part of what he calls "psychics."

In *A Treatise on Probability*, he had identified the "individual consciousness" as the "unit" to be taken as the starting point for study of what he there called "mental events." The *Treatise* treats this as an "atomic" unit in the sense of a unit whose relations are "external." So conceived, its identity is independent of changes in its relations; it is a "substance" in two senses, one derived from Aristotle and one from Descartes. The Aristotelian sense designates an entity that bears qualities without being itself a quality; the Cartesian, an entity that needs nothing but itself in order to exist, its essential qualities being conceived as independent of its relations and as not changing with changes in them.

The first part of the chapter aims to demonstrate that Keynes subsequently abandoned the atomic hypothesis on which *A Treatise on Probability* had been based as invalid in psychics. He replaced it with the hypothesis of "organic unity" meaning by this the idea of the relations of the individual consciousness as "internal" rather than "external." It was now conceived as an "adjective" of its social conditions with its essential qualities dependent on them.

Keynes's idea of "organic unity" in this sense is very close to A.N. Whitehead's, the main exponent in his early Cambridge context of an ontology of internal relations. Whitehead had criticized atomism both in the form given to it by Bertrand Russell in his elaboration of formal logic in *Principles of Mathematics* as "logical atomism," and in the form appropriated from Russell by Keynes and then amended with the addition of "logical probability relations" as a means of enlarging Russell's idea to include judgments of probability as part of formal logic. Whitehead had developed a foundation for such judgments of his own grounded in his particular idea of organic unity. This foundation, a form of "frequency" theory, had been explicitly considered by Keynes in the *Treatise*. Very soon after its publication, Whitehead proceeded to answer, by

DOI: 10.4324/9781003138655-7

means of an elaboration of its relation to the hypothesis of organic unity, the questions Keynes had raised in his discussion of it.

The chapter also treats Alfred Marshall as an important source of these ideas for Keynes, particularly as the developer of an economics based on them. The influences from which he had himself appropriated them were mainly German, specifically, as Keynes points out, Hegel. Keynes makes it clear in his elaboration of the role of these ideas in Marshall's economics that they are ideas he shares.

The second part of the chapter examines another foundational idea of Keynes, the idea of an objective and knowable "good." The original source of this idea was G.E. Moore's *Principia Ethica*, but this was later modified, partly in terms of its content, but mostly in terms of the idea of the methods by which the content was known and developed. These modifications replaced an "atomic" with an "organic" view of relations and, relatedly, replaced Keynes's original idea of "experience" with the idea of it Whitehead claimed could rationally ground both the idea of "organic unity" and the idea (and content) of an objective and knowable "good." The idea of such a "good" is the basis of Keynes's idea of "rationality" as characteristic of the "reliable, rational, decent people" who will populate "the ideal social republic of the future" (XXI 241). This social republic will not be capitalist.

This part also examines in more detail the essential feature of Keynes's idea of human nature pointed to above, the fact of there "being insane and irrational springs of wickedness in most men." This is the major obstacle in the way of the development of "reliable, rational, decent people."

The third and final part examines Keynes's "general theory" as a theory of capitalism treated as an historically and culturally limited form of economy having the "essential characteristic" specified above. His understanding of it is underpinned by the hypothesis of organic unity in the sense of internal relations that limits the idea of "general" involved.

One key aspect of this understanding is his treatment of capitalism as an interim form that, though inconsistent with "the ideal social republic of the future," works, without conscious intent, in the still more specific form of irrationality characteristic of the "entrepreneur" as a "strenuous purposive money-maker," to bring about the development of science and technology that, objectified in productive forces, will make possible the "material abundance" required to make the ideal practicable. Its realization, however, will require a different form of "individual consciousness," the form Keynes identifies with "reliable, rational, decent people" able to make the abundance the basis of "good lives" actualizing non-economic aesthetic, intellectual and ethical "goods." This is the sense in which the "ideal commonwealth" (VII 374) will not be capitalist.

Another key aspect deriving from the treatment of interdependence as "organic" is the very limited role this allows for mathematical representation of the knowable order involved. It does allow, however, for a kind of order able to provide a basis for rational induction, rational judgments of probability and, based on these, rational predictions.

Finally, this last part of the chapter uses Keynes's analysis of and activity in financial markets to illustrate the role given to these ideas in a very concrete part of his economics, a part providing a foundation for his own activity in them. This, the rational form of speculation as "the activity of forecasting the psychology of the market" (VII 158), bases its forecasting on the rational forms of inductive and probability judgments made possible by knowledge of the interdependence involved as a specific form of organic unity in the sense of internal relations.

Formal logic and the hypothesis of organic unity

A Treatise on Probability appropriated its idea of formal logic from Bertrand Russell's *Principles of Mathematics* (X 438–9, 445). The latter was based on the atomic hypothesis, *i.e.* on the hypothesis that, as Russell would state it in 1956 in the context of reaffirming his belief in it, "the world is made up of an immense number of bits and each bit would be exactly what it is if all the other bits did not exist" (Russell 1956: 42). Keynes's *Treatise* attempted to extend the range of reasonable judgments included in formal logic in this sense by means of the idea of "logical probability relations."

He had also there (VIII 276–8), in a discussion of the requirements for rational induction, addressed the validity of the hypothesis by comparing and contrasting the "atomic" and "organic" ideas of natural law. He tentatively opted for the atomic idea on the ground that the organic could not provide a rational basis for induction because it was inconsistent with any stability in such laws. Consequently, if law was organic, "prediction would be impossible and the inductive method useless." In this discussion he identifies two ultimate atomic "units," one for "mental," the other for "material events." He claims that:

> We do habitually assume, I think, that the size of the atomic unit is for mental events an individual consciousness, and for material events an object small in relation to our perceptions.
>
> (VIII 278)

He subsequently explicitly abandoned these beliefs. In his essay on Frank Ramsey, he says of the subsequent development of formal logic:

> The first impression conveyed by the work of Russell was that the field of formal logic was enormously extended. The gradual perfection of the formal treatment at the hands of himself, of Wittgenstein and of Ramsey had been, however, gradually to empty it of content and to reduce it more and more to mere dry bones, until finally it seemed to exclude not only all experience, but most of the principles, usually reckoned logical, of reasonable thought.
>
> (X 338)

Having excluded from rational treatment by formal logic "not only all experience, but most of the principles, usually reckoned logical, of reasonable thought," Keynes now goes on to explicitly abandon it as a foundation for probability.

> Wittgenstein's solution was to regard everything else as a sort of inspired nonsense, having great value indeed for the individual, but incapable of being exactly discussed. Ramsey's reaction was towards what he himself described as a sort of pragmatism, not unsympathetic to Russell but repugnant to Wittgenstein. "The essence of pragmatism", he says, "I take to be this, that the meaning of a sentence is to be defined by reference to the actions to which asserting it would lead, or, more vaguely still, by its possible causes and effects. Of this I feel certain, but of nothing more definite."
>
> Thus he was led to consider "human logic" as distinguished from "formal logic". Formal logic is concerned with nothing but the rules of consistent thought. But in addition to this we have certain "useful mental habits" for handling the material with which we are supplied by our perceptions and by our memory and perhaps in other ways, and so arriving at or towards truth; and the analysis of such habits is also a sort of logic. The application of these ideas to the logic of probability is very fruitful. Ramsey argues, as against the view which I had put forward, that probability is concerned not with objective relations between propositions but (in some sense) with degrees of belief, and he succeeds in showing that the calculus of probabilities simply amounts to a set of rules for ensuring that the system of degrees of belief which we hold shall be a consistent system. Thus the calculus of probabilities belongs to formal logic. But the basis of our degrees of belief—or the *a priori* probabilities, as they used to be called—is part of our human outfit, perhaps given us merely by natural selection, analogous to our perceptions and our memories rather than to formal logic. So far I yield to Ramsey—I think he is right. But in attempting to distinguish "rational" degrees of belief from belief in general he was not yet, I think, quite successful. It is not getting to the bottom of the principle of induction merely to say that it is a useful mental habit. Yet in attempting to distinguish a "human" logic from formal logic on the one hand and descriptive psychology on the other, Ramsey may have been pointing the way to the next field of study when formal logic has been put into good order and its highly limited scope properly defined.
>
> (X 338–9)

As Keynes points out here, Ramsey elaborated "human logic" as providing a rational objective ground for probability and induction and, hence, as distinct from "formal logic" and "descriptive psychology."

> Let us therefore try to get an idea of a human logic which shall not attempt to be reducible to formal logic. Logic, we may agree, is concerned

not with what men actually believe, but what they ought to believe, or what it would be reasonable to believe. What then, we must ask, is meant by saying that it is reasonable for a man to have such and such a degree of belief in a proposition?

(Ramsey 1931: 193)

Thus, in agreeing that the idea "may have been pointing the way" to such a ground, while dissenting from Ramsey's attempt to find this in Peirce's pragmatism, Keynes was accepting that there might be such a ground. He explicitly abandons, however, his *Treatise* attempt to provide it in the form of the formal logical idea of "logical probability relations."

Linked to this, Keynes also subsequently abandoned the atomic hypothesis as valid in psychics, replacing it with the hypothesis of organic unity. The person in Keynes's (and Russell's) Cambridge context who provided an elaboration of the hypothesis that justified both this move and, relatedly, Keynes's abandonment of a formal logic approach to probability and induction was A.N. Whitehead. The latter's ideas appear explicitly in *A Treatise on Probability* in the form of a frequency theory of probability (VIII 110–20).[3] Keynes's discussion of it does not explicitly treat it as based on Whitehead's particular elaboration of "organic unity" in the sense of "internal relations," the idea that, in contrast to the external relations idea found in Russell's claim above, treats the characteristics of individuals as the outcome of their relations so that any change in the latter alters to some degree the former. He indicates what he sees as difficulties with the theory, but does not outright reject it.

Shortly after its publication in 1921, Russell reviewed the *Treatise* in *The Mathematical Gazette* (Russell 1922). The review explicitly addressed Keynes's treatment of Whitehead's frequency theory. Russell claimed that Keynes's objections to it were not addressed to its "principle," but consisted instead "in showing technical difficulties which, one feels, might be overcome by ingenuity and skill."

He [Keynes] is less convincing in arguing against a modified form of the [frequency] theory suggested to him by Dr. Whitehead. His objections here are not addressed to the principle, but consist in showing technical difficulties which, one feels, might be overcome by ingenuity and skill.

(Russell 1922: 124)

Russell's 1956 memoir, "Beliefs: Discarded and Retained," focused on Whitehead's having convinced him that the grounds on which he and G.E. Moore had rejected Hegel's version of the idea of organic unity as "internal relations," along with the claim about experience (as essentially vague) Hegel made in support of it, were mistaken. Whitehead, Russell reports, used his own version of these ideas to critique the atomic foundations of Russell's treatment of formal logic. He acknowledges that he was persuaded by this critique that the atomic hypothesis did not have the "metaphysical necessity" his initial use of it as a basis for formal logic implied, though, as pointed out above, he did not abandon the hypothesis.

Whitehead himself elaborated the implications of the hypothesis for the problem of induction in "Uniformity and Contingency," his presidential address to the Aristotelian Society on November 6, 1922 (Whitehead 1923). He explicitly connects the argument he makes there to Keynes's *Treatise*. His elaboration aimed to ground the argument in "direct intuitive observation," the idea of experience as essentially vague he had defended in his criticism of Russell and which, he argued, could provide rational grounding for this and other propositions in the field of "speculative Metaphysics."[4]

Without explicitly mentioning them, the paper addresses questions Keynes had raised about Whitehead's version of a frequency theory. At the end of the *Treatise*'s chap. 18, connecting his own treatment of induction to the idea of "logical probability relations," Keynes had concluded:

> The validity and reasonable nature of inductive generalisation is, therefore, a question of logic and not of experience, of formal and not of material laws. The actual constitution of the phenomenal universe determines the character of our evidence; but it cannot determine what conclusions given evidence rationally supports.
>
> (VIII 246)

In his own copy of the book (see Keynes 1921: 121), Whitehead had made the following annotation:

> Induction ultimately depends on the belief that information about one matter of fact affords some information about other matters of fact. If there be no such derivative information, all induction lacks any justification.

"Uniformity and Contingency" begins with this as the problem to be addressed, namely, does our experience give us knowledge of internal relations?

> The general problem is to examine, whether any isolated portion of our experience has any character which of itself implies a corresponding character, extending beyond the domain of that immediate example. In other words, we ask whether, on the ground of experience, we can deduce any systematic uniformity, extending throughout any types of entities, or throughout the relations between them.
>
> (Whitehead 1923: 1)

He then sets out his own answer as, yes it does.

> My own position is that consciousness is a factor within fact and involves its knowledge. Thus apprehended nature is involved in our consciousness. But in its exhibition of this character our consciousness exhibits its significance of factors of fact beyond itself.
>
> (ibid: 11–12)

This is elaborated as an organic unity of "consciousness" and "nature" that enables "consciousness" to both exist and provide an objective rational basis for induction. The elaboration makes it possible to separately "abstract" consciousness and nature from their "embeddedness in all-embracing fact."

At the end of the address, Whitehead provides the following summary of the "evidence" he has argued "experience" in his sense provides of a rational basis for an inductive argument. "Perceptual objects" are the "objectifications" of the internal relations of an "event." An "Aristotelian adjective" is the adjective of something that is not itself an adjective, namely, an "event" during its activity as conditioned by its internal relations in the form of these "perceptual objects." These, though "objectifications" of these relations, are, as present in the event, "Aristotelian adjectives," *i.e.* an "event" during its activity as conditioned by its internal relations in the form of these "perceptual objects" is not an "adjective." There is "a break down in the reign of relativity" in the sense that this activity, while internally related before and after it begins and ends, is not in its "duration" internally related.

> The evidence is summed up in the statement that the ingression of sense-objects into nature involves events analysable into space-time qualified by pervasive Aristotelian adjectives. The sensoria are always indicated in this way as the loci of perceptual objects, and also in general so are the situations of the sense-objects. But what are the perceptual objects – tables, trees, stones, etc. – which are thus signified? For unbiassed evidence of their character we must have recourse to the general popular idea, and not to scientific accounts, elaborated in the interest of theories, and vitiated by faulty analyses of nature. The popular evidence is unanimous: – The modes of ingression of sense-objects in nature are the outcome of the perceptual objects exhibiting themselves. The grass exhibits itself as green, the bell exhibits itself as tolling, the sugar as tasting, the stone as touchable. Thus the ultimate character of perceptual objects is that they are Aristotelian pervasive adjectives which are the controls of ingression. Now an Aristotelian adjective marks a breakdown of the reign of relativity; it is just an adjective of the event which it qualifies. And this relation of adjective to subject requires no reference to anything else. Accordingly, a perceptual object is neutral as regards events, other than those which it qualifies. It is thus sharply distinguished from a sense-object, whose ingression involves all sorts of events in all sorts of ways. Furthermore, the contingency of ingression, with its baffling tangle, is now simplified into the contingency attaching to the simpler relations of perceptual objects to the events which they qualify. But, if the very nature of perceptual objects is to be controls, have we not in them those missing characters of events, whose supposed absence led Hume to remove causation from nature into the mind? A control is necessarily the control of the process, or transition, in finite events. It thus means, in its essential character, a control of the future from the basis of the present. Thus in modern scientific phraseology, a

perceptual object means a present focus and a field of force streaming out into the future. This field of force represents the type of control of the future exercised by the perceptual object – which is, in fact, the perceptual object in its relation to the future, while the present focus is the perceptual object in its relation to the present. But the present has also a duration. What we observe is the control in action during the specious present. There are a finite number of perceptual objects within any region of space-time relevant to our experience. This finiteness still remains as we pass from the somewhat vague perceptual objects to the more precise scientific objects such as electrons.

Accordingly, there are a finite number of such controls of the future, which are in any way relevant to our experience. The latest and subtlest analysis of the difficulties which luster round the notion of Induction is to be found in Part III of J. M. *Keynes's Treatise on Probability*. I will conclude with a quotation from his profound discussion:

"The purpose of the discussion, which occupies the greater art of this chapter, is to maintain that, if the premises of our argument permit us to assume that the facts or propositions, with which the argument is concerned, belong to a finite system, then probable knowledge can be validly obtained by means of an inductive argument."

(*Treatise on Probability*, Ch. XXII) [VIII 280] (Whitehead 1922: 17–18)

Whitehead thus defended an idea of organic unity consistent with a limited form of uniformity that would, he claimed, provide a rational objective foundation for induction, also in a limited form, that the atomic hypothesis on which Keynes was relying could not (the address: 12–14, gives reasons for this in its discussion of Hume and Russell on induction). Moreover, he had also attempted to ground this in an idea of "direct knowledge" different from, and, he claimed, more descriptively accurate than, the idea on which the *Treatise* had itself been based.

Keynes had acknowledged in the *Treatise* (VIII 291–3) that, given his idea of it as a form of "direct acquaintance," "experience" (identified with "atomic" sense data (VIII 12)) could not justify various hypotheses required for the existence of a rational basis for induction. Specifically, experience so conceived could not justify belief in the "uniformity of nature," "the law of causation" and what he calls "the inductive hypothesis – the assumption "that *all* systems of fact are finite." He suggested other aspects of his concept of direct acquaintance might be able to do this, but acknowledged he was unable to provide a fully persuasive account of how this was so.

I do not pretend that I have given any perfectly adequate reason for accepting the theory [of how direct acquaintance in his *Treatise* sense might be able to justify the inductive hypothesis] I have expounded, or any such theory.

(VIII 293)

He looked forward to a "proper answer" being "given to the inquiry—of what sorts of things are we *capable* of direct knowledge?" as finally providing a "conclusive or perfectly satisfactory answer."

> I do not believe that any conclusive or perfectly satisfactory answer to this question can be given, so long as our knowledge of the subject of epistemology is in so disordered and undeveloped a condition as it is in at present. No proper answer has yet been given to the inquiry—of what sorts of things are we capable of direct knowledge? The logician, therefore, is in a weak position, when he leaves his own subject and attempts to solve a particular instance of this general problem. He needs guidance as to what kind of reason we could have for such an assumption as the use of inductive argument appears to require.
>
> (VIII 291)

He had, however, already pointed to the idea of "vague knowledge" as possibly relevant to this question:

> I cannot attempt here to analyse the meaning of vague knowledge. It is certainly not the same thing as knowledge proper, whether certain or probable, and it does not seem likely that it is susceptible of strict logical treatment. At any rate I do not know how to deal with it, and in spite of its importance I will not complicate a difficult subject by endeavouring to treat adequately the theory of vague knowledge.
>
> (VIII 17–18)

The relation of the ideas elaborated in "Uniformity and Contingency" to Keynes's *Treatise* is explicitly pointed to again in 1929 in *Process and Reality* (Whitehead 1985: 203–6). There, the hypothesis of organic unity is further elaborated as providing an objective rational basis for induction. He explicitly indicates that the essence of induction based on the hypothesis is not "the divination of general laws."

> You will observe that I do not hold induction to be in its essence the divination of general laws. It is the derivation of some characteristics of a particular future from the known characteristics of a particular past. The wider assumption of general laws holding for all cognizable occasions appears a very unsafe addendum to attach to this limited knowledge. All we can ask of the present occasion is that it shall determine a particular community of occasions, which are in some respects mutually qualified by reason of their inclusion within that same community.
>
> (Whitehead 1985: 204)

This argument closes with an elaboration of the hypothesis as providing an objective rational basis for a frequency theory of probability, an elaboration answering further questions about that theory raised by Keynes in the *Treatise*. The relation to the *Treatise* is again made explicit in a concluding note:

> Note.—By far the best discussion of the philosophical theory of probability is to be found in Mr. J. Maynard Keynes' book, *A Treatise on Probability*. This treatise must long remain the standard work on the subject. My conclusions in this chapter do not seem to me to differ fundamentally from those of Mr. Keynes as set out towards the conclusion of his Chapter XXI. But Mr. Keynes here seems to revert to a view of probability very analogous to that form of the "frequency theory" which, as suggested by me, he criticized acutely (and rightly, so far as concerned that special form) in his Chapter VIII.
>
> (Whitehead 1985: 206)

Still further elaboration of this concept of organic unity for induction and probability is found in Whitehead's account, in *Adventures of Ideas* (Whitehead 1933: 142–3), based on the hypothesis of organic unity, of the "the doctrine of Law as immanent." This doctrine itself requires "the doctrine of Internal Relations."

> the doctrine of Immanent Law is untenable unless we can construct a plausible metaphysical doctrine according to which the characters of the relevant things in nature are the outcome of their interconnections, and their interconnections are the outcome of their characters. This involves some doctrine of internal relations.
>
> (ibid: 143–4)

Understood in terms of this doctrine:

> the order of nature expresses the characters of the real things which jointly compose the existences to be found in nature. When we understand the essences of these things, we thereby understand their mutual relations to each other. Thus, according as there are common elements in their various characters, there will necessarily be corresponding identities in their mutual relations. In other words, some partial identity of pattern in the various characters of natural things issues in some partial identity of pattern in the mutual relations of things. These identities of pattern in the mutual relations are the Laws of Nature. Conversely, a Law is explanatory of some commonality in character pervading the things which constitute Nature. It is evident that the doctrine involves the negation of "absolute being". It presupposes the essential interdependence of things.
>
> (ibid: 142)

Whitehead next elaborates the rational basis this idea of "law" provides for inductive and probability judgments (ibid: 143). Finally, on this understanding of them, the laws of nature are not fixed:

the laws of nature depend on the individual characters of the things constituting nature, as the things change, then correspondingly the laws will change. Thus the modern evolutionary view of the physical universe should conceive of the laws of nature as evolving concurrently with the things constituting the environment. Thus the conception of the Universe as evolving subject to fixed, eternal laws regulating all behaviour should be abandoned.

(ibid)

Whitehead claimed that, because the relevant relations, particularly contemporary relations, changed much more quickly in the case of the "individual" foundational for social theory, including political economy, it was essential both to understand the nature of this individual's internal relations and to take account of relevant changes in them in order to keep assumptions about the character of this individual realistic. Since this character was shared by individuals within the same internal relations, it provided a rational basis for induction and generalization but only so long as the relevant relations themselves remained stable.

> Our sociological theories, our political philosophy, our practical maxims of business, our political economy, and our doctrines of education, are derived from an unbroken tradition of great thinkers and of practical examples, from the age of Plato in the fifth century before Christ to the end of the last century. The whole of this tradition is warped by the vicious assumption that each generation will substantially live amid the conditions governing the lives of its fathers and will transmit those conditions to mould with equal force the lives of its children. We are living in the first period of human history for which this assumption is false.

(Whitehead 1933: 117–18)

Consequently:

> In the present age, the element of novelty which life affords is too prominent to be omitted from our calculations. A deeper knowledge of the varieties of human nature is required to determine the reaction, in its character and its strength, to those elements of novelty which each decade of years introduces into social life.

(Whitehead 1933: 120)

As indicated by his critical engagement with Russell's "logical atomism," Whitehead traced out the implications of these ideas for the validity of axiomatic deductive, including mathematical, reasoning. A summary of them is found in *Modes of Thought* (Whitehead 1938: 144–7).

Whitehead begins by pointing out that deduction cannot be the method by means of which its own use can be justified. The latter is a subject for the field he calls "speculative Metaphysics" whose ultimate ground is experience as "direct intuitive observation," an idea of experience claiming, when elaborated, to point to an essential aspect of experience ignored by the conventional idea of it as atomic sense data. The intuitive aspect of such observation concerns non-sensuous experience, an example of which is direct experience of the body, *e.g.* the eyes as the cause of visual sense experience.[5]

This then provides the foundation for "special sciences" such as economics by justifying the narrower assumptions from which each can start. The assumptions are "narrower" because they specify particular characteristics of the "individual" at issue in the "special science." These are the outcome of specific internal relations. The validity of the assumptions depends, therefore, on these relations remaining stable. This makes the validity of deductive reasoning based upon them itself dependent on the relevant relations remaining stable. This requires direct knowledge both of the dependence and of the stability of the relations. Whitehead gives as an example reasoning that requires a particular kind of identity between a person at birth and at forty. For some purposes, *e.g.*, deciding who is named in a will, the person at forty can reasonably be treated as the same as at birth, for other purposes the person cannot.

Finally, he examines the implications for forms of deductive reasoning that make use of the logical idea of a "variable." This is an element in reasoning assumed to maintain its identity through changes in its relations. Whitehead points, as an example, to the "variables" of algebra. Such reasoning is not validly applicable to the representation of order where elements having the properties of variables in this sense do not exist. A knowable order that can be the basis for valid inductive judgments and predictions based on them may be present, but it will not be an order representable by a system of "variables" in the above sense, *e.g.*, by algebra.

Though Whitehead was the only person in Keynes's context to provide a detailed response to Keynes's *Treatise* arguments based on a very developed and philosophically complex idea of organic unity, he was not the only one to have appropriated the idea and employed it in a way directly relevant to Keynes's employment of it in his economics. In his biographical essay on Marshall (first published in *The Economic Journal*, March 1924), Keynes associates "the profundity of his [Marshall's] insight into the true character of his subject in its highest and most useful developments" (X 188) with his organic unity view of its subject matter.

> Marshall ... arrived very early at the point of view that the bare bones of economic theory are not worth much in themselves and do not carry one far in the direction of useful, practical conclusions. The whole point lies in applying them to the interpretation of current economic life. This requires a profound knowledge of the actual facts of industry and trade. But these and the relation of individual men to them are constantly and rapidly changing.
>
> (X 196)

Keynes follows this with some extracts from Marshall's Inaugural Lecture at Cambridge (1885) in which Marshall criticizes classical political economy for ignoring the fact that "man himself is in a great measure a creature of circumstances and changes with them (Marshall, as cited by Keynes, X 196).

In reaching this idea, Marshall had, as Keynes points out, been very significantly influenced by Hegel's idea of organic unity, particularly as elaborated in Hegel's *Philosophy of History*. This idea allowed for "abstracting" from more or less of this form of interdependence so long as the relevant relations and the characteristics of individuals to which they gave rise could be treated as stable, *i. e.* as what Keynes, in *The General Theory*, calls "given" (VII 245–7).

Marshall makes this same point in the *Principles*, again as a criticism of "Ricardo and his followers." He claims that, as a result of the development of understanding of "the nature of organic growth" by Goethe, Hegel and others, it was recognized that, "if the subject-matter of a science passes through different stages of development, the laws which apply to one stage will seldom apply without modification to others; the laws of the science must have a development corresponding to that of the things of which they treat" (Marshall 1961: Vol. 1, 762–4).

In his biographical essay, Keynes connects this idea of "the nature of organic growth" to Marshall's critical attitude to conventional uses of mathematics in economics. Agreeing with this, he writes:

> Unlike physics, for example, such parts of the barebones of economic theory as are expressible in mathematical form are extremely easy compared with the economic interpretation of the complex and incompletely known facts of experience, and lead one but a very little way towards establishing useful results.[6]

In a footnote to this, Keynes claims that "those whose gift mainly consists in the power to imagine and pursue to their furthest points the implications and prior conditions of comparatively simple facts which are known with a high degree of precision" find "the amalgam of logic and intuition and the wide knowledge of the facts, most of which are not precise, which is required for economic interpretation in its highest form ... overwhelmingly difficult" (X 186 note).

> Professor Planck, of Berlin, the famous originator of the Quantum Theory, once remarked to me that in early life he had thought of studying economics, but had found it too difficult! Professor Planck could easily master the whole corpus of mathematical economics in a few days. He did not mean that! But the amalgam of logic and intuition and the wide knowledge of the facts, most of which are not precise, which is required for economic interpretation in its highest form is, quite truly, over-whelmingly difficult for those whose gift mainly consists in the power to imagine and pursue to their furthest points the implications and prior

conditions of comparatively simple facts which are known with a high degree of precision.

An "amalgam of logic and intuition and the wide knowledge of the facts, most of which are not precise" is required because the "facts" are an organic unity. This raises the question of the basis on which Keynes thinks he knows this. The basis pointed to by Whitehead is the form of experience revealed by "direct perceptual observation" as "essentially vague" and revealing "facts" that, as embedded in internal relations, are themselves "essentially vague" requiring for their description "notions" that are also "essentially vague." In "My Early Beliefs," Keynes critically describes and rejects his own early ideas of experience, facts and language as ignoring what he now claims are these essential features.

One of the main criticisms he makes there of his and his friends' initial understanding of the "good" concerns "method." The first such criticism concerns the method by which knowledge of its content was to be ascertained and disputes about this content resolved. The second concerns the method for "handling" this "material" once known. Keynes identifies the first with Moore's method in *Principia Ethica* and the second with Bertrand Russell's *Principles of Mathematics*.

Initially, he and his friends treated the good as knowable through "direct unanalysable intuition" (X 437). To direct knowledge of the good attained in this way they then applied "logic and rational analysis." In doing so, they mistakenly, he now claims,

> regarded all this as entirely rational and scientific in character. Like any other branch of science, it was nothing more than the application of logic and rational analysis to the material presented as sense data. Our apprehension of good was exactly the same as our apprehension of green, and we purported to handle it with the same logical and analytical technique which was appropriate to the latter. Indeed we combined a dogmatic treatment as to the nature of experience with a method of handling it which was extravagantly scholastic. Russell's *Principles of Mathematics* came out in the same year as *Principia Ethica*; and the former, in spirit, furnished a method for handling the material provided by the latter.
>
> (X 438)

By "scholasticism" Keynes means Frank Ramsey's definition of it as "treating what is vague as if it were precise and trying to fit it into an exact logical category" (X 343).

This, he now claims, characterized "Moore's method according to which you could hope to make essentially vague notions clear by using precise language about them and asking exact questions" (X 440). Rejecting "direct unanalysable intuition" (which he describes as a method in which "victory was [unreasonably] with those who could speak with the greatest appearance of clear, undoubting conviction and could best use the accents of infallibility" (X: 438)), he implicitly substitutes for it "actual experience" as follows: "I see no reason to shift from the fundamental intuitions of *Principia Ethica*, though they are much too few and too narrow to fit actual experience which provides a richer and more various content" (X: 444).

This, however, is not "actual experience" as atomic sense data, the *Treatise on Probability* view (VIII 12) he now rejects as "dogmatic." This view was also scholastic in Ramsey's sense; it excluded that part of actual experience that was "essentially vague."

In his biographical essay on Edgeworth, in the context of criticizing Edgeworth's use of mathematics in *Mathematical Psychics*, Keynes explicitly reports his abandonment of the atomic hypothesis in favour of the hypothesis of organic unity as the realistic idea of relations in psychics, *i.e.* of the relations of the individual consciousness.

> Mathematical Psychics has not, as a science or study, fulfilled its early promise. In the 'seventies and 'eighties of the last century it was reasonable, I think, to suppose that it held great prospects. When the young Edgeworth chose it, he may have looked to find secrets as wonderful as those which the physicists have found since those days. But, as I remarked in writing about Alfred Marshall's gradual change of attitude towards mathematico-economics (pp. 186–7 above), this has not happened, but quite the opposite. The atomic hypothesis which has worked so splendidly in physics breaks down in psychics. We are faced at every turn with the problems of organic unity, of discreteness, of discontinuity—the whole is not equal to the sum of the parts, comparisons of quantity fail us, small changes produce large effects, the assumptions of a uniform and homogeneous continuum are not satisfied.
>
> (X 262)

It is this organic unity understanding of interdependence that underpins Keynes's criticism of attempts to understand and represent it in systems of "variables": in his discussion of "Tinbergen's method" (XIV 285–320); in his treatment of interdependence on pp. 245–7 of *The General Theory*; in his explicit criticism there of mathematical economics on pp. 297–8; *etc*. All are underpinned by the assumption that the interdependence involved in "psychics" is the "essential interdependence" involved in organic unity as "internal relations."

Keynes on "rationality" and "irrationality"

The "real thing" at the basis of social, including economic, phenomena, according to Keynes, is the "individual consciousness." He elaborates a "rational" form of this consciousness that will become dominant in "the ideal social republic of the future." It is the consciousness of what, in "My Early Beliefs," he describes as, reliable, rational, decent people influenced by truth and objective standards who can be safely released from the outward restraints of convention and traditional standards and inflexible rules of conduct, and left, from now onwards, to their own sensible devices, pure motives and reliable intuitions of the good.

(X 447)

His own idea of this "good" is delineated in the first part of the memoir as a critical appropriation of the idea set out in G.E. Moore's *Principia Ethica* as non-economic aesthetic, intellectual and ethical "goods."

In "Economic Possibilities for Our Grandchildren" its actualization is represented as what the solution to the "economic problem" will make economically practicable. We will then, he claims, be free

> to return to some of the most sure and certain principles of religion and traditional virtue—that avarice is a vice, that the exaction of usury is a misdemeanour, and the love of money is detestable, that those walk most truly in the paths of virtue and sane wisdom who take least thought for the morrow. We shall once more value ends above means and prefer the good to the useful. We shall honour those who can teach us how to pluck the hour and day virtuously and well, the delightful people who are capable to taking direct enjoyment in things, the lilies of the field who toil not, neither do they spin.
>
> (IX 330–1)

This idea of rationality incorporates an idea of "rational choice," but, as these short summaries of its foundation in "reliable intuitions of the good" demonstrate, it is an idea very different from the idea taken as the starting point in contemporary economics. In "My Early Beliefs," Keynes says the following about the "Benthamite tradition" from which the currently dominant idea derives:

> It can be no part of this memoir for me to try to explain why it was such a big advantage for us to have escaped from the Benthamite tradition. But I do now regard that as the worm which has been gnawing at the insides of modern civilisation and is responsible for its present moral decay. We used to regard the Christians as the enemy, because they appeared as the representatives of tradition, convention and hocus-pocus. In truth it was the Benthamite calculus, based on an over-valuation of the economic criterion, which was destroying the quality of the popular Ideal.
>
> (X 445–6)

The second main focus of "My Early Beliefs" is what Keynes describes as a "disastrously mistaken" early belief about "reliable, rational, decent people." This belief was that "the human race already consists of" such people.

This ignored, he now claims, the fact of there being "insane and irrational springs of wickedness in most men." In believing it, he and his friends

> repudiated all versions of the doctrine of original sin, of there being insane and irrational springs of wickedness in most men. We were not aware that civilisation was a thin and precarious crust erected by the personality and the will of a very few, and only maintained by rules and conventions skilfully put cross and guilefully preserved.
>
> (X 447)

The claim that his early beliefs ignored the fact of irrationality and its implication that "civilisation" was "a thin and precarious crust" in need of defending by the rational few creating and then maintaining "rules and conventions" is inconsistent with the very similar beliefs recorded in his 1904 essay on Burke.

Keynes there accepts Burke's defense of "customary morals, conventions and conventional wisdom" on the basis that "the part that reason plays in motive is slight." He stresses Burke's "disbelief in men's acting rightly, except on the rarest occasions, because they have judged that it is right so to act." It is "just prejudices" rather than reason that must be the guide of life. Moreover, given the role such prejudices play in defending civilization from forms of irrationality that threaten it, they themselves have to be defended from critical attack (*i.e.* in 1904 he sets out "a *dictum* in which," according to "My Early Beliefs," "we should have been unable to discover any point or significance whatever" (X 448)).

Keynes attributes to Burke the view that, since reason plays such a small role in motivation,

> those who would govern men must consequently, rely upon other aids; they must foster and preserve just prejudices; they must discountenance the exposure even of those prejudices which are based upon misapprehension but are beneficial in their immediate results.
>
> (Keynes 1904: 82)

His disagreement with Burke concerned the stability of the "just prejudices," the "rules and conventions," required to protect civilization from what in *The General Theory* he calls "dangerous human proclivities" (VII 374). He argued that the nature of the danger involved changed through time so the protections had to be subject to revision to maintain their effectiveness in the face of such changes. Political reforms with this in mind are a frequent subsequent concern[7] as in the following passage from his 1927 review of H.G. Wells's *The World of William Clissold*.

> The extreme danger of the world is, in Clissold's words, lest, "before the creative Brahma can get to work, Siva, in other words the passionate destructiveness of labour awakening to its now needless limitations and privations, may make Brahma's task impossible". We all feel this, I think.
>
> (IX 319)

A common misinterpretation of *A Treatise on Probability* is that Keynes intended it as a general theory of human belief and action. Apart from what ought to be the obvious inconsistency of this interpretation with his claims in this 1904 essay on Burke and his *Two Memoirs*, he explicitly denies this in the *Treatise* itself.

> The theory of probability is logical, therefore, because it is concerned with the degree of belief which it is rational to entertain in given conditions, and not merely with the actual beliefs of particular individuals, which may or may not be rational.
>
> (VIII 4)

Keynes claimed the implication of the fact of irrationality for rational "discussion of practical affairs" was that such discussion had to take account of the essential and very significant role it played in them (X 449). The first memoir, "Dr Melchior: A Defeated Enemy" (originally a presentation to the Memoir Club on February 2, 1921), illustrates this, as had *The Economic Consequences of the Peace* itself, by examining the essential role it played in the negotiations ending in the Treaty of Versailles. Consistent with these ideas, Keynes's economics gives an essential and significant role to irrationality.

The General Theory as a general theory of capitalism

The General Theory takes as its starting point an idea of the "individual consciousness" it treats as dominating capitalist economic motivation. Keynes claims "the essential characteristic of capitalism" is "the dependence upon an intense appeal to the money-making and money-loving instincts of individuals as the main motive force of the economic machine" (IX 293).

In "Economic Possibilities for Our Grandchildren," he elaborates these "instincts" as the irrational "love of money as a possession" and irrational "purposiveness." The former, he claims, is "one of those semi-criminal, semi-pathological propensities which one hands over with a shudder to the specialists in mental disease" (IX 329). The latter,

> means that we are more concerned with the remote future results of our actions than with their own quality or their immediate effects on our own environment. The "purposive" man is always trying to secure a spurious and delusive immortality for his acts by pushing his interest in them forward into time.
>
> (IX 329–30)

Keynes says of the irrational "love of money as a possession" that,

> When the accumulation of wealth is no longer of high social importance, there will be great changes in the code of morals. We shall be able to rid

ourselves of many of the pseudo-moral principles which have hag-ridden us for two hundred years, by which we have exalted some of the most distasteful of human qualities into the position of the highest virtues. We shall be able to afford to dare to assess the money motive at its true value.

(IX 329)

Similarly, he says of the treatment of irrational "purposiveness" when that future arrives:

Of course there will still be many people with intense, unsatisfied purposiveness who will blindly pursue wealth—unless they can find some plausible substitute. But the rest of us will no longer be under any obligation to applaud and encourage them. For we shall inquire more curiously than is safe today into the true character of this "purposiveness" with which in varying degrees Nature has endowed almost all of us.

(IX 329)

However,

The time for all this is not yet. For at least another hundred years we must pretend to ourselves and to everyone that fair is foul and foul is fair; for foul is useful and fair is not. Avarice and usury and precaution must be our gods for a little longer still. For only they can lead us out of the tunnel of economic necessity into daylight.

(IX 331)

In the final chapter of *The General Theory*, he ties the idea of the irrational motivation he identifies with capitalism to the "insane and irrational springs of wickedness in most men." They appear in the passage as the source of "dangerous human proclivities."

For my own part, I believe that there is social and psychological justification for significant inequalities of incomes and wealth, but not for such large disparities as exist to-day. There are valuable human activities which require the motive of money-making and the environment of private wealth-ownership for their full fruition. Moreover, dangerous human proclivities can be canalised into comparatively harmless channels by the existence of opportunities for money-making and private wealth, which, if they cannot be satisfied in this way, may find their outlet in cruelty, the reckless pursuit of personal power and authority, and other forms of self-aggrandisement. ... The task of transmuting human nature must not be confused with the task of managing it. Though in the ideal commonwealth men may have been taught or inspired or bred to take no interest in the stakes, it may still be wise and prudent statesmanship to allow the game to be played, subject to rules and limitations, so long as the average man, or even a significant section of the community, is in fact strongly addicted to the money-making passion.

(VII 374)

The General Theory resolves this general idea of capitalism's "essential characteristic" into its "three fundamental psychological factors, namely, the psychological propensity to consume, the psychological attitude to liquidity and the psychological expectation of future yield from capital-assets" (VII 246–7). The specific forms taken by them vary historically and culturally so "models" based on them must also vary, as is claimed in the material dealing with "Professor Tinbergen's Method," his elaboration of Marshall's method, *etc.*

Thus, the much lower nineteenth century "psychological propensity to consume" is tied by Keynes to saving having become the focus of "all those instincts of puritanism which in other ages has withdrawn itself from the world and has neglected the arts of production as well as those of enjoyment" (II 11). In *The General Theory*, he claims "the history of India at all times has provided an example of a country impoverished by a preference for liquidity amounting to so strong a passion that even an enormous and chronic influx of the precious metals has been insufficient to bring down the rate of interest to a level which was compatible with the growth of real wealth" (VII 337).

Also in *The General Theory*, he says of an earlier form of the role of "the psychological expectation of future yield" that:

> In former times, when enterprises were mainly owned by those who undertook them or by their friends and associates, investment depended on a sufficient supply of individuals of sanguine temperament and constructive impulses who embarked on business as a way of life, not really relying on a precise calculation of prospective profit.
>
> (VII 150)

Even within a specific historical and cultural form of capitalism the psychological factors vary as a feature of the particular forms of individual consciousness involved. They vary in ways that prevent their variation being described with a system of "variables" in Whitehead's sense. An example is the changes in "the psychological expectation of future yield from capital-assets" and "the psychological attitude to liquidity" characteristic of trade cycles as "waves of irrational psychology."

The main concern in "Economic Possibilities for Our Grandchildren" is to examine the future possibilities that will exist when what he calls the "economic problem" has been solved; a time he places at least one hundred years into the future. The problem will be solved by the development of the science and technology that will create the productive forces required to produce the "material abundance" that, properly organized, will "yield up the fruits of a good life" in the sense specified above.

The positive form of capitalist motivation (the form that will undertake the "valuable human activities" that will, without conscious intent, solve this problem by bringing about the development of science and technology it requires) is the "entrepreneurial" form. Keynes explicitly ties this form to the ideas of irrational "purposiveness" and the irrational "love of money as a possession" he elaborates in the same essay.

He characterizes such individuals as "strenuous purposive money-makers" and explicitly contrasts them with the "reliable, rational, decent people" "who will be able to enjoy the abundance when it comes."

> The strenuous purposeful money-makers may carry all of us along with them into the lap of economic abundance. But it will be those peoples, who can keep alive, and cultivate into a fuller perfection, the art of life itself and do not sell themselves for the means of life, who will be able to enjoy the abundance when it comes.
>
> (IX 328)

As "purposeful" the entrepreneur is "trying to secure a spurious and delusive immortality for his acts by pushing his interest in them forward into time." His accumulation of capital is the means of doing this. It is also money-making as an end in itself, *i.e.*, "the love of money as a possession" as opposed to "the love of money as a means to the enjoyments and realities of life" (IX 329). "Enterprise" as "the activity of forecasting the prospective yield of assets over their whole life" (VII 158) is an essential aspect of this activity. It underpins the third of the "three fundamental psychological factors" of *The General Theory*, "the psychological expectation of future yield from capital-assets" (VII 247).

Most clearly and explicitly in the 1937 *Quarterly Journal of Economics* article, "The General Theory of Employment" (XIV 109–23), Keynes claims the future of concern in enterprise is normally "uncertain" in the sense of unknowable (particularly when, as with the "'purposive' man," it is "the accumulation of wealth for an indefinitely postponed future") (XIV 113). There is not sufficient currently available relevant evidence on which to base rational "enterprise." There is, however, sufficient currently available relevant evidence on which to base certain rational belief in one's future death. As conceived by Keynes, the accumulation of capital is a means of denying this certain fact, *i.e.* the certain fact that, "*In the long run* we are all dead" (IV 65).

Associated with this, the uncertainty involved in the accumulation must itself be denied. It arouses "the thought of ultimate loss," *i.e.* in the case of this accumulation, the "ultimate loss" of accumulated money. For the purposive man, putting aside this thought is a means of avoiding fear of death by suppressing the thought of death unconsciously identified with it. In contrast, the "healthy," *i.e.* "the reliable, rational, decent," man, self-consciously puts aside the thought of death itself. He is *not* purposive, *i.e.* "those walk most truly in the paths of virtue and sane wisdom who take least thought for the morrow" (IX 331),[8] and treats money instrumentally as a "means to the enjoyments and realities of life" (IX 329).

Consequently, it is "purposiveness" that explains the role Keynes gives to "animal spirits" in enterprise.

> It is safe to say the enterprise which depends on hopes stretching into the future benefits the community as a whole. But individual initiative will only be adequate when reasonable calculation is supplemented and supported by animal spirits, so that the thought of ultimate loss which often overtakes pioneers, as experience undoubtedly tells us and them, is put aside as a healthy man puts aside the expectation of death.
>
> (VII 162)

It is not accurate to describe "animal spirits" as a "supplement" to rational calculation given that Keynes explicitly assumes such calculation is not possible in this context.

The denial of uncertainty takes the form of the forecasting "conventions" (XIV 114). Their psychological function, like the purposive activity itself, is avoidance of fear of death, of the "disquietude" (XIV 116) the thought of inevitable future death provokes (a method different from, but serving the same function as, "pyramids" and "masses for the dead" (VII 131)). These connect entrepreneurship to "knowledge"; they are a "substitute for the knowledge that is unattainable."

The irrational nature of "the psychological attitude to liquidity" is made clear in the account of the role it plays when these "more precarious conventions have weakened."

> Partly on reasonable and partly on instinctive grounds, our desire to hold money as a store of wealth is a barometer of the degree of our distrust of our own calculations and conventions concerning the future. Even though this feeling about money is itself conventional or instinctive, it operates, so to speak, at a deeper level of our motivation. It takes charge at the moments when the higher, more precarious conventions have weakened. The possession of actual money lulls our disquietude; and the premium which we require to make us part with money is the measure of the degree of our disquietude.
>
> (IV 116)

The "reasonable" grounds are associated with "calculations" where the "degree of distrust" is measured by the rational concept of "weight," a concept that continues to be relevant in Whitehead's version of a frequency theory of probability. In that theory successive occasions of actual experience in which the frequency remains stable enable relevant evidence ("weight") to increase. In contrast, a significant change in the frequency makes this accumulated evidence irrelevant, significantly reducing weight. The movement into money is rational in the latter context because of the irrational liquidity preferences of others. These make money a relatively safe place in which to temporarily store investible funds while accumulating relevant evidence about the new frequency.

The calculations in question cannot be calculations of "the prospective yield of capital assets over their whole life" because this is "uncertain" in the sense of not rationally calculable. In fact, they concern the rational calculations possible in rational speculation in financial markets where by "speculation" is meant "the activity of forecasting the psychology of the market" (VII 158).

For the same reason, the "conventions" cannot be reasonable "calculations" of this prospective yield, though they are means of forecasting it. As described, they are a more rational, but still irrational, way of dealing with instinctively anchored fear of death. It is in this sense that they operate at a "higher, more precarious" "level of our motivation."

The link between the two psychological factors elaborated here involves a change in the "feeling about money" to one that "operates, so to speak, at a deeper level of our motivation." This changed feeling serves, as did "the higher, more precarious [forecasting] conventions" before they "weakened," to enable the possession of money to "lull" "disquietude," the "degree" of which is measured by the increase in interest rates caused by the sudden sharp increase in the irrational "propensity to hoard." This is a change in the identity of the individual consciousness involved; it cannot be accurately represented by a system of "variables."

This link between "the psychological expectation of future yield of capital-assets" and "the psychological attitude to liquidity" is accompanied by a psychologically linked change in the "psychological propensity to consume." Taken together, these links constitute trade cycles as "waves of irrational psychology" with their accompanying waves of output and employment.

These waves have their counterpart in the individual consciousness Keynes treats as characteristic of participants in financial markets. This involves a significantly greater degree of irrationality than that characteristic of entrepreneurs. Keynes claims of such participants that:

> The vast majority of those who are concerned with the buying and selling of securities know almost nothing whatever about what they are doing. They do not possess even the rudiments of what is required for a valid judgment, and are the prey of hopes and fears easily aroused by transient events and as easily dispelled. This is one of the odd characteristics of the capitalist system under which we live, which, when we are dealing with the real world, is not to be overlooked.
>
> (VI 323)

This has the result that, as he puts it in *The General Theory*, "conventional valuation" in these markets is the outcome of "the mass psychology of a large number of ignorant individuals" (VII 154). This provides a basis for rational "speculation" meaning by speculation "the activity of forecasting the psychology of the market." The "calculations" involved will be rational inductive and probability judgments. His own judgments are underpinned by the ideas of them derived from the organic unity idea of interdependence in "psychics."

In *A Treatise on Money*, Keynes claims this irrational "mass psychology" is understandable and predictable by the "wisest" market participants, *i.e.* by those not themselves subject to it. Given the influence of mass psychology on conventional valuations, it pays these "wisest" participants "to anticipate mob psychology rather than the real trend of events, and to ape unreason proleptically" (VI 323).

> So long as the crowd can be relied on to act in a certain way, even if it is misguided, it will be to the advantage of the better-informed professional to act in the same way—a short period ahead.
>
> (VI 324)

In both the *Treatise* and *The General Theory*, he claims this forecasting can be rationally grounded in experience. In the *Treatise* he says the "wisest" are able to make forecasts "on the basis of past experience of the trend of mob psychology" (VI 323). This is repeated in *The General Theory*.

> The professional investor is forced to concern himself with the anticipation of impending changes, in the news or in the atmosphere, of the kind by which experience shows that the mass psychology of the market is most influenced.
>
> (VII 155)

Keynes's own approach to investment in these markets was rational speculation in this sense. In his case he was applying ideas of rational inductive and probability judgments based on an organic unity idea of interdependence in "psychics." As pointed out above, the probabilities remain probabilities of propositions. They continue to change with changes in circumstances, they can be based on more or less weight, and it may not be possible to form numerically precise judgments, but the probabilities themselves are numerical "truth frequencies."

In the following April 10, 1940 letter (XII 76–8) to F.C. Scott explaining a particular investment in the American stock market, he sets out a uniform feature of the irrational psychology present in that market as the basis of rational speculation.

> My latest information is that this rise [in the price of United Gas First Preferred] is probably due to a change for the better in the prospects of the funding scheme for the arrears of United Gas First Preferred. There is now said to be a much better chance of this. But I am not backing this in the very near future. I am only saying that it is bound to happen sooner or later. Very few American investors buy any stock for the sake of something which is going to happen more than six months hence, even though its probability is exceedingly high; and it is out of taking advantage of this psychological peculiarity of theirs that most money is made.
>
> (XII 78)

Similar claims are made about opportunities for rational speculation in the bond market created by the sudden sharp anxiety-provoked increase in irrational liquidity preference characteristic of financial crises. Keynes claimed (VII 207–8) "a financial crisis or crisis of liquidation" of this kind occurred in the U. S. in 1932. This had created a psychological atmosphere in which "scarcely anyone could be induced to part with holdings of money on any reasonable terms." Letters he wrote at the time indicate he believed this had created a practically certain opportunity for rational speculative profit, a judgment backed by great evidential "weight." The rational inductive judgment involved was that the anxiety would dissipate significantly in the rationally predictable future with a consequent very substantial increase in bond prices.

For example, in a July 7, 1932 letter to C.L. Baillieu he claimed that

> the most striking feature of the immediate situation is the extraordinary disparity between yields in London and yields in New York of comparable securities. It seems to me quite impossible that the present situation can long persist. And I should have supposed it to be probable that the readjustment would be brought about by a substantial rise in the prices of prime fixed-interest securities in New York. The present may be the chance of a lifetime for the purchase of the latter. Obviously everyone in New York is scared so stiff as to be unable to move. But that may be the opportunity of others away from any unsettling influence of the local atmosphere. No serious risk can arise unless the existing financial system in America is going to peg out altogether. I suppose that that is just possible, but I cannot believe that it is probable.
>
> (XXI 113)

He provides a detailed examination of the price differences between London and New York and of the psychological factors underpinning them (XXI 117–18).

By August 19 there had, according to Keynes, been signs of this predicted turnaround in bond prices. In another letter to Baillieu, he writes:

> Since the above was written [letter of July 20], there are abundant indications that the change in the United States has actually commenced. I do not so much refer to the fact, though it is truly remarkable, that the paper value of all the railways and public utilities, after having fallen to one tenth of what it had been two years previously, has then proceeded to double itself within five weeks. For this is no more than a vivid illustration of the disadvantages of running a country's development and enterprise as a by-product of a casino. I refer, rather, to the indications of a reversal of the upward trend of the long-term rate of interest as shown by a rise of 16 per cent in the index number of bonds between July 8 and August 19, 1932.
>
> (XXI 121)

In a March 1934 letter to Walter Case, Keynes repeats this analysis of the American bond market.

> Unless the recovery plans break down completely and end in universal disorder and discredit and fear, interest rates in America are almost certain, sooner or later, to take the same course they [that] they have over here. It seems to me that it must be right to back this opinion, since, if this is wrong, all other forms of investment in America, except possibly the flight of capital from the country, are certain to turn out disastrously. It seems to me almost absurd to suppose that an investment either in common stocks or in actual cash can turn out well and that an investment in fixed-interest securities of the second class can turn out badly. There are innumerable instances of profits on that scale in this country during the last two years on the most steady going securities. It is obvious, looking back, that opportunities which offered profit out of all proportion to possible loss were missed. My feeling is that this is now the position in the United States. If you have any belief in your own prospects at all, this strikes me as the outstanding certainty.
>
> (XXI 319)

Here he stresses the role of mistaken and irrational beliefs about the determination of interest rates.

> The whole subject has, of course, many more ramifications than can be discussed in a letter, but almost everyone who has any pretensions to being a sound or orthodox thinker on financial problems in New York probably has his brain stuffed with fallacies on this particular matter. So there is an opportunity for anyone, if there is anyone, who can think (or so it seems to me) scientifically straight on this issue.
>
> (XXI 320)

Conclusion

Keynes's economics is based on ideas radically different from those now dominant. It treats economics as part of "psychics" for which the foundational unit is the "individual consciousness."

The character of this unit is the outcome of its relations as "internal relations." The structure of these provides a foundation for the limited stability of this character. This in turn allows for limited forms of "general theory," namely, forms tied to the limited stability of forms of character. These features of the relations are consistent with a rational basis for inductive and probability judgments.

The method that provides a rational grounding for these claims, also grounds an idea of an objective and knowable "good." Keynes identifies "rationality" with a rational self-consciousness able to know this good and actualize it in activity. Such an individual consciousness can be "immoralist" (X 446–7) in the sense of "safely released from the outward restraints of convention and traditional standards and inflexible rules of conduct, and left, from now onwards, to their own sensible devices, pure motives and reliable intuitions of the good." This idea of "reliable, rational, decent people" is the basis of his idea of "an ideal social republic of the future" where it will have become the dominant form of individual consciousness. He also, however, places the time when this might, if at all, be an actually possible society very far into the future.

There were two main obstacles to this practicability. The first was what Keynes called the "economic problem." This was the need for a capacity to produce the "material abundance" required to meet the instrumental "material" needs of such individuals, the meeting of these being instrumental to "good lives" actualizing non-capitalist, non-economic, aesthetic, intellectual and ethical ultimate "goods." He places a solution to this problem, a solution he assumes will be provided by capitalism, more than one hundred years into the future (*i.e.* on or after 2030 given the date of publication of "Economic Possibilities for Our Grandchildren").

The main problem however, and the one most difficult to solve, was "spiritual."

> There is no reason, therefore, why the inhabitants of Europe, if they have wisdom, need fear their material surroundings. They can still see a Golden Age in front of them and travel towards it. If Europe is to suffer a decline, it will be due, not to material, but to spiritual causes.
>
> (XVII 449)

This was the problem of developing the "reliable, rational, decent people" who would create and live in this "ideal commonwealth."

This was the source of "the profound moral and social problems of how to organise material abundance to yield up the fruits of a good life" (XXVI 260). The main obstacle in the way was "the insane and irrational springs off wickedness in most men." These were not only obstacles in the way of developing the rational self-consciousness the future ideal society required; they were also a constant threat to the "civilisation" already existing. The danger posed by these "springs" made it a "thin and precarious crust" requiring for its protection "rules and conventions wisely put across and guilefully preserved."

The General Theory is a general theory of capitalism understood in terms of these ideas. It is an historically and culturally specific form of organic unity whose "essential characteristic" is the domination of economic motivation by a specific form of *irrational* individual consciousness, one itself dominated by the "money-making and money-loving instincts." Keynes claimed capitalism, by providing "opportunities for money-making and private wealth," served to "canalise" the "dangerous human proclivities" originating from "the insane and irrational springs" into the "relatively harmless" "money-making and money-making instincts" and, in this way, protect the "thin and precarious" crust. He also claimed, however that, in their most positive form, they motivated "valuable human activities." These were the activities of "entrepreneurs" as "strenuous purposive money-makers."

This idea of capitalist irrationality provides the psychological foundation of *The General Theory*. There, it is resolved into the theory's "three fundamental psychological factors." Their role in the theory is illustrated by, on the one hand, the relation between "the psychological attitude to liquidity" and "the psychological expectation of future yield from capital-assets" in the "waves of irrational psychology" with which Keynes identified trade cycles, and, on the other, by the opportunities the less canalized form of irrationality dominant in financial markets created for rational "speculation."

In the first case, Keynes describes the "conventional" basis of the "psychological expectation of future yield" as operating at a "higher" and, hence, "more precarious" "level of motivation" than the "conventional or instinctive" "feeling about money, which operates at a "deeper level" and "takes charge" when the "higher, more precarious" forecasting conventions "weaken." Both are irrational means of avoiding "disquietude." They reinforce each other in bringing about the falling off of investment in new physical productive forces and of expenditure on research and development aimed at improving them. This falling off is amplified somewhat by the "multiplier" linked to the more stable, but still varying in a way that reinforces the variation in the other two psychological factors, "psychological propensity to consume." Taken together, this linked behaviour of the irrational psychological factors causes a falling off in output and employment.

The second illustration concerns two features of financial markets.

The first is the irrational form taken by the expectations that determine prices in the American stock market. These are irrationally focused on the current yield. They also ignore, however, predictable events more than six months into the future that will significantly influence this yield. The opportunity for rational speculative profits arises from knowing about this "psychological peculiarity" and its degree of stability and, on this basis, making stock market investments based on rational inductive and probability judgments.

The second is the linked form of irrationality characteristic of bond markets. Keynes claimed that this explained the movement of bond prices during and following a financial crisis. Initially this took the form, similar to what occurs with the weakening of the conventional basis of expectations of "future yield of capital assets," of a sudden increase in the "degree of disquietude" in the market, met, as an irrational means of dealing with this, with an equally sudden change in the "psychological attitude to liquidity." This motivated a sudden sharp increase in the "propensity to hoard" and a precipitous drop in bond prices, the extent of the latter depending on the degree of disquietude involved. The opportunity for rational speculative profit arises from knowledge, grounded in actual experience, of this irrationality that the disquietude will dissipate significantly in the rationally forecastable future with a resulting significant increase in bond prices. In this case as well, the idea of rational "speculation" at work is Keynes's general idea of the nature of rational belief.

In "My Early Beliefs," Keynes implicitly acknowledged having failed to take adequate account of the degree to which irrationality anchored in "the insane and irrational springs of wickedness" opposed the understanding, let alone the persuasiveness, of the actual ideas on which *The General Theory* had been based. He wrote:

> I still suffer incurably from attributing an unreal rationality to other people's feelings and behaviour (and doubtless to my own, too). There is one small but extraordinarily silly manifestation of this absurd idea of what is "normal", namely the impulse to protest—to write a letter to The Times, call a meeting in the Guildhall, subscribe to some fund when my pre-suppositions as to what is "normal" are not fulfilled. I behave as if there really existed some authority or standard to which I can successfully appeal if I shout loud enough—perhaps it is some hereditary vestige of a belief in the efficacy of prayer.
>
> (X 448)

Notes

1 For earlier interpretive treatments by the author of the ideas of Keynes examined in this chapter, see (Winslow 1986, 1989, 1993a, 1993b and 2003).
2 References to Keynes's *Collected Writings* take the form of the volume number followed by the page number[s].
3 "In what follows I am much indebted for some suggestions in favour of the frequency theory communicated to me by Dr Whitehead; but it is not to be supposed that the exposition which follows represents his own opinion" (VIII 110 note 1).
4 For an explanation of Whitehead's idea of "speculative metaphysics" see (Gare 1999).
5 For an explanation of Whitehead's idea of "intuition," see Johnson 1947.
6 X 186, see also the critique, implicitly based on an organic unity view of interdependence, of mathematical economics in *The General Theory* (VII 297–8).
7 For an account of this concern, its basis and the advocacy of political reforms reflecting it, see Winslow 1990.
8 This does not mean they take *no* "thought for the morrow." They take the amount of thought that is reasonable. This is the "least" amount because it is instrumental to the end in itself activity that defines the "good life."

References

Gare, Arran. 1999. "Speculative Metaphysics and the Future of Philosophy: The Contemporary Relevance of Whitehead's Defence of Speculative Metaphysics." *Australasian Journal of Philosophy*, 77, 2, 127–145. doi:10.1080/00048409912348891.

Johnson, A.H. 1947. "A.N. Whitehead's Theory of Intuition." *The Journal of General Psychology*, 37, 61–66.

Keynes, John Maynard. 1904. "Essay on Edmund Burke" on deposit in The Papers of John Maynard Keynes: JMK/UA/20, The Archive Centre, King's College, Cambridge.

Keynes, John Maynard. 1921. *A Treatise on Probability*. London: Macmillan and Co. Archives of the Johns Hopkins Libraries. Container: 6 [aspace.31043.box.6] (Mixed

Materials). Alfred North Whitehead collection, MS-0282. Special Collections. https://a space.library.jhu.edu/repositories/3/archival_objects/31205. Accessed August 5, 2021.

Keynes, John Maynard, Moggridge, D.E., Johnson, Elizabeth S., and Royal Economic Society (Great Britain). 1971. *The Collected Writings of John Maynard Keynes*. London; New York: Macmillan; St. Martin's Press for the Royal Economic Society.

Marshall, Alfred. 1961. *Principles of Economics*, 2 vols. Ninth (Variorum) Edition. Edited and annotated by C.W. Guillebaud. London: Macmillan and Co.

Ramsey, Frank Plumpton. 1931. *The Foundations of Mathematics and other Logical Essays*. Edited by R.B. Braithwaite. London: Routledge.

Russell, Bertrand. 1922. "Review of *A Treatise on Probability*," *The Mathematical Gazette*, 11, 159, 119–125.

Russell, Bertrand. 1956. "Beliefs: Discarded and Retained." In *Portraits from Memory, and Other Essays*. London: G. Allen and Unwin.

Whitehead, Alfred North. 1923. "Uniformity and Contingency: The Presidential Address." *Proceedings of the Aristotelian Society*, 23, new series, 1–18.

Whitehead, Alfred North. 1927. *Symbolism: Its Meaning and Effect*. Cambridge: Cambridge University Press.

Whitehead, Alfred North. 1929. *The Function of Reason*. Princeton: Princeton University Press.

Whitehead, Alfred North. 1933. *Adventures of Ideas*. Cambridge: Cambridge University Press.

Whitehead, Alfred North. 1938. *Modes of Thought: Six Lectures*. Cambridge: Cambridge University Press.

Whitehead, Alfred North. 1985. *Process and Reality: An Essay in Cosmology: Gifford Lectures Delivered in the University of Edinburgh during the Session 1927–28*. New York: The Free Press.

Winslow, E.G. 1986. "'Human Logic' and Keynes's Economics." *Eastern Economic Journal*, 12, 413–430.

Winslow, E.G. 1989. "Organic Interdependence, Uncertainty and Economic Analysis." *The Economic Journal*, 99, 1173–1182.

Winslow, E.G. 1990. "Bloomsbury, Freud, and the Vulgar Passions." *Social Research*, 57, 785–819.

Winslow, E.G. 1993a. "Keynes on Rationality." In W.J. Gerrard (ed.) *The Economics of Rationality*. London: Routledge.

Winslow, E.G. 1993b. "Atomism and Organicism." In Geoff Hodgson, Warren Samuels and Marc Tool (eds.) *Handbook of Institutional and Evolutionary Economics*. Cheltenham: Edward Elgar.

Winslow, E.G. 2003. "Foundations of Keynes's Economics." In Jochen Runde and Mizuhara Sohei [eds.] *Perspectives on the Philosophy of Keynes's Economics: Probability, Uncertainty and Convention*. London: Routledge.

8 Unintended order and self-organization in the evolutionary social theory of Friedrich Hayek

Hilton L. Root

Introduction

Friedrich Hayek viewed the economic system as a "living" system of interacting parts, whose principles of global order he spent a lifetime attempting to grasp. Human social orders, even when they conform to a definite pattern, he insists are not consciously designed by anyone: much of the order we observe results from the unintended consequences of human action. Most popular interpretations of Hayek relate the concept of "spontaneous order," and his belief that the economy is best left to its own self-organizing dynamics, with the classical liberal idea of the free market and the invisible hand. Although he never systematically addressed the properties the economy shared with other natural systems, his thinking penetrates beyond the visible evidence of spontaneous order into questions about the source of order itself. The interaction of human volition and intentionality with self-organization is among the most provocative themes in Hayek's reasoning and we will attempt to link his notion that the economy self-organizes according to its own rules of complexity with the methodological concerns of contemporary scholarship on complex systems. We will explore how Hayek developed an endogenous, evolutionary and organic account of moral change that is conceptually akin to the complex adaptive systems thinking that has revolutionized our understanding of the origins of order in the natural world.

The origin of the economy's structure is what Hayek considered to be the biggest unanswered question facing economics and social science more generally. In *The Counter-Revolution of Science*, a collection of essays published in 1952 he discusses the urgency for the social sciences to become better at understanding the origins and functioning of compositive wholes, and to single out from the totality of observed phenomena the groups of elements which are structurally connected. This structure cannot be investigated "mechanically" as if it was caused by objectively observable external events. Nor can the conditions under which they emerged be attributed to the knowledge or consent of individual actors. He questioned the efficacy of seeking explanations for the ordering of human society by analogy with the working of the human mind or probing its psychology. The search for a purposeful design or for proof of a

DOI: 10.4324/9781003138655-8

designing mind would only lead people to interpret the events in the external world after their own image. The orderly structures of human society are the product of the actions of the many, and are not the result of coordinated human design or action by any one group or authority. Human intention and volition are not sufficient to explain the construction of systems that have enabled human beings to adapt successfully to changes in their environment.

The endogenous nature of moral change

Hayek understood that human communities perceive the world and each other through concepts or mental constructs that are common to the group they belong to. Thus, he probes: "What can we say about the whole network of activities in which men are guided by the kind of knowledge they have and a great part of which at any time is common to most of them?" (1952: 23). Human cognition is limited because "everything which determines their actions, including science itself" is determined by "the views and concepts people hold as part of what they know and believe about themselves" (ibid: 24). This in turn limits the potential of humans to fully grasp and shape their environment. To grasp the formation of long-lived structures of historical regimes we must go beyond what actors know or believe can motivate conscious action.

> If social phenomena showed no order except in so far as they were consciously designed, there would indeed be no room for theoretical sciences of society and there would be, as is often argued, only problems of psychology. It is only in so far as some sort of order arises as a result of individual action but without being designed by any individual that a problem is raised which demands a theoretical explanation.
>
> (ibid: 39)

To understand where the structure of the economy comes from, we must be able to explain the unintended or undesigned results of the actions of many individuals and how they are related to one another.

> If the social structure can remain the same although different individuals succeed each other at particular points, this is not because the individuals which succeed each other are completely identical, but because they succeed each other in particular relations, in particular attitudes they take towards other people and as the objects of particular views held by other people about them.
>
> (1952: 34)

It is the "network of relationships" of which individuals are a part "which form the recurrent, recognizable and familiar elements of the structure" that we must seek to understand. Thus:

if one policeman succeeds another at a particular post, this does not mean that the new man will in all respects be identical with his predecessor, but merely that he succeeds him in certain attitudes towards his fellow man and as the object of certain attitudes of his fellow men which are relevant to his function as policeman. But this is sufficient to preserve a constant structural element which can be separated and studied in isolation.

(ibid)

Hayek did not possess a methodology to *discover* "principles of structural coherence of the complex phenomena which had not (and perhaps could not) be established by direct observation" (ibid: 38). Network science, in its early stages of development when Hayek was writing, is perhaps a way that contemporary social scientists will be able to detect the "unintended and often uncomprehended results of the separate and yet interrelated actions of men in society" (ibid: 34) that Hayek was seeking. When better understood, network structure can perhaps reveal the essential determinants of long-term historical change and confirm what Hayek describes as the mystery of the economy's organized complexity, and how it is embedded in society.

Economic outcomes are the result of many people holding certain views and acting according to those beliefs. Hayek contrasts ideas that drive action, and the ideas which people form about that phenomenon, and criticized his contemporary social scientists for constantly failing to keep these two classes of ideas distinct. He warned that if we do not distinguish between conscious action and the structures it produces, we will not fully grasp the role of the individual in society. The attitudes and actions of individuals are the familiar elements in the historical record, but how they combine to produce the complex phenomena is much less well understood. Should we begin by studying the complex phenomena of nature and work backwards to infer the elements from which they are composed? Hayek cautions against this approach if we want to understand the place where the individual stands in the order of things. So much of the world we inhabit is order for free rather than the result of conscious action.

Hayek's organic theory of morality

Hayek's ideas about the formation of structure in human society are fundamentally organic in that he posits *a definite order that is not the result of any conscious design*. Being unable to control what produced that order or predict its precise course or result, leaves us with an ethical challenge. If the independent actions of individuals will produce an order which is not part of their intentions, then what should be our moral priority? Hayek's response is that liberty and freedom must take priority over comfort, for its pursuit will instill a willingness to bear risks. There is no reason to believe that economic insecurity will ever be eliminated or solved, Hayek reasons, and even in aspiring to solve it, we put our larger human values of independence and self-reliance at risk. He invites us to put our most human values first and to fulfill our individual potential for liberty and freedom even before, and regardless of, the economic costs. Human virtues don't derive from solving the problem of economic scarcity; freedom for the individual should guide public policy and be the basis of public ethics. Waiting for a time when all toil ceases may even blunt our moral senses and produce a society prone to collectivism, obedience and corrupted values, with little taste for individual responsibility and individual social action. "Freedom to order our own conduct in the other sphere where material circumstances force a choice upon us, and responsibility for the arrangement of our own life according to our own conscience," he wrote in *The Road to Serfdom,*

> is the air in which alone moral sense grows and in which moral values are daily recreated in the free decision of the individual. Responsibility, not to a superior, but to one's conscience, the awareness of a duty not exacted by compulsion, the necessity to decide which of the things one values are to be sacrificed to others, and to bear the consequence of one's own decision, are the very essence of any morality which deserves the name.
>
> (1944: 212)

Freedom is the ultimate gift of civilization and its preservation requires independence, self-reliance and local responsibility, regardless of whether the problem of economic scarcity is, or ever will be, solved.

Hayek and the organic roots of complexity economics

The desire to understand the elements from which human beings construct different patterns of social relationship continued to motivate the later Hayek and in this regard his thinking foreshadowed many great innovations in contemporary social science. Whereas professional economists were increasingly drawn to mechanical notions of how the economy derived its order, Hayek's thinking moved increasingly in the direction of organic conceptions of order in which social institutions, such as the state, are not built; they grow. Thus Hayek sought a public policy designed "to cultivate growth by providing the appropriate environment, in the manner in which the gardener does this for his plants" (1989: 7). His later thought (1952, 1967) raised perspectives on knowledge diffusion, emergence, systems theory, cognition, evolution and agent behavior that were rarely discussed among his peers and that place him close to the core concerns of contemporary research in complexity science, which have guided research in foundational science and increasingly in economics since his death (Bienhocker, 2006; Arthur, 2014, 2021; Root, 2020).

(1) Hayek's vision of economic and political liberty was closely connected to his belief that social order emerges through processes of self-organization out of the interactions of dispersed, heterogeneous agents; that "if left free, ... will often achieve more than individual human reason could design or foresee"

(1948: 11). He lamented the inadequacy of conventional methods for addressing problems of economic policy and moral philosophy, based as they were on models of linear change. He emphasized that an economy forms from the interactions and adaptive reactions among agents, in which individuals that populate the system are continually adapting, acquiring new characteristics as they adjust their behaviors to new sets of rules and to the anticipated reactions of nearby agents. In his Nobel acceptance speech (Hayek 1974) he highlights the need to understand the economy as an "organized complexity" whose characteristics depend "not only on the properties of the individual elements of which they are composed, and the relative frequency of which they are composed, and with which they occur, but also on the manner in which the individual elements are connected with each other".

(2) He sketched out an idea, elaborated later by Herbert Simon's "bounded agent rationality." For Simon, the limitation arises in decision making because when making a decision, people don't maximize on only one dimension: They consider outcomes on different dimensions that must be traded against each other (1969: 54). Hayek recognized that knowledge is distributed among interacting agents, but not equally throughout the system. This "bounded" knowledge was a constant in his thinking: human cognition "cannot be guided … by full knowledge and evaluation of all the consequences" (1948: 19). Recent findings in evolutionary social psychology confirm Hayek's belief that local culture, community, acquired beliefs and institutions are the filters through which people frame essential issues. People don't consider all information when making decisions because they search for new information selectively and are vulnerable to biases, dismissing information that contradicts their personal or collective goals.

(3) The later Hayek expressed ideas about cultural evolution that are often misconstrued and criticized, incorrectly, on the grounds that he presumed that evolution through self-organization is a process that produces optimal fitness. In fact, he repeatedly distanced himself from the view that something is efficient because it exists (Whitman, 1998). Like Adam Smith he was aware that individuals continue to act according to habit and custom even after the circumstances from which that habit arose have changed. Cultural evolution in the later Hayek shares with evolutionary biology an understanding that suboptimal or maladapted traits, and the polities or cultures in which they reside, can persist for long periods of time. But he was also aware that micro level changes in behavior accumulate to transform the macro level institutional regime.

(4) In his later years, Hayek went against the grain of the economics profession and its embrace of equilibrium-based methodologies. Instead, he increasingly referred to social agents coevolving and adapting continually in a decentralized space, and with distributed knowledge, producing an economy without equilibrium and comprising many interacting parts that change over time ([1981] 2012: 338–339). Thus he writes:

> It is tempting to describe as an "equilibrium" an ideal state of affairs in which the intentions of all participants precisely match and each will find a

partner willing to enter into the intended transaction. But because for all capitalist production there must exist a considerable interval of time between the beginning of a process and its various later stages, the achievement of an equilibrium is strictly impossible. Indeed, in a literal sense, *a stream can never be in equilibrium*, because it is disequilibrium which keeps it flowing and determining its directions. Even an apparent momentary state of balance in which everybody succeeds in selling or buying what he intended, may be *inherently* unrepeatable, irrespective of any change in the external data, because some of the constituents of the stream will be results of past conditions which have changed long ago.

([1981] 2012, 338–339)

In a similar vein, he frequently criticized mainstream economics for limiting the notion of competition to an equilibrium state of affairs. He doubted the utility of equilibrium on grounds that it excludes change in the structure of production, minimizing both the role of innovation and the importance of incentives for entrepreneurial discovery. In an equilibrium system, there would be no reason for any one agent to act differently from any other. Instead, Hayek insisted that competition was a process that encourages the discovery of new knowledge rather than an outcome.

Hayek's micro level account of how macro level moral beliefs emerge organically from individual moral judgments has much in common with Adam Smith. In both Hayek and Smith moral beliefs evolve in an organic fashion and are embedded within the societies that produce them. These emerge organically from individual moral judgments, often resulting in unintended consequences at the macro level. Over a period of time, as a new standard of behavior is internalized another cycle of change at the macro level initiates. Then practices once universally accepted gradually fall from use, and are considered to be improper and anachronistic. The gradual shift in the conventional behavior within the group propels feedback into the next period of social learning, crystalizing into new macro-level codes of behavior, and a continuous reformulation of beliefs rather than moral equilibrium.

(5) He emphasized that social order emerges without a central "controller" or a global optimum design. The idea that a small number of influential thought and culture leaders can control and direct social process jars with his belief in cognitive fallibility.

(6) When Hayek refers to the "impersonal and anonymous social processes by which individuals help to create things greater than they know," and when he describes outcomes that are not products of individual reason or "consciously designed ... or ... fully intelligible to it" (1948: 8), he is describing what modern evolutionary science calls *emergence*, often resulting in outcomes that lie outside of the range of human intention and beyond the precognition of the agents. Emergence describes the process through which a system acquires new structures and behaviors that its individual components did not possess.

(7) He recognized that early cultural adaptations or mutations can place populations around the world on paths that differ from the prior and unique

circumstances that paved the way for Western development. In any ecology, multiple adaptive peaks are possible. Populations, he suggested, are more likely to attain the highest adaptability along a local trajectory than by switching from one adaptive peak to another (1976: 27).

(8) Indeed, he was skeptical of social engineering, based on his understanding that perception and cognition are bottom-up processes. Hayek postulated that laws belonging to "lower," more fundamental levels of a system cannot be used to reconstruct the universe in which they form only one part and that top-down institutional transplants rarely survive. Yet he also saw a dynamic relationship between top-down and bottom-up *causality*, e.g., in his writing about how the creation of money altered the behavior of agents and organizations (Rosser 2015). The theme of downward causation cannot be disregarded when reflecting that throughout history there are instances when states that win wars are positioned to decide the legitimate order for other states and, in certain rare cases, might change the order or ecology in which those states exist. This occurred via the U.S. occupation of Germany to ensure its democratic orientation after World War II.

(9) He was very aware of what is currently depicted in political economy analysis as path dependence, writing that:

> The way in which footpaths are formed in a wild broken country is such an instance. At first everyone will seek for himself what seems to him the best path. But the fact that such a path has been used once is likely to make it easier to traverse and therefore more likely to be used again; and thus, gradually more and more clearly defined tracks.
>
> (1952: 40)

Bounded rationality, dispersed knowledge, self-organization, cognitive limitations, ecologies with no central controller—these ideas that are central concerns of Hayek are also core premises of complexity approaches in economics. He came to these conceptions from his belief that the market economy is an information-increasing algorithm in which spontaneous order arises from the independent action of market participants, through the coordination made possible by prices. Hayek's foundational contributions to economic reasoning can stand on their own, as distinct from the assumption that is attributed to him, that all forms of governmental activism will inevitably end in a loss of freedom for the individual (Bowles, Kirman and Sethi, 2017).

Conclusion: is the economy mechanistic or organic?

Unlike many of his colleagues that expressed Keynesian optimism that an economy, like a mechanism, could be decoded and reconfigured via wholesale social engineering, Hayek believed in piecemeal, gradual reform and that an economy is organic, but an "organism" that could never be controlled with tools based on rational mechanics, for no matter how sophisticated the tools, they could eventually be exploited, and used for evil. His pessimism also stems from his doubts that humankind would ever possess the mechanisms or knowledge to control the self-organizing cycles of economic growth and decline. An economy could take on a life of its own and thus show organic life, having the global properties of what scientists today call a complex adaptive system.

References

Arthur, Brian. 2014. *Complexity and the Economy*. Oxford: Oxford University Press.
Arthur, Brian. 2021. "Foundations of Complexity Economics." *Nature Reviews Physics* 3, 136–145.
Beinhocker, Eric D. 2006. *Origins of Wealth: Evolution, Complexity, and the Radical Remaking of Economics*. Cambridge, MA: Harvard University Press.
Bowles, Samuel, Alan Kirman and Rajiv Sethi. 2017. "Retrospectives: Friedrich Hayek and the Market Algorithm." *Journal of Economic Perspectives* 31 (3): 215–230. doi:10.1257/jep.31.3.215.
Hayek, Friedrich August. 1994/1944. *The Road to Serfdom: Fiftieth Anniversary Edition*. Chicago: University of Chicago Press.
Hayek, Friedrich August. 1948. *Individualism and Economic Order*. Chicago: University of Chicago Press.
Hayek, Friedrich August. 1952. *The Counter-Revolution of Science: Studies on the Abuse of Reason*. University Park: Liberty Fund.
Hayek, Friedrich August. 1967. "The Theory of Complex Phenomena." In *Studies in Philosophy, Politics, and Economics*, 22–42. Chicago: University of Chicago Press.
Hayek, Friedrich August. 1974. Nobel Prize Lecture. Nobel Prize Outreach AB 2021. https://www.nobelprize.org/prizes/economic-sciences/1974/hayek/lecture/. Accessed August 5, 2021.
Hayek, Friedrich August. 1976. *Law, Legislation and Liberty, Vol. 2: The Mirage of Social Justice*. Chicago: University of Chicago Press.
Hayek, Friedrich August. 1989. "The Pretence of Knowledge." *American Economic Association* 79 (6): 3–7.
Hayek, Friedrich August. 2012. "The Flow of Goods and Services." In *The Collected Works of F. A. Hayek. Volume 8. Business Cycles. Part II*, edited by H. Klausinger, 331–346. Chicago: University of Chicago Press.
Root, Hilton L. 2020, *Network Origins of the Global Economy: East vs. West in a Complex Systems Perspective*. Cambridge: Cambridge University Press. doi:10.1017/9781108773607.
Rosser, Barkley J.Jr. 2015. "Complexity and Austrian Economics." In *The Oxford Handbook of Austrian Economics*. New York: Oxford University Press. doi:10.1093/oxfordhb/9780199811762.013.27.
Simon, Herbert A. 1969. *The Sciences of the Artificial*. Cambridge, MA: MIT Press.
Whitman, Douglas Glen. 1998. "Hayek Contra Pangloss on Evolutionary Systems." *Constitutional Political Economy* 9: 45–66. doi:10.1023/A:1009058615310.

9 The politics of naturalizing the economy

Organic aspects in the economic thought of Karl and Michael Polanyi[1]

Gábor Bíró

Introduction

Karl and Michael Polanyi were raised in their mother's well-known *fin-de-siècle* salon in Budapest. *Tante Cécile*'s salon was a gathering point for all kinds of Budapest radicals from fanatical communists to liberal and social democratic progressives and the Polanyi siblings were at home exposed to a diverse and changing set of thinkers and ideologies (Tyson 2005/6: 19–22). During their university years, they were among the founding members of the Galileo Circle (1908–1918, 1918–1919), a student organization fostering anti-dogmatism and studies of social theory. The Circle centered around the ideas of Gyula Pikler, a professor of legal theory who became the target of right-wing conservative Christian students for publicly discussing concepts of religion and nation as nonsense and harmful for the society. Even though Pikler's radical leftist ideas became the engine for mobilizing the opposition, the subsequently established discussion groups and other gatherings, including *Tante Cécile*'s salon and the Galileo Circle, were not merely different institutions with a single ideology. They were part of a diverse network connected by a commitment to the principle that addressing any topic properly requires consideration of social aspects. Demeter (2008, 2011, 2020) has recently identified a sociological tradition in Hungarian philosophy which had deep roots in this network. However, besides this commitment to social aspects, the network was loose and heterogenous: it included future hardcore communists such as Georg Lukacs and Mátyás Rákosi, socialists such as Karl Mannheim and Karl Polanyi, as well as socially sensitive liberals such as Oscar Jaszi and Michael Polanyi.

The Polanyis had a good relationship with Count Mihály Károlyi who became president of the new Hungarian Republic after the Aster Revolution of October 1918. After the social democratic–civic radical coalition government of Károlyi was dethroned by the Hungarian Soviet Republic in March 1919, its supporters, including Karl and Michael Polanyi, found themselves in an extremely heated political situation. Béla Kun, leader of the Hungarian Soviet Republic, imported and forced an artificial economic and political system on the country to please his foreign masters. To strengthen his power, he unleashed the Red Terror, which allowed the capture, torture and killing of

DOI: 10.4324/9781003138655-9

people likely to be anti-communist or counter-revolutionary. Kun took little interest in the existing political culture, the economic situation or the people living in the country. He was primarily interested in building a new Soviet republic. The short reign (March–August 1919) of the Red Terror was followed by the White Terror (1919–1921) of Miklós Horthy whose government was fueled by nationalistic sentiments that had been stimulated by the shock from the Treaty of Trianon. Austro-Hungary lost two-thirds of its territory and one-third of its Hungarian-speaking citizens. In the White Terror, groups again swept across the country, but this time hunting likely communist sympathizers. Horthy's government, like that of Kun, approved the killing of many citizens of its own country. Free-thinking intellectuals were a threat in the brutal environment of postwar Hungary and both Polanyi brothers recognized they were in danger.

The Polanyi brothers were among those Jewish-Hungarian intellectuals who left the country in a "double exile" (Frank 2009), that is, they first moved from Hungary to Austria and Germany, and then later moved on once again to escape the Third Reich. Karl first went to Austria to become an economic journalist (1924–1933) of the *Der Österreichische Volkswirt*, then to England to work as a lecturer on international relations and economic history (1933–1940) in university extension programs and at the Workers' Educational Association (hereafter WEA). Eventually he moved from England to North America to teach, first at Bennington College (early 1940s) and then later at Columbia University (1947–1953). Michael went to Karlsruhe (1919–1920) and then to Berlin (1920–1933) to join the prestigious Kaiser Wilhelm Institute as a chemist. Later he moved on to the Victoria University of Manchester (1933–1959) and to the University of Oxford (1959–1961).

The Polanyi brothers purportedly had a famously strained relationship, mostly due to their conflicting ideological commitments – Karl was a staunch socialist and Michael was a steadfast liberal. This divide was reflected in their economic theorizing. While Karl worked on a socialist economic theory resting on the claim that free market capitalism, with its fallacious social constructs, was the bane of contemporary social life, Michael was developing a liberal approach to economic thought which might be aptly described as Keynesianism with a monetary twist. Despite all these differences, Michael's *Full Emloyment and Free Trade* (1945a) happened to earn him the rare approval of his brother (Polanyi 1945b: 3). Inspired by this unlikely revelation, this chapter will delve into the economic thought of the two brothers to explore what might lie behind this brief comment.

Making and taming of the economic

Karl Polanyi suggested that there is no such thing as the "economic" per se. When speaking about "economic interests," "economic reasons" or "economic means" people are speaking about fictitious constructions because these things do not have anything inherently "economic" in them. Karl blamed the capitalist system and its theoreticians for these popular fallacies which, for him, seemed to foster the interests of a specific establishment. Liberal economists are, whether they are aware of it or not, working for this establishment which rules by defining what "economic" does and does not mean. Karl gave a historical treatment to reveal how this so-called "economic sphere" (Karl Polanyi 2014: 35)[2] was developed and how utilitarian philosophers enmeshed the "economic" (ibid: 36) and the "rational" in order to be able to describe everything which they consider "non-economic" as "irrational" and therefore "inmoral" and "insane" (ibid). In this "machine civilization" (ibid: 33) of ours, people have forgotten that they have both the right and the responsibility to figure out the actual "requirements of social justice" (ibid) in their community. Its not something which was replaced by the market mechanism. But this responsibility remains hidden in modern market societies. The task ahead is to make modern human beings conscious again, and then, to find the balance between "freedom" (ibid: 34) and "justice" (ibid) in specific social settings.

Michael Polanyi wrote several pieces in the thirties and forties which resonate quite well with these important ideas articulated by Karl. Michael argued that there is a need for "social consciousness" (Polanyi 1936: 5; Polanyi 2014a: 56) in modern market societies and this should be addressed if liberal thought was to resist the lure of socialism. He suggested that there are multiple "standards of economic justice" (Polanyi 1945a: 146) within which liberal capitalism can operate, so members of the community should decide on appropriate standards. Like Karl, he was not pleased with the impact of laissez-faire liberalism and utilitarianism on the public mind. Unlike his brother, however, he did not think of "economic" as a fictitious or nonexistent category and did not paint with such an overly broad brush to enmesh the evolution of capitalism with that of economics. Michael was working from a liberal approach and was trying to find the best way to channel social aspects into economics;[3] Karl was working from a socialist approach and was trying to show that the social system of capitalism and the discipline of economics must both be abandoned.

Volition of market, volition of war

According to Karl, the market as it has developed in the modern West is not a natural phenomenon and does not have its own volition. Theoreticians of capitalism have reframed nature and man as land and labor, fictional commodities pretending to work as "an automaton running in its own grooves and governed by its own laws" (Karl Polanyi 2014: 35). But "economic determinism" (ibid: 36) is a "delusion" (ibid). People are not being driven by an "economic motivation" (ibid: 37), the concept of economic man does not properly describe the real people out there and a society is much more than the people being engaged in an economic system. The idea of the market society being an "autonomous and automatic" (ibid: 50) system is, in Karl's view, fallacious and has never been realized in its pure form. The working of such a "Satanic mill" (ibid: 51)[4] would result in "destroying the human society" (ibid: 50). For Karl, a society run by the market would be "a tower of Babel whirling itself to destruction" (ibid).

But how could such a grand delusion enchant the scholarly community for so long? Karl contended that historians like Cunningham or Schmoller "rejected Ricardian economism" (ibid: 58), and because of this, economists ignored the works of historians. Thinking about the economy became increasingly axiomatic and accounts of historians have systematically downplayed economic aspects. According to Karl, there is an urgent need to change the approach of scholarly inquiries into the economy. Formal or scarcity economics should be replaced by a substantive economics, which is a kind of institutional economics focusing on economic aspects of human societies (ibid). Rather than focusing on the formal meaning of "economic" which attends to the allocation of scarce means having alternative uses, Karl's substantive approach focuses, more broadly, on what is in connection with the satisfaction of material wants. He defined the economy itself as being an aggregation of economic elements – that is, "elements being listed as needs and wants, material resources, services" (ibid: 59) – and activities connected to the "production, transportation and consumption of goods." Economic elements are "embodied in economic institutions" (ibid) which do not only consist of economic elements and are not only concerned about economic matters. If our inquiries are to go beyond the "incubus of an economistic or modernizing misinterpretation of the past" (ibid: 60) which postulates the selfish, profit-seeking nature of man, we should redefine our notions of economic institutions by using cultural anthropology.[5] When taking an institutional approach, we realize that the "assumed logical triad of trade, money and markets" (ibid: 61) is fallacious and that the "market assumption" (ibid) has mislead most accounts about earlier economies.

Michael was also working on a new kind of economics in the 1940s. While his diagnosis seems somewhat similar to that of his brother, that is, economics becoming too abstract and decontextualized, his proposed remedy was different. Michael did not want to replace formal economics with a substantive economics focusing on the satisfaction of material wants. He rather focused on the role of the human mind in knowing the economy. In *What to Believe* (1947), Michael suggested that "the process of knowing has three inherently interrelated aspects: understanding, believing and belonging" (Bíró 2020b: 29) which he also called *theoretical, confessional* and *social* aspects of knowing (Polanyi 1947: 6). Michael's claim is that it is the social aspect that "principally determines, which knowledge is true, and which is false" (ibid: 12); he thus perhaps should be seen as laying down the foundations of a novel, post-critical economics which he, unfortunately, never fully developed, although Michael's later thought works out carefully what he calls both a "fiduciary" and a "post-critical" philosophical perspective. His *Social Capitalism* (1946) offers a less radical alternative, "a capitalism with a human face" (Mullins 2019: 17) which performs better in finding "a balance between freedom and social justice" (Tartaro 2019: 27). It is tempting to claim that Karl's *liberal socialism* and Michael's *social capitalism*, from almost contradictory starting points, were developed towards the same end. But this is an oversimplification. Although both of them were working on a more humane economics that can help build a more humane economy, their approaches starkly differed on whether this humanization necessarily comes with more or with less market.

Karl's radical anti-market approach is particularly strange in light of his attitude to war. In his *The Nature of International Understanding* (Karl Polanyi 2014: 67–76),[6] he argued that there are situations in which the outbreak of a war between two nations is very likely, even if the communities of both prefer peace. He suggested that war is an institution, but it's not true that "its existence is a mere function of our volition." (ibid: 72) It has its own volition coming from the situation. But why did Karl acknowledge the volition of war coming from the situation and did not acknowledge the volition of market coming from the situation? Was war a special institution for him in this respect? It does not seem so. He gave the following general summary about institutions: "it is not true that, because something is a human institution, it depends only upon us whether we will have it or not" (ibid: 71). Elsewhere he wrote that "very few institutions exist because individuals wish them to exist" (ibid: 80). Apparently, one can be drawn into a war without wanting it (e.g., by living in one of the countries around a political vacuum) but one cannot be drawn into a market without wanting it (e.g., by producing a good that raises the interests of others). Entering into an unwanted war can be a rational strategy to follow in order to be able to avoid an even worse outcome, but entering into a market without wanting it cannot be? Karl's claims about whether institutions can have their own volition seem to be inconsistent.

According to Michael's pro-market approach, the market has its own volition which is actually a desirable method for organizing social matters. For him, the rise of the market was inherent to the rise of democracy: it fostered replacing autocracy with democracy and replacing feudalism with capitalism. In Michael's view, the market was an instance of spontaneous order, an order which emerged spontaneously and which was free from any kind of discriminative external intervention or control. Spontaneous order was not tied to the volition of anyone specifically. It had its own "volition" emanating from the very principle constituting the spontaneous order. If there was any interference with this volition, the order ceased to be spontaneous.

Explaining and transforming society

Market as an organ, society as an organism

Karl argued that a new international economic order should come to replace the class structure of society and the free movement of capital, labor and commodities. In order to be able to do this, communities should be "united in the service of transcending ideals" (ibid: 83) which makes "the coming of socialism inevitable in our age." Karl suggested transforming capitalist nation states into socialist communities by "bringing economic life under the control of the common people" (ibid). He contended that human consciousness is reformed again and again in history, and now is the time to reform it through the socialist transformation, that is, to lead people out from their "self-estrangement" (ibid: 84) by helping them in "reclaiming personal life in a complex society" (ibid). According to Karl, the socialist transformation is the only way to do such a timely reenchantment (Michael argued that there are several ways for doing so, and that socialist transformation is one of the worst). But this transformation for Karl was not simply socialist, but liberal socialist.

Karl perceived the school of liberal socialism to have arisen from various nineteenth century intellectuals including Anne Robert Jacques Turgot, Adam Smith, Henry Charles Carey, Pierre-Joseph Proudhon, Eugen Karl Dühring, Claude-Frédéric Bastiat, Henry George, Herbert Spencer, Peter Kropotkin, Theodor Hertzka and Franz Oppenheimer (ibid: 166). He noted that freedom gives rise to the "natural condition, whose harmony is grounded in itself, and is solid as unshakeable" (ibid: 167): a condition that represents "true and genuine freedom"; a condition that represents a state without violence and coercion. According to Karl, the English–French Revolution only did half of the job as it did not destroy the "feudal institution of monopoly on land" that would have been necessary to build a system which brings "work and natural forces into a free relation" (ibid). In his view, exploitation of the laborers comes from the "political law of coercive property in land that actually prevails and nullifies free competition" (ibid: 168). Competitors are not free or equal in their economic status to participate in a fair competition. Property thus acts as a coercive device smashing competition and keeping property owners in control of the propertyless class. If we were living in an economy without surplus value, "supply and demand [would] function as harmonious regulators of production and distribution" (ibid: 169). Without surplus value, there won't be any crises since the driving force of profit-seeking could not be in tension with the driving force to satisfy social needs.

For Karl Polanyi, the "unjust economic constitution" spearheaded by contemporary capitalism should be replaced with a just one, based on free cooperation. However, this requires "an organic form of organization – no longer a mechanical one." Production and consumption should be organized "in an organic structure of autonomous cooperatives" solely by the market without any kind of "parasitic practices" such as intermediate trade or speculation. In the economy, each and every person is "able to survey his position in relation to his environment within the narrow scope" of the related cooperative economic enterprises. He continually re-examines impulses of both economic self-interest and cooperative altruism and uses his "vivid intuition" to "preserve and nourish them with his entire personality." Economic institutions are "rectified in an organic way, without in the process destroying the active individual, the invisible driving cell of the whole organism." As Karl summarized it, "the image of social life … is an image of an organic entity." He argued that "the economy is a living process that can by no means be replaced by a mechanical apparatus, however subtly and ingeniously conceived." Karl suggested that the "statistical determination" of the needs, capabilities and interests of people is "completely unfounded" (ibid) from the approach of liberal socialism. Things such as the "intensity and quality" (ibid: 170) of work or the "technical possi-bilities of an invention" cannot be quantified. And these are pivotal aspects, "the only factors that [really] count in the life process of the economy." The market is not to be mistaken for the working of the economy. The market is only a "sense organ," but its "perceptual function" is being accomplished by free price formation. Without the market the "circulatory system of the econ-omy would collapse." In his view, the market does not show "manifest" needs and work efforts, but moments of change behind these manifestations. It does not show "real magnitudes as such, but differentials of the organic life processes of the economy." Prices do not really tell us anything about the products, but about the relationships of producers. However, the modality of these relation-ships is hidden by "the dense web of myriads of economic cells." All we get in the market is the result in the form of prices. But there is no economy without market. That would be like having a "collection of limbs with an active cir-culatory system, or a living human being with an artificial heart mechanism."

The market economy is "synonymous with" (ibid) cooperative socialism. And, unlike the profit economy of the capitalist system, it is not based on sur-plus value but on the "organically structured market of equivalent products of free labor" (ibid: 171). In his view, liberal socialism is a physiocratic doctrine because of "the dependence of production as a whole on agricultural yields." Karl distinguished between enforced and free (or voluntary) cooperation and suggested that, in case of cooperative socialism, only free cooperation is tenable. His contrasting of enforced and free cooperation offers several vitalistic ele-ments. He described them as "different as a living human being is from the panopticon mannequin" as "their construction, their efficient cause, their metabolism, and hence their durability and vital function are fundamentally different" (ibid). Despite what certain communist thinkers suggest, cooperatives are not subsidiaries of a state economy but are vital components. As the fol-lowing quotation suggests, for Karl, the state should not intervene to hamper the organic economic activities of individuals:

> Liberal socialism is fundamentally *hostile to force*. For liberal socialism, not only the state as an organism exercising domination over persons, but also the state as an administrator of things is, practically speaking, a necessary evil, and theoretically speaking, a superfluous and harmful construct. Any attempt to use state power to replace what can arise through the life and activity of the individual inevitably has devastating consequences.
>
> (ibid: 172)

The state should not act as an organ, since that role is to be taken by the workers' councils and other cooperatives. The ownership of large-scale indus-trial enterprises should be passed "to the economic autonomy of all, as repre-sented by the organs of the organised economy" (ibid: 173). Liberal socialism should separate institutions of "organic economic autonomy (council and curia system)" from institutions of representative democracy. The representation of economic autonomy should realize the "complete organic equalization of mental and physical work" (ibid), that is, having equal representation for the two kinds of work. Regulations on prices and wage should be abolished; land should be requisitioned and divided between those who are willing to cultivate it. Karl gave an unusual picture of the Russian economy. He argued that market, private property and free cooperation are actually there affecting what is happening in the economy. Karl suggested that the political triumph of the Soviet Government came at the expense of the "complete collapse of the centralized state economy" (ibid: 174). He made a general statement from this instance claiming that "the political success of the dictatorship of the proletariat and the economic success of the dictatorship of the proletariat are mutually exclusive." Karl thought that the Hungarian Soviet Republic would not have failed and "would still be in control today" if its leaders had realized this connection and eased their insistence of a communist state economy. Interestingly, Karl perceived the Russian agricultural cooperatives as an example of grassroots initiations forming a "voluntary, mighty colossus," while Michael saw them as pars construens of the all-consuming Leviathan. Karl stated that "every other socialist economy, except the communist, is compatible with the political power of the working class" (ibid). He noted that as the rise of the bourgeoisie brought forth nation-states, the rise of the working class will bring forth the "world state" (ibid: 175), realizing "free cooperation among free workers, on the liberated land of the world" (ibid).

Humanistic reasons for an organic economics

According to Karl, there is a crisis in a moral and social sense which has its roots in the Industrial Revolution during which the "relation of man to nature, his craft, his family, his tradition was utterly destroyed" (ibid: 186). The extension of *laissez aller* increased the tension between the "traditional feudalist classes" and the "new industrial classes" (ibid). In Karl's view, there is a trade-off between economic liberalism and political democracy, or, in other words, between laissez-faire and popular government. Too much from the first would "destroy society" (ibid: 185), too much from the latter would destroy the economy. The task ahead is to find the right balance between the two tendencies – or as Karl called them, philosophies: *Democratic philosophy*, which "tends to be socialist" (ibid: 188), and *laissez-faire philosophy*, which "tends to be antidemocratic" (ibid). In the current crisis, the "capacity for adaptation" (ibid: 187) was "diminishing" in national economies. This capacity should be restored, because "major adaptations [are] needed" (ibid) to find a new niche in the postwar international economic environment. The "dissolution of the international system upon which our civilization had unconsciously depended in its life and growth" (ibid: 211) made it necessary to establish a new international system.

Labor is not a commodity, but a human activity, a "part of man's functions as a physiological, psychological and moral being" (ibid: 206). It is not "produced" for sale but for "an entirely different set of motives" (ibid). And, "land is produced for sale as little as man: it is a part of nature" (ibid: 207), "man's habitation, the site of all his activities, the source of his life" (ibid). Society of the nineteenth century separated the economic and the political sphere but this cannot last long. A "society containing within its orbit a separate, self-regulating, and autonomous economic sphere is a utopia" (ibid: 214). Karl used the famous gun–butter example with a twist: one might prefer guns to butter or butter to guns, but "he will never *mistake* [Karl Polanyi's italics] the guns for the butter" (ibid). For him, guns are a placeholder for "political needs" (ibid: 215) and butter is a placeholder for economic needs, thus he argued that, in general, one does not simply mistake political needs with economic needs and vice versa. The "dogmatism of the liberal economist" (ibid: 216) understood the market as being "independent of human volition, of sentiments and ideals" and having its own volition. Any kind of intervention affects the whole system through the volition of the market. Karl suggested that liberal thinkers developed the concept of "*economic society* [Karl Polanyi's italics] – that is, a human community based on the assumption that society depends for its existence on material goods alone" (ibid: 217). They proposed a system in which the "Satanic mill" of the market runs the economy "according to the whims of a blind mechanism removed by its very nature from the needs of the living community embodied in every human society." A system that is "extremely artificial" and "bound for destruction" (ibid). Of course, liberal economists never believed in a society run by purely economic means. This is a *reductio ad absurdum* of their approach. Apparently, Karl was not attentive enough to spot the several disclaimers and explicit assumptions of liberal economic theories. He was painting with an overly broad brush – not only in his critique but also in his own argument. He argued that economics and politics were never completely separated. Nevertheless, two paragraphs later, he suggested that the separation of economics and politics caused a "catastrophic internal situation" (ibid: 218) in postwar Europe. There is a strange dialectic between what liberals say is nonsense and has nothing to do with reality and of liberals messing up the economy out there. He failed to grasp that both cannot be true. Liberal theories either have or do not have a relation to economic reality. His argument is like quarrelling with a close friend both for not coming to our party and for coming and ruining it. Liberalism cannot be both the villain and the silly sidekick.

Similarly to his brother, Michael Polanyi was devoted to showing the humanistic side of the economy. He joined his brother in claiming that the roots of the then contemporary moral and social crisis was based in a flawed way of thinking about people. Michael proposed that, unlike what mainstream theories suggest, knowers cannot be *detached* from acts of knowing (Polanyi 1998/1958). Knowers of the economy were, of course, no exception. They were embedded in a community of fellow knowers, as it was described in Polanyi's early piece, *What to Believe* (1947). Later Michael went into details about the relation of the knower and the known in general. He developed his famous idea of *tacit knowing* to emphasize the inexplicable content of knowing by borrowing the twin terms of *focal* and *subsidiary awareness* from Gestalt psychology (Polanyi 2009/1966). While a thorough analysis of Michael's philosophical inquiries into the realm of the tacit would undoubtedly lie outside the scope of this chapter, it seems adequate to note here that his thinking about the tacit was inspired by bringing back humanistic elements into thinking about the society and its constituents.

Historical reasons for an organic economics

Karl thought that economic history should reset its scope. It should not focus on studying economic data, but on studying "the place occupied by the economy in society as a whole" (Karl Polanyi 2014: 133), or, in other words, the "changing relation of the economic to the noneconomic institutions in society" (ibid). The concept that the market economy encapsulates "man and nature into a self-regulating system" (ibid: 136) was a utopian fantasy inducing a crisis and a grand-scale "transformation of the institutional set-up connected with the world economy" (ibid). The dominant form of integration, exchange, gives way to others, reciprocity and redistribution, which do not mirror such belief in the power of self-regulation. Karl argued that "the production and distribution of material goods was embedded in social relations of a noneconomic kind" (ibid: 141). Moreover, he suggested that the economic system is "simply a byproduct" (ibid) of the functioning of noneconomic institutions. Economics is embedded in society and not vice versa, as proponents of market economy suggest. Thus, when studying economic history, one should study the "relation of economic and noneconomic factors" (ibid: 146) in connection to "society as a whole." The embeddedness of the economic system to society is "time-bound" (ibid); it changes over time, so using an eighteenth century economic theory in the twentieth century and pretending that society did not change at all in the meantime can lead to dangerous conclusions.

Karl identified three *institutional patterns* (Karl Polanyi 2001 [1944]: 50–51) which can be found in various forms in human communities: symmetry, centricity and autarky. These institutional patterns facilitate certain *principles of behavior* (ibid: 49–51, 57). Symmetry facilitates *reciprocity*. Centricity facilitates *redistribution*. Autarky facilitates *householding*. Modern capitalist economies, however, are dominated by a fourth institutional pattern called market which facilitates *barter/exchange*. Market is different than the other institutional patterns. It is "capable of creating a specific institution [also called market]" (ibid: 60) based on a specific motive (that of truck or barter). Neither of the three other patterns is capable of this feat. None of them can create an institution which has (or is presumed to have) its own economic motive. To build a system based on this economic motive, one should separate the economic from the social sphere. And, separating these spheres requires the subordination of the social sphere to the needs of an autonomous economic sphere. What follows is that, in market economies, "instead of economy being embedded in social relations, social relations are embedded in the economic system" (ibid).

Economic gain, whatever that means, became the ultimate measure of social performance.

While market, the institution, is only compatible with one principle of behavior, barter/exchange, market, the institutional pattern, is compatible with all principles of behavior. The market pattern can not only facilitate barter/exchange but also reciprocity, redistribution and householding. Moreover, in Karl's view, these three latter principles of behavior were actually more dominant than barter/exchange in realizing the institutional pattern of the market before the Industrial Revolution. The Industrial Revolution brought forth ideas suggesting the separation of the economic from the social. Ideas suggesting that the economic system is no more "absorbed in the social system" (ibid: 71) and that markets are not only "accessories" but the most important elements of economic life. Market has started to be seen as a "self-regulating mechanism" run by humans seeking "maximum money gains" (ibid), and, by doing so, producing and distributing goods with the highest efficiency. All production is production for the market and all gain comes from the market. One cannot produce for other purposes or achieve gains by other means than from the market. To ensure this, society must be subordinated to the economy. A "market economy can exist only in a market society" (ibid: 74). Commodifying labor and land, human beings and their natural surroundings is "to subordinate the substance of society itself to the laws of the market" (ibid: 75). But if commodities are those objects produced for sale, then how can labor and land be treated as commodities? Neither nature nor human beings are generally considered to be made for sale on the market (or anywhere else). Money is "merely a token of purchasing power" (ibid), so also not an object produced for sale. Labor, land and money are *fictitious commodities* which, as Karl warned, are not to be mistaken for Marx's *commodity fetish*. Fictitious commodities are not real commodities. Fetishized commodities are real commodities being treated in a fictitious way. There is a "satanic mill" (ibid: 35, 77)[7] destroying the "human and natural substance" (ibid: 3) by supporting belief in fictitious commodities.

Machines of production became more expensive and sophisticated, transforming industrial production. To keep up with the increased pace of production, supply of certain elements – including land, labor and money – had to be provided. And the most efficient way of doing so was commodifying them in order to be able to sell them on the market. But industrial improvement comes with a huge cost: social dislocation. In Karl's view, "human society would have been annihilated but for the protective counter-moves which blunted the action of this self-destructive mechanism" (ibid: 79). There was a *double movement*: efforts to extend the scope of the market institution to all social relations, went in parallel with efforts to restrict this scope in relation to land, labor and money (ibid: 79).[8] The latter were natural counter-measures of a "society [which] protected itself against the perils inherent in a self-regulating market system" (ibid: 80). To emphasize the importance of economic history for understanding the economy, Karl went into details regarding the British case.

In the United Kingdom, the "destruction of the traditional fabric of society" (ibid: 81) was prevented by the Speenhamland Law (1795) which hampered the commodification/mobilization of labor. In England, the commodification of both land and money was already done before the commodification of labor. Karl argued that in the new realm of the economic man, "nobody would work for a wage if he could make a living by doing nothing (or not much more than nothing)" (ibid: 82). The wage system and the "right to live" (ibid: 82–83) were incompatible with each other, which lead to dire results: the Speenhamland Law ruined the people whom it intended to help. Speenhamland was, of course, "designed to prevent the proletarianization of the common people" (ibid: 86), but what it did was pauperize the masses. The Poor Law reform (1834) taking away this "right to live" was also extremely harmful to the people but it worked in the opposite direction: "If Speenhamland had overworked the values of neighborhood, family and rural surroundings, now man was detached from home and kin, torn from his roots and all meaningful environment" (ibid: 87). These quick and radical changes "shifted the vision of men toward their own collective being as if they had overlooked its presence before" (ibid: 88). And this created puzzlement about how people should organize society: "social consciousness was cast in its mold" (ibid: 87). The political economy became the main place to discuss this new phenomenon called society, and to figure out how to make the two principles of "unbounded hope and limitless despair" (ibid: 88), or the vision of hope and the vision of doom, compatible with each other.

Both harmony and conflict were said to be inherent principles in the economy. Harmony was mirrored by the necessary compatibility of the interests of the individual and those of the community. Conflict was mirrored by the struggle of individuals and social classes which was eventually a "vehicle of a deeper harmony" (ibid: 89). Political economists have started to make universal statements about society from two perspectives: the perspective of "progress and perfectibility" and the perspective of "determinism and damnation" (ibid). These perspectives gave rise to policies embracing the idea of self-regulation/noninterventionism and the idea of competition/conflict to let the economy work out its natural harmony instead of chaos or some unnatural harmony. According to Karl, political economists have developed a keen eye for the occurrences of these two principles but became inattentive to those instances which did not fit to this scheme.[9] They failed to see that the interests of an individual might be in conflict with interests of a community and that conflict does not necessarily lead to a deeper harmony.

Karl was struck by the "icy silence" (ibid: 103) of Malthus and Ricardo about the hardships of the poor. In his reading, their "philosophy of secular perdition" (ibid) mirrored insensitivity and ignorance towards the suffering of the masses. And there was unprecedented suffering. The "coming of the machine" (ibid: 128) caused social dislocation to a great degree. People were now "condemned to serve" (ibid: 103) the machine and by doing so being "transformed into a nondescript animal of the mire" living in "physical conditions which denied the human shape of life." Instead of empowering laborers, Speenhamland actually prevented their escape from "the fate to which they were doomed in the economic mill." It was "an unfailing instrument of popular demoralization" (ibid). Karl noted that "if a human society is a self-acting machine for maintaining the standards on which it was built, Speenhamland was an automaton for demolishing the standards on which any kind of society could be based" (ibid: 103–104). Karl discussed the Bentham brothers' plan of a convict- and then pauper-run machine and that recently their "private business venture merged into a general scheme of solving the social problem as a whole" (ibid: 112). The government planned 250 Industry Houses with more than 500,000 inmates in South England by "the commercialization of unemployment on a gigantic scale" (ibid: 113). Michael was also very critical of utilitarianism and orthodox economic liberalism which he thought to have four major weaknesses: the inability to see that the just reward for the factors of production does not necessarily lead to the just distribution of these rewards (i); the inability to see the limits of the free market as an organizing principle in human relations (ii); the inability to explain trade cycles (iii); and the inability to develop a widely accessible economic thought (iv).[10]

According to Karl, wealth was "merely an aspect of the life of the community, to the purposes of which it remained subordinate" (ibid: 116) in the Smithian political economy. This means that despite the fact that Smith's *Wealth of Nations* (1776) was primarily concerned with how to increase wealth, it treated this issue as only one aspect of the "nations struggling for survival in history" (ibid). There is no distinct separation of the economic and social spheres. Following our self-interest serves society best. There is no need to think about the social consequences of our everyday doings as these would lead us to even worse results than following a selfish moral compass. Karl interpreted the Smithian reading of the field as "political economy should be a human science; it should deal with that which was natural to man, not to Nature" (ibid: 117). Karl further explained this reading as the following: "natural is that which is in accordance with the principles embodied in the mind of man; and the natural order is that which is in accordance with those principles" (ibid). Thus, the source of Nature is not some objective reality out there, but the human mind. Karl perceived Malthus and Ricardo as developing a distinct economic society free from Smith's humanistic concerns. This society rests on two constitutive elements, the fertility of people (Malthus' law of population) and the fertility of soil (Ricardo's law of diminishing returns). This led to the artificial naturalization of certain social disorders, including poverty, for "poverty was Nature surviving in society" (ibid: 122). The "discovery of economics … hastened greatly the transformation of society" (ibid: 124–125) at the dawn of machine civilization. Thus, according to Karl, "not the natural but the social sciences should rank as the intellectual parents of the mechanical revolution which subjected the powers of nature to man" (ibid: 125).

Naturalizing and re-naturalizing the economy

Karl described the Ricardian law of diminishing returns as a "law of plant physiology" (ibid: 130) and the Malthusian law of population as a concept connecting the "animal instinct of sex and the growth of vegetation in a given soil" (ibid). Nature provides a limit, a border that cannot be crossed without grave consequences. Who "disobeyed the laws" (ibid: 131) of a competitive society, must face "the sanction of the jungle." Economic realities were constrained by the grim laws of Nature. This marked a milestone in social thought. "From this time onward naturalism haunted the science of man, and the reintegration of society into the human world became the persistently sought aim of the evolution of social thought" (ibid).

In Karl's view, the creation of the labor market was not a natural tendency but an "act of vivisection performed on the body of society" (ibid: 132). He welcomed Owen's approach which aimed to explain human motives with their social origins. According to Karl, Owen's socialism was "based on a reform of human consciousness to be reached through the recognition of the reality of society" (ibid: 133). He joined Owen in claiming that "what appeared primarily as an economic problem was essentially a social one" (ibid: 134). From the perspective offered by the market economy it was impossible to spot the destruction of the social fabric caused by the working of the profit-driven system. It is worth quoting here Karl's assessment of the social costs of this fallacy:

> the trading classes had no organ to sense the dangers involved in the exploitation of the physical strength of the worker, the destruction of family life, the devastation of neighborhoods, the denudation of forests, the pollution of rivers, the deterioration of craft standards, the disruption of folkways, and the general degradation of existence including housing and arts, as well as the innumerable forms of private and public life that do not affect profits.
>
> (ibid: 139)

Karl thought that the harmful social effects were due to the spread of a liberal creed which started "as a mere penchant for nonbureaucratic methods" (ibid: 141) and "evolved into a veritable faith in man's secular salvation through a self-regulating market" (ibid). He argued that both laissez-faire and economic liberalism in general evolved in response to the needs of a rapidly developing economic system. Regarding laissez-faire, he noted that it only started to mean the three essential tenets, that is, the competitive labor market, the automatic gold standard and international free trade, from the 1820s. Economic liberalism did not act as a "crusading passion" (ibid: 143) and the belief in laissez-faire was not a "militant creed" (ibid) being spread with "evangelical fervor" (ibid: 141) and "uncompromising ferocity" (ibid: 143) before this decade. According to Karl, "there was nothing natural about laissez-faire" (ibid: 145). It was not discovered but made. By stating that "[l]aissez-faire was planned; planning was not" (ibid: 147) he meant that the theoretical and social system of laissez-faire was consciously developed while the counteractions eventually leading to the planning movement in the 1930s were ad hoc responses from the people driven by their social hardships. Karl suggested that while several authors have acknowledged what he called a *double movement*, they had a different interpretation. In his view, the double movement referred to the progress of the utopian concept of the self-regulating market and to the process of how this progress was hampered by the "realistic self-protection of society" (ibid: 148). The other authors rather deemed this progress realistic and the concept that society can and should be protected from it utopian. Karl argued that the core of the liberal defense was that the "intellectual and moral weaknesses" (ibid: 151) of the people who failed to comprehend the new economic system (and to play according to its rules) urged them to fight against the system itself.

Dehumanizing and rehumanizing society

Karl suggested that one cannot have both a self-regulated market and free competition because an unregulated market gives rise to flaws of competition (e.g., monopolies). The state is needed to establish and maintain markets (e.g., with regulations and restrictions), a prerequisite of free competition.

Karl thought that although "human society is naturally conditioned by economic factors, the motives of human individuals are only exceptionally determined by the needs of material want satisfaction" (ibid: 160). People are not driven by money-mongering or profit-mongering but by various motivations.

Economic processes may disintegrate the cultural environment of an individual, inflicting a "lethal injury to the institutions in which his social existence is embodied" (ibid: 164). People might find themselves in a "cultural vacuum" (ibid: 165) after a "cultural debasement" destructing their social embeddedness without offering a viable alternative. One should not "expect that economic needs would automatically fill that void and make life appear livable under whatever conditions" (ibid). People are getting uprooted from their social environment due to "economistic prejudice" (ibid: 166). By making land, labor and money commodities, "which, again, is only a short formula for the liquidation of every and any cultural institution in an organic society" (ibid: 167), people did not only follow an "economistic prejudice" but also a "materialistic fallacy" (ibid: 169) ignoring spiritual and moral aspects of economic thinking. In Karl's view, "man and nature are practically *one* [not my italics] in the cultural sphere" (ibid: 170). And the "laws of the market was to annihilate all organic forms of existence and to replace them by a different type of organization, an atomistic and individualistic one" (ibid: 171). That was to completely wipe out the cultural sphere. There was no place for "organizations of kinship, neighborhood, profession and creed" anymore and attempts for their "spontaneous reformation" (ibid) were met with ideological obstacles. Humanity was sacrificed on the altar of economic progress. And Karl claimed to know the identity of the chief cultist: David Ricardo. Besides what Schumpeter called the *Ricardian vice*, that is, the tendency to develop abstract theories of analytical beauty and practical insignificance, Karl identified a second Ricardian vice, that is, the tendency to develop theories postulating that thinking about economic and social aspects of life can and should be separated. Karl's grasp of this second Ricardian vice deserves to be quoted here:

> Hobbes's grotesque vision of the state – a human Leviathan whose vast body was made up of an infinite number of human bodies – was dwarfed by the Ricardian construct of the labor market: a flow of human lives the supply of which was regulated by the amount of food put at their disposal.
>
> (ibid: 172)

In Karl's view, theories should treat "man as a whole" (ibid: 176), addressing the "organic and traditional forms of life among the laboring people" (ibid: 181). He suggested that, "land and labor are not separated; labor forms part of life, land remains part of nature, life and nature form an articulate whole" (ibid: 187). Land is inseparable from social institutions of "kinship, neighborhood, craft and creed," being interwoven with several aspects of life. The economic function is "but one of many vital functions of land." Land is much more than a "site" (ibid) of wealth. With the global spread of "free trade the new and tremendous hazards of planetary interdependence sprang into being" (ibid: 190) and people have started to look for ways "to protect their habitation against the juggernaut, improvement" (ibid: 191). The market system carrying the "liberal virus" (ibid: 196) was "more allergic to rioting [that is, interference with regular functioning] than any other economic system we know" (ibid: 195). In Karl's view, the minds of liberals became "insensitive to the phenomena of nation and of money" (ibid: 212) and failed to grasp that these two new institutions (nation state, national currency) are "inseparable" (ibid). In a political sense, national identity was established by the government; in an economic sense it was established by the central bank. Monetary policy was not just a way to adjust the value of money, it was also a way to adjust the life of people. With globalization, the system went too large to be controlled:

> World trade now meant the organizing of life on the planet under a self-regulating market, comprising labor, land, and money, with the gold standard as the guardian of this gargantuan automaton. Nations and peoples were mere puppets in a show utterly beyond their control.
>
> (ibid: 226)

Western civilization itself was "being disrupted by the blind action of soulless institutions the only purpose of which was the automatic increase of material welfare" (ibid: 228). Self-interest driven economic life is "unnatural" (ibid: 257) in the sense that it is inconsistent with human nature. Economic histories portraying the "gradual and spontaneous emancipation of the economic sphere from governmental control" (ibid: 258) were fallacious. It was not the social dislocation of economic phenomena but the countermovement that was spontaneous. Karl suggested that if we want freedom and peace, "we will have consciously to strive for them in the future if we are to possess them at all; they must become chosen aims of the societies toward which we are moving" (ibid: 263). Planning, regulation, control and power are not necessarily evil. They are ever present in a complex society. The market view of society had a very narrow definition of freedom, as an individual freedom to make contractual relations. It implies that "there is nothing in human society that is not derived from the volition of individuals and that could not, therefore, be removed again by their volition" (ibid: 266). Karl proposed instead an organic view of society implying that it is much more than a sum of its individual parts. This view would acknowledge that a modern individual wants to know her place in the society. This is now a "constitutive element" (ibid: 268) of our consciousness that we cannot escape from. We should stay committed to our aim, that is, to create "more abundant freedom for all." If we stay true to this commitment, we "need not fear that either power or planning will turn against" freedom (ibid).

Michael's pro-market approach at first glance seems to be rather insensitive to social issues compared to Karl's anti-market approach. But only at first glance. He also sought a way to rehumanize society. Michael was critical about liberal capitalism and wanted to reform it to have stronger ties to laypeople. His proposal was twofold: fostering a renewal of economics to become more comprehensible (i); and fostering a renewal of economic policies to avoid corruption and favouritism (ii). Michael Polanyi's economics film project was at the center of this proposal. It was made to educate the masses in economics by using comprehensible visual symbolism,[11] and its central message was about a corruption-free economic policy, a neutral Keynesianism (Bíró 2020a). This economic policy was imagined by Polanyi to operate only through budget deficit and tax remissions and not through financing public works and infrastructural investments. The film had two main takeaways. First, if there is no discretionary decision, there is no opportunity for corruption. If the economic policy can only adjust the volume of money in circulation but cannot define exactly where the money goes, there is no room for corruption. And second, there is no single optimal volume of the money in circulation. Members of society could and should choose (that is the reason why the educated opinion of the general public matters in issues of economic policy) from various inflation–unemployment pairings and within certain limits each of these alternatives are rational choices. A society can prefer a lower level of unemployment that necessarily comes with a higher level of inflation or a lower level of inflation that necessarily comes with a higher level of unemployment. It depends on the actual standard of economic justice in a given society. There is no single optimal alternative that is only discernible to top experts or politicians. There are several alternatives to choose from and all members of the society should have a voice in making the decision because it affects everyone. This was part of Michael's liberal way to rehumanize society.

Similarly to his brother, Michael was very critical of laissez faire liberalism. He thought that economic liberalism was derailed by "utilitarian exigencies" (Michael Polanyi 1944: 3) and lost touch with the humane side of the economy. Michael even used the Dickensian portrayal of liberal economics as it was presented in *Hard Times* (2005) [1854] to argue against the social insensibility of extreme liberalism (Bíró 2019: 17–18). Utilitarianism, along with scepticism, Michael believed, have corrupted the modern mind which is now without adequate moral anchorage. The problem is not that economics took a different path than many other social sciences (see the second Ricardian vice in the discussion of Karl Polanyi in the previous section) but that natural and human sciences in general became seen as empty in a moral and metaphysical sense. Michael urged the replacement of this misplaced critical philosophy with a post-critical one that is better at addressing the relation between the knower and the known. For Michael, the knower and the known have an organic relationship in which the context of knowing has great importance. Perhaps, the most striking example of this is the Polanyian parallel in *The Logic of Liberty* (1951) between the meaninglessness of central plans and the meaninglessness of summarizing multiple games of chess by the steps taken by each kind of pieces. Michael argued that "the moving of any particular castle or bishop constitutes a 'move in chess' only in the context of the moves (and possible moves) of the other pieces in the same game" (Polanyi 1951: 135). A similar thing happens when economic outputs are "taken out of their economic context" and regarded "merely as processes of physical change" (ibid). Moving a chess piece is not a "move in chess" in itself. Similarly, physical production is not economic production in itself. One is tempted to identify the influence of certain twentieth century German holistic philosophies here, particularly the work of Jakob Johann von Uexküll who "envisioned the organism and its environment as a single, integrated system (the so-called *Umwelt*)" (Harrington 1996: 34). Polanyi seems to be suggesting that the meaning and the rationality of economic actions, as well as the purpose of economic activity comes from the interaction of economic agents and their environment. One cannot extract an output from its economic context without deconstructing its meaning. While this influence remains speculative without a direct Polanyian reference to Uexküll, there are further clues suggesting this so far unnoticed influence in Michael's examples of spontaneous order. Polanyi discussed that in a vessel, "particles are free to obey the internal forces acting between them, and the resultant order represents the equilibrium between all the internal and external forces" (Polanyi 1951: 155). He also portrayed evolution as a spontaneous order with an Uexküllian flavour: the "evolution of a polycellular organism from the fertilized cell" (ibid: 156) was presented as "arising from the continuous tendency of its particles, interacting with the nutrient medium, to come to an internal equilibrium." He noted that "the entire evolution of species is commonly thought to have resulted from a continued process of internal equilibration in living matter, under varying outside circumstances" (ibid). Thus, particles filling up a vessel and cells evolving to adapt to their environment are akin to economic agents interacting with each other and their environment: their interactions are meaningless without the context.

Polanyi was also inspired by another holistic approach, Gestalt psychology (on Polanyi and Gestalt psychology see Goodman 2000; Hull 2007; Jacobs

2015; Mullins 2010; Mullins 2013; Mullins 2016). This approach emphasized that knowing a part always already implies knowing a whole, yet to a different degree. Polanyi even borrowed Köhler's Gestalt term, "dynamic order," to denote a specific kind of order which he later renamed as spontaneous order (Goodman 2000; Mullins 2013; Jacobs 2015; Mullins 2016). These orders emerge from independent atomistic interactions which are always already inherent parts of the order they are constituting. This happens in the case of the market. By making an autonomous transaction, the agent is also contributing to the constitution of the market. And, the existence of the market implies a swarm of autonomous transactions made by several agents. There is an organic relation between the constituting parts and the constituted whole. And the main influence of this Polanyian relation seems to be Köhler's dynamic order. Both Polanyi's borrowing of the Uexküllian relation of the organism and its environment and his reliance on the Gestalt relation of the part and the whole can be interpreted as being constitutive of his attempts to rehumanize thinking about society.

Conclusion

It was shown in this chapter that, when talking about the economy, the Polanyi brothers both saw mechanic problems and organic solutions. Yet they disagreed on what are these problems and how to solve them. In Karl's view, the main problem was the economization of social relations mirrored in theories and practices of liberal economics. His arch villain was David Ricardo, whom he saw as initiating a century old fissure between economic and social studies (this was termed the second Ricardian vice). According to Karl, economics is embedded in society (and not vice versa) thus economists should pay more attention to the social layers of economic activity. He relied on the findings of cultural anthropology in his critique and suggested taking a similar approach when making inquiries into modern economies. On the historical scale he perceived a double movement, a twin process of economizing all social relations (i) and of providing some protection against social disruption (ii). He considered the first process, the economization of the social world, to be supported and perhaps induced by two kinds of mechanization: the theoretical mechanization of people by political economists through the concept of economic man; and the practical mechanization of production by capitalists through the introduction of advanced machines in mass production. The latter, of course, meant a departure from labor-intensive towards capital-intensive ways of production, leading to unemployment and other harmful social effects. He discussed how this artificial process was framed by some theoreticians as an instance or an extension of the concept of struggle for survival in order to lend legitimacy from the laws of Nature itself. But Karl argued that it had nothing to do with Nature. And even if it had, we should not simply be concerned about Nature but what is "natural to man" (Karl Polanyi 2001 [1944]: 117). We should take the economic sphere as an inherent part of the social sphere which developed in an organic way conditioned by the local natural and social environment. He fostered an "organic form of organization" (Karl Polanyi 2014: 169) based on free cooperation which would build up "an organic structure" supporting the economy as "a living process." He contrasted the passive economic man of liberal capitalism with the "active individual" of his liberal socialism who is the "invisible driving cell of the whole organism" (ibid). He proposed the separation of institutions of "organic economic autonomy" (ibid: 173) from institutions of political autonomy and emphasized that a political power which limits the first cannot endure based on the second. The "economistic" (Karl Polanyi 2001 [1944]: 169) and "materialistic" prejudice of liberal theoreticians "was to annihilate all organic forms of existence and to replace them by a different type of organization, an atomistic and individualistic one" (ibid: 171). What the world needs, in his view, is a "spontaneous reformation" of the "organizations of kinship, neighborhood, profession and creed" (ibid) which would regenerate the organic tissues of society. He rejected the liberal naturalization of the economy and offered a new one that would rehumanize society in an organic way.

Unlike his brother Karl, Michael did not want to replace but to reform liberal capitalism. He also perceived a mechanistic problem in how liberal economists (and utilitarians) addressed people. Their atomistic, individualistic and desocialized accounts did not seem to be plausible for Michael either, who sought to address the people's need for a "social consciousness" (Polanyi 1936: 5; Polanyi 2014a: 56), their craving to understand how their everyday doings fit into a larger economic and social scheme. He believed that addressing this craving is the key for more popular social thought and that "the struggle for it will dominate public life until it has found reasonable satisfaction" (Polanyi 1937b: 32). Michael did not blame industrial mechanization for the social dislocation/disenchantment of people as Karl did, but the Enlightenment which unleashed the principles of scepticism and utilitarianism that eventually went too far and corrupted the modern mind. To heal this corruption people should find a reattachment to spiritual and moral realms without dogmatism and coercion. This is also a call for an organic return to what is "natural to man" (Karl Polanyi 2001 [1944]: 117). Michael designed an economics film[12] for laypeople and urged using this and other motion pictures to enlighten people, that is, to make them conscious of the social entanglements of economic activity. The main message is that there is always already a standard of economic justice working behind the economy, whether we are aware of it or not, so we should rather make this conscious and establish democratic ways to decide on this standard. Michael thought that capitalism can be made to conform to any standards of economic justice so members of society should decide on the one which fits to their moral compass the most (Karl thought that a capitalist system can only be based on economic injustice). After Michael's programme of "democracy by enlightenment through the film" (Michael Polanyi 1935: 1) failed to have societal effects, he turned to arguing that spontaneous orders are not only more efficient in ordering economic affairs but also more acceptable in a moral sense than corporate orders. They were better both in adjusting economic relations and in empowering people. Spontaneous orders are developed in an organic way, that is, growing out from the society they intended to order without having any kind of coercion from authorities. Corporate orders are not grown out spontaneously but designed for a purpose which is often to suppress a certain group of people. The only way towards a good society is to have good institutions. And those can only be developed in an organic way to rehumanize society.

Michael and Karl Polanyi perceived mechanic problems and organic solutions in the economy. The Budapest roots of their education and intellectual socialization, and most importantly, the sociological tradition in Hungarian philosophy (Demeter 2008, 2011, 2020) apparently made its mark on the economic thought of the two brothers. However, while Karl saw an artificially crafted dogmatism in the desocialized nature of liberal economics, Michael spotted a spontaneous disciplinary flaw which has gone a very long way. Karl embraced liberal socialism and suggested putting down the foundations of a novel system based on cooperatives. Michael did not want to replace but to reform liberalism by revisiting the role of people in economic circulation. The Polanyi brothers were working on renaturalizing the economy and rehumanizing society and their parallel endeavours, while being very different, both relied on a resurrection of organic aspects in thinking about the economy.

Notes

1 Thanks are due to Tamás Demeter, Phil Mullins, Martin Turkis, Charles Lowney, Roope O. Kaaronen and Thomas Dillern. This chapter contributes to the research programme of MTA Lendület Morals and Science Research Group.
2 Resta and Catanzariti (Karl Polanyi 2014) found this undated conference paper in the Karl Polanyi archives (37–34) with the title "Economics and the Freedom to Shape our Social Destiny." They also discovered that Karl Polanyi used parts of this paper in his "Our Obsolete Market Mentality: Civilization Must Find a New Thought Pattern," which was published by *Commentary* in 1947 (3): 109–117 (Karl Polanyi 2014: 33).
3 On a detailed comparison of Michael Polanyi's liberalism to that of his contemporaries see Allen 1998 and Beddeleem 2017.
4 "Satanic Mill" is also the title of the first Section of "Part Two: Rise and Fall of Market Economy" in Karl Polanyi's *The Great Transformation: The Political and Economic Origins of Our Time* (2001) [1944].
5 Michael Polanyi's work also mirrored anthropological insights, particularly his "Scientific Beliefs" (1950) and "The Stability of Beliefs" (1952) which explicitly dealt with the diversity of beliefs and the organic relation of beliefs and their social contexts. See more on this topic in Jacobs 2003, Jacobs and Mullins 2017.
6 Also found by Resta and Catanzariti in the Karl Polanyi Archives (17–29) who made some great editing to make the text more readable (Karl Polanyi 2014: 67).
7 See note 2.
8 Also on Karl Polanyi 2001 [1944]: 136, 138, 148, 151, 156–157, 223.
9 A similar idea was mirrored in Michael Polanyi's proposal for a new liberal journal, *Civitas*. Michael urged the rewriting of the political theory of liberalism to provide "a new radically sharpened theory of democracy and civic liberties" (Polanyi 1945c: 6). See more on this in Mullins 2014.

10 Discussed in detail in Polanyi's *On Popular Education in Economics* 1937a: 4–6 [or in Polanyi 2015: 20–21]. See more on this in Beira 2015 and in Bíró 2019: 14–15.
11 Michael Polanyi argued that "a complex structure that cannot be seen cannot be understood" (Polanyi 1936: 1), and that the economy is very complex, so if one wants people to understand it one needs to make it visible. His *Visual Presentation of Social Matters* (1937c) [2014b], *Suggestions for a New Research Section* (1937d) and *Memorandum on Economic Films* (1938b) constituted the programmatic basis from which Polanyi launched an actual educational project, his economics film. See more on this in Beira 2014, Moodey 2014, Mullins 2014, Bíró 2017, Bíró 2019, Bíró 2020a.
12 The first version of the film premiered as *An Outline of the Working of Money* in 1938, the second as *Unemployment and Money: The Principles Involved* in 1940. The film was rediscovered by Eduardo Beira, who made the first comments about it. The film has recently been addressed in detail in Bíró 2020a.

References

Allen, Richard T. 1998. *Beyond Liberalism: The Political Thought of F. A. Hayek and Michael Polanyi*. New Brunswick, NJ: Transaction Publishers. doi:10.4324/9781351290807.

Beddeleem, Martin. 2017. *Fighting for the Mantle of Science: The Epistemological Foundations of Neoliberalism, 1931–1951*, PhD dissertation, Montréal: Université de Montréal.

Beira, Eduardo. 2014. "'Visual Presentation Of Social Matters' as a Foundational Text of Michael Polanyi's Thought," *Tradition & Discovery* 41(2): 6–12.

Beira, Eduardo. 2015. "'On Popular Education in Economics': Another Foundational Text Of Michael Polanyi's Thought," *Tradition & Discovery* 42(3): 8–24.

Bíró, Gábor István. 2017. *Projecting the Light of Democracy: Michael Polanyi's Efforts to Save Liberalism via and Economics Film, 1933–48*, PhD dissertation, Budapest: Budapest University of Technology and Economics.

Bíró, Gábor István. 2019. *The Economic Thought of Michael Polanyi*. London: Routledge.

Bíró, Gábor István. 2020a. "Michael Polanyi's Neutral Keynesianism and the First Economics Film, 1933 to 1945," *Journal of the History of Economic Thought* 42(3): 335–356.

Bíró, Gábor István. 2020b. "Toward a Postcritical Economics: Comment on Michael Polanyi's 'What to Believe'," *Tradition & Discovery* 46(2): 29–35.

Demeter, Tamás. 2008. "The Sociological Tradition of Hungarian Philosophy," *Studies in East European Thought* 60(1–2): 1–17. doi:10.1007/s11212-11008-9043-9041.

Demeter, Tamás. 2011. *A szociologizáló hagyomány. A magyar filozófia főárama a XX. Században*. Budapest: Századvég.

Demeter, Tamás. 2020. "New Class Theory as Sociology of Knowledge." In Tamás Demeter, ed., *Intellectuals, Inequalities and Transitions. Prospects for a Critical Sociology*. Leiden: Brill. doi:10.1163/9789004400283_004.

Dickens, Charles. 2005 [1854]. *Hard Times*. Webster's German Thesaurus Edition for ESL, EFL, ELP, TOEFLL®, TOEIC®, and AP® Test Preparation. San Diego: ICON Classics.

Frank, Tibor. 2009. *Double Exile: Migrations of Jewish-Hungarian Professionals through Germany to the United States, 1919–1945*. Oxford: Peter Lang.

Goodman, C.P. 2000. "A Free Society: The Polanyian Defence," *Tradition & Discovery* 27(2): 8–25.

Harrington, Anne. 1996. *Reenchanted Science: Holism in German Culture from Wilhelm II to Hitler*. Princeton: Princeton University Press. doi:10.2307/j.ctv14163kf.

Hull, Richard. 2007. "The Great Lie: Markets, Freedom and Knowledge." In Dieter Plehwe, Bernhard J.A. Walpen and Gisela Neunhöffer, eds., *Neoliberal Hegemony: A Global Critique*. London: Routledge.

Jacobs, Struan. 2003. "Two Sources of Michael Polanyi's Prototypal Notion of Encommensurability: Evans-Pritchard on Azande Witchcraft and St Augustine on Conversion," *History of the Human Sciences* 16(2): 57–76. doi:10.1177/0952695103016002003.

Jacobs, Struan. 2015. "Hayek, the 'Spontaneous' Order and the Social Objectives of Michael Polanyi." In Robert Leeson, ed., *Hayek: A Collaborative Biography: Part IV, England, the Ordinal Revolution and the Road to Serfdom, 1931–50*. New York: Palgrave Macmillan. doi:10.1057/9781137452603_5.

Jacobs, Struan and Mullins, Phil. 2017. "Anthropological Materials in the Making of Michael Polanyi's Metascience," *Perspectives on Science* 25(2): 261–285. doi:10.1162/POSC_a_00243.

Moodey, Richard W. 2014. "'Visual Presentations of Social Matters' and Later Changes in Polanyi's Social Theory," *Tradition & Discovery* 41(2): 25–34.

Mullins, Phil. 2010. "Michael Polanyi's Use of Gestalt Psychology." In Tihamér Margitay, ed., *Knowing and Being: Perspectives on the Philosophy of Michael Polanyi*. Newcastle upon Tyne: Cambridge Scholars Publishing.

Mullins, Phil. 2013. "Michael Polanyi's Early Liberal Vision: Society as a Network of Dynamic Orders Reliant on Public Liberty," *Perspectives on Political Science* 42(3): 162–171. doi:10.1080/10457097.2013.793525.

Mullins, Phil. 2014. "Comments on Polanyi's 'Visual Presentation of Social Matters'," *Tradition & Discovery* 41(2): 35–44.

Mullins, Phil. 2016. "Polanyi on 'public liberty' and 'dynamic order'." In R.T. Allen, ed., *Freedom, Authority and Economics: Essays on Michael Polanyi's Politics and Economics*. Wilmington, DE: Vernon Press.

Mullins, Phil. 2019. "From Countering Utilitarianism to Countering Planning: Michael Polanyi's 'Social Capitalism' and Its Place in His Social Philosophy," *Polanyiana* 28(1–2):3–19.

Polanyi, Karl. 2001 [1944]. *The Great Transformation: The Political and Economic Origins of Our Time*. Boston: Beacon Press.

Polanyi, Karl. 2014. *For a New West: Essays, 1919–1958*, edited by Giorgio Resta and Mariavittoria Catanzariti. Cambridge: Polity Press.

Polanyi, Michael. 1935. A Letter of 13th December 1935 from Michael Polanyi to John Grierson, Michael Polanyi Papers, Box 3, Folder 5, Special Collections, University of Chicago Library.

Polanyi, Michael. 1936. "Notes on a Film," Michael Polanyi Papers, Box 25, Folder 10, Special Collections, University of Chicago Library.

Polanyi, Michael. 1937a. "On Popular Education in Economics," Michael Polanyi Papers, Box 25, Folder 9, Special Collections, University of Chicago Library.

Polanyi, Michael. 1937b. "Historical Society Lecture," Michael Polanyi Papers, Box 25, Folder 10, Special Collections, University of Chicago Library.

Polanyi, Michael. 1937c. "Visual Presentation of Social Matters," Michael Polanyi Papers, Box 25, Folder 9, Special Collections, University of Chicago Library.

Polanyi, Michael. 1937d. "Suggestions for a New Research Section," Michael Polanyi Papers, Box 25, Folder 9, Special Collections, University of Chicago Library.

Polanyi, Michael. 1938a. *An Outline of the Working of Money*. London: G.B. Instructional.

Polanyi, Michael. 1938b. "Memorandum on Economic Films," Michael Polanyi Papers, Box 3, Folder 6, Special Collections, University of Chicago Library.

Polanyi, Michael. 1940. *Unemployment and Money: The Principles Involved*. London: G.B. Instructional.

Polanyi, Michael. 1944. A letter of 9th July 1944 from Michael Polanyi to Toni Stolper, Michael Polanyi Papers, Box 4, Folder 11, Special Collections, University of Chicago Library.

Polanyi, Michael. 1945a. *Full Employment and Free Trade*. Cambridge: Cambridge University Press.

Polanyi, Michael. 1945b. A letter of 20th December 1945 from Michael Polanyi to Toni Stolper, Michael Polanyi Papers, Box 4, Folder 13, Special Collections, University of Chicago Library

Polanyi, Michael. 1945c. "Civitas." *Collected Articles and Papers of Michael Polanyi*. 1963. Compiled by Richard L. Gelwick. Berkeley, CA: Pacific School of Religion. Available online on the Polanyi Society website (polanyisociety.org).

Polanyi, Michael. 1946. "Social Capitalism," *Time and Tide* 27 (April 13): 341–342.

Polanyi, Michael. 1947. "What to Believe," Michael Polanyi Papers, Box 31, Folder 10, Special Collections, University of Chicago Library.

Polanyi, Michael. 1950. "Scientific Beliefs," *Ethics* 61: 27–37.

Polanyi, Michael. 1951. *The Logic of Liberty: Reflections and Rejoinders*. London: Routledge and Kegan Paul.

Polanyi, Michael. 1952. "The Stability of Beliefs," *British Journal for the Philosophy of Science* 3: 217–232.

Polanyi, Michael. 1998/1958. *Personal Knowledge: Towards a Post-Critical Philosophy*. London: Routledge.

Polanyi, Michael. 2009/1966. *The Tacit Dimension*. Chicago: The University of Chicago Press.

Polanyi, Michael. 2014a [1936]. "Notes on a Film," *Polanyiana* 23(1–2): 56–65.

Polanyi, Michael. 2014b [1937]. "Visual Presentation of Social Matters," *Tradition & Discovery* 41(2): 13–24.

Polanyi, Michael. 2015 [1937]. "On Popular Education in Economics," *Tradition & Discovery* 42(3): 18–24.

Tartaro, Alessio. 2019. "Capitalism with a human face: a comment on Michael Polanyi's 'Social Capitalism'," *Polanyiana* 28(1–2): 20–27.

Tyson, Ruel. 2005/6. "From Salon to Institute: Convivial Spaces in the Intellectual Life of Michael Polanyi," *Tradition & Discovery* 32(3): 19–22.

Index

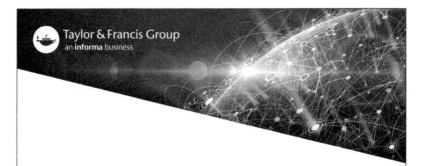

Printed in the United States
by Baker & Taylor Publisher Services